IMAGES
of America

Jacksonville's Gullah Geechee Heritage

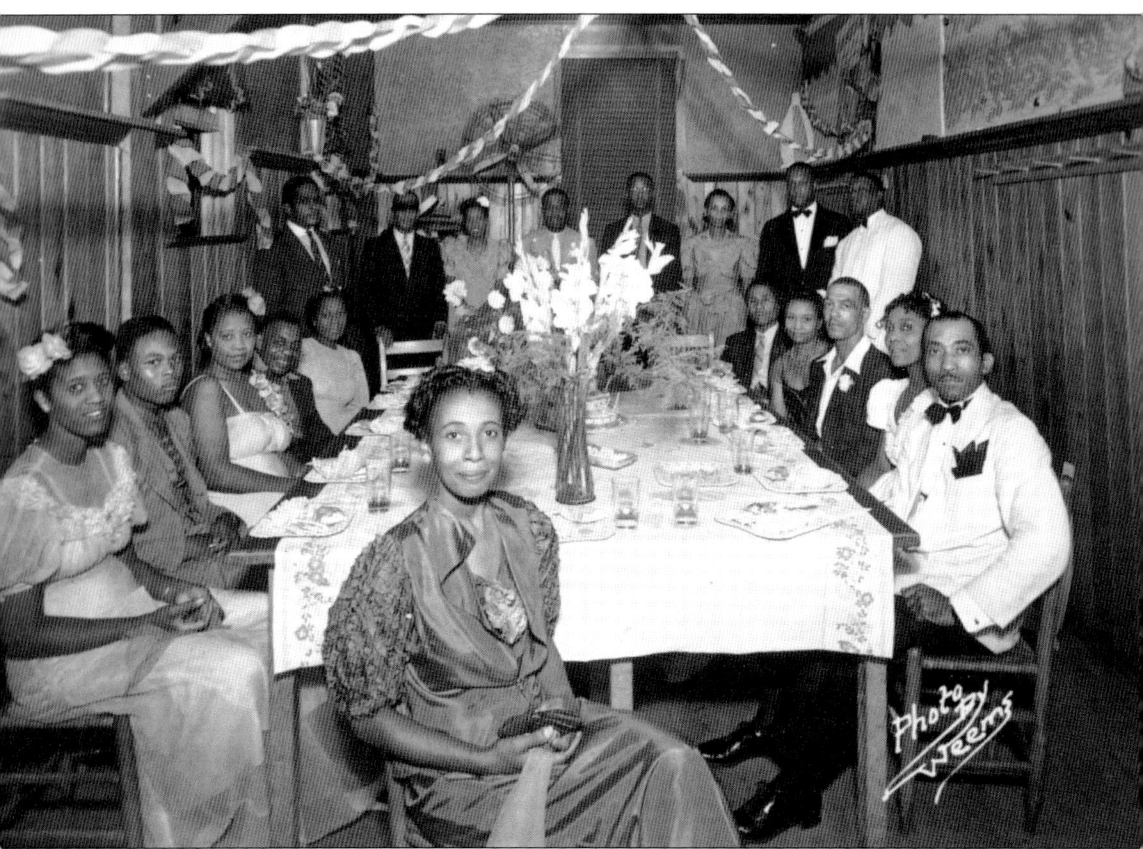

In this photograph, likely dating to the late 1930s or early 1940s, a group of Jacksonville residents enjoys a celebratory meal featuring deviled crabs. This culinary dish is representative of Gullah Geechee foodways that one can still find in town today. The people assembled around the table tell a story of economic prosperity in Jacksonville's Black community, a demonstration of excellence that is repeated throughout the city's Gullah Geechee history up until the present time. (Courtesy of the Ritz Theatre & Museum.)

On the Cover: The segregated Black waiting room at the Jacksonville Terminal is pictured in 1921. In 1916, the *Chicago Defender* published Jacksonville poet Matthew Ward's poem "Bound for the Promised Land." The poem encouraged Black Americans to leave the racially discriminatory South and move to the North. That year, more than 6,000 Black Americans left Jacksonville alone, starting one of the largest movements of people in the United States. This movement is now recognized as the Great Migration. (Courtesy of the State Archives of Florida.)

IMAGES
of America

JACKSONVILLE'S GULLAH GEECHEE HERITAGE

Ennis Davis and Adrienne Burke
Foreword by Saundra Morene

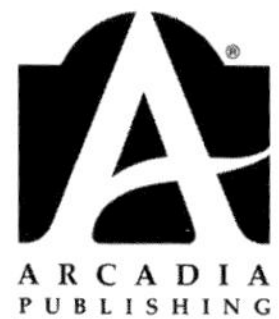

ISBN 978-1-4671-6334-7
Hardcover ISBN 978-1-5402-9948-2

Published by Arcadia Publishing
Charleston, South Carolina

Printed in the United States of America

Library of Congress Control Number: 2025948916

For all general information, please contact Arcadia Publishing:
Telephone 843-853-2070
Fax 843-853-0044
E-mail sales@arcadiapublishing.com

Visit us on the Internet at www.arcadiapublishing.com

Dedicated to our family and friends, whose steadfast support, patience, and encouragement made this work possible and whose belief in us carried it forward.

Contents

Foreword

The Gullah Geechee people are descendants of West and Central Africans who were enslaved and brought to the coastal regions of the southeastern United States. Their distinctive culture developed over centuries on the isolated Sea Islands and coastal plantations of North Carolina, South Carolina, Georgia, and Florida. Designated in 2006, the federal Gullah Geechee Cultural Heritage Corridor was established to recognize and preserve this unique heritage. Jacksonville maintains its position within the Heritage Corridor as being the home of the largest number of Gullah Geechee descendants.

The foundations of Gullah Geechee culture lie in the geography and agricultural practices of the antebellum South. The hot, humid, and disease-ridden climate of the coastal rice, indigo, and Sea Island cotton plantations made it difficult for White plantation owners and overseers to live there year-round. As a result, enslaved people often worked with minimal White supervision, allowing them to maintain and pass down many of their indigenous African traditions. Language, arts, crafts, and foodways that exist today are cultural continuations from the Gullah Geechee ancestors.

Beginning in the colonial era, enslaved Africans were brought to the Jacksonville area to work on plantations and in the city's maritime industry. After the Civil War, Jacksonville's Black population expanded significantly as newly freed people flocked to the city for economic opportunities. This brought an increase in Gullah Geechee people who migrated to Jacksonville for work from many parts of the southeastern states. During Reconstruction, newly freed Black residents in Jacksonville established communities and crucial community institutions.

In the modern era, Gullah Geechee people face significant challenges to their land, culture, and economic stability. Coastal development, tourism, and gentrification threaten traditional communities and land ownership. Climate change poses a severe existential threat, with rising sea levels and more frequent, intense storms endangering the coastal communities and their traditional livelihoods. Despite these pressures, Gullah Geechee communities have shown remarkable resilience, continuing to preserve and celebrate their unique cultural heritage. Organizations and cultural heritage programs like the Jacksonville Gullah Geechee Community Development Corporation work to document, research, and protect Gullah Geechee history and traditions for future generations.

Within this landscape, Jacksonville's historic Gullah Geechee time line is an all-American story. The story of Black residents here is one of resilience, cultural vibrancy, and struggle, shaped by slavery, the Jim Crow era, and the fight for civil rights. From the plantation fields of the 19th century to Black-owned businesses and political representation today, Gullah Geechee descendants have profoundly influenced the city's history and development.

—Saundra Morene
Jacksonville Gullah Geechee Nation Community Development Corporation

ACKNOWLEDGMENTS

We are indebted to the following staff and institutions whose collections, expertise, and commitment to preservation made this work possible: the Library of Congress, State Archives of Florida, Florida State College at Jacksonville, National Archives, Jacksonville Public Library, University of Florida, University of North Florida, Ritz Theatre & Museum, and City of Jacksonville, among others as noted. Each of these repositories holds invaluable stories that connect the city's people and places to a broader understanding of American history. We recognize Zora Neale Hurston and Viola B. Muse, who played a significant role in collecting stories of Florida's Black heritage.

Inspiration for this work also came from visits to national institutions, including the National Museum of African American History and Culture in Washington, DC; the A. Philip Randolph Pullman Porter Museum in Chicago, and the Schomburg Center for Research in Black Culture in Harlem. Each of these sites underscores the significance of Jacksonville's people and stories in contributing to the national narrative. This encourages us to continue making Jacksonville's rich and enduring history more widely known.

We thank local historians, archivists, and advocates Adonnica Toler, Lloyd Washington, Jerry Urso, Mitch Hemann, Imani Phillips, Peri Frances Betsch, Carol Alexander, Jennifer Grey, Heather Hodges, and Theodore Johnson for being dedicated stewards of Jacksonville's Black history. To all librarians, especially at the Jacksonville Public Library Special Collections, our sincere gratitude for the incredible work you do in making knowledge accessible. We recognize the efforts of Gullah Geechee leaders Saundra Morene and Glenda Simmons Jenkins, whose dedication to preserving the Gullah Geechee legacy in Northeast Florida is inspiring.

We are especially grateful to the communities whose stories are represented throughout these pages. Their resilience, creativity, and faith continue to define Jacksonville's cultural identity.

Finally, Ennis extends his deepest gratitude to his Gullah Geechee ancestors, known and unknown. He is humbled to contribute to telling a story that celebrates their culture and history and ensures that their legacies are shared.

Introduction

The story of the Gullah Geechee people is deeply tied to the land and waters of the southeastern coast of the United States. From the Carolinas to Northeast Florida, this region has been home to generations of people who have maintained connections to African languages, beliefs, and ways of life. Enslaved Africans forcibly brought to the coastal plantations of the Southeast and free people of color shaped a new, distinct culture that combined West and Central African traditions with the realities of life in the Americas. Over time, this shared heritage became known as Gullah Geechee, a living culture that continues to evolve while holding firm to its roots.

Jacksonville's place in the Gullah Geechee story is significant but often overlooked. It is part of the southern anchor of the federally designated Gullah Geechee Cultural Heritage Corridor. It is a city shaped by the hands of free and enslaved Africans brought to Florida and those who carried culture from Georgia and South Carolina.

The origins of this story reach back centuries to a time when the Timucua people first called this region home since time immemorial, laying foundations for a relationship with the natural environment and introducing ways of cooking, agriculture, and living with the coastal landscape. With the arrival of European colonizers in the 16th century, other cultural influences were inserted into this landscape. During Northeast Florida's first Spanish colonial period, laws were more flexible toward people of African descent, allowing some to gain freedom and establish communities. Spanish Florida also became a refuge for freedom seekers from British colonies to the north. They found protection under Spanish rule and often converted to Catholicism as part of that alliance. These early settlements laid the groundwork for the later presence of free Black communities in Florida.

When the British gained control in Northeast Florida in 1763, conditions changed. The British colonial period brought stricter racial hierarchies and the expansion of plantation agriculture. Enslaved Africans were brought in greater numbers, and the legal rights of free Black people were limited. The system of enslavement deepened during this time, shaping the labor and culture of the region. Even within this system, people resisted through cultural retention, preserving language, crafts, and spiritual practices that reflected African origins.

Maroon communities, groups of escaped enslaved people, lived in remote areas of Florida's wetlands and forests, often allying with Indigenous people. These connections were powerful acts of resistance and survival. Together, they created new societies that challenged the institution of slavery and told early stories of resistance. The United States' wars against the Seminole people were, in part, efforts to suppress these Black and Native alliances. After Spain regained control in 1784, the Gullah Geechee presence continued to evolve, and it continued to do so after Florida's entrance into the United States in 1821.

When freedom came, formerly enslaved people established settlements and neighborhoods across Northeast Florida. Gullah Geechee people built new lives on the same lands and near waterways where they had once labored. The rivers and creeks that flow through Jacksonville could be both barriers and lifelines. The water provided access, defense, and sustenance through an abundance of food. Many of these communities still exist today, linking generations who worked, worshipped, and raised families there.

In the years following the Civil War, Jacksonville became a central destination for freed people seeking opportunity in one of the growing cities along the southeast coast. They built homes, churches, and schools, creating the foundation of today's Black Jacksonville. The legacy of their work is visible in neighborhoods such as LaVilla, Durkeeville, Eastside, and Sugar Hill, among others.

Jacksonville became a center of Black excellence and advancement led by Gullah Geechee descendants. The establishment of schools was one of the community's earliest priorities. Stanton School, founded in 1868 with support from the Freedmen's Bureau, became Florida's earliest public schools for Black children. Education represented hope and progress in a world still marked by inequality. Black teachers were deeply respected community leaders, providing not only academic instruction but also civic guidance and mentorship.

Churches also stood at the center of community life. From the Reconstruction era through the 20th century, Black congregations in Jacksonville offered spiritual grounding, social support, and leadership opportunities. Churches were places where faith met action. The influence of spiritual traditions, many with deep African roots, extended beyond the church walls into the daily rhythms of life.

As the city grew, so did its neighborhoods. Gullah Geechee descendants continued establishing communities throughout Jacksonville. Each had its own character, but all reflected a shared spirit of connection. Neighborhoods were built on trust, where families looked after one another, and the front porch symbolized community. The front porch, with roots in West African design, became a hallmark of Southern homes and a continuation of the communal values that define Gullah Geechee life.

Work has always been central to the Gullah Geechee story. Gullah Geechee labor has fundamentally shaped the economic and cultural landscape of Jacksonville. Enslaved Africans brought agricultural expertise that was essential to the region's development. After emancipation, Black workers continued to build the city by laying streets, constructing buildings, starting businesses, and providing skilled labor and knowledge that fueled Jacksonville's growth.

During the early 20th century, Gullah Geechee descendants in Jacksonville found employment in a range of occupations. Many worked as domestics, cooks, railroad porters, or laundresses, while others became teachers, nurses, ministers, or entrepreneurs. The Jacksonville Red Caps, a Negro League baseball team active during the 1930s and 1940s, symbolized athletic talent and the organizational strength of Black Jacksonville. Fraternal lodges and civic groups offered structure, social support, and collective purpose during a time of segregation.

Women of Gullah Geechee descent played essential roles in the community. As one example, Black midwives, long trusted within the community, continued traditions that dated back to enslavement. Midwives provided care and cultural connection at a time when access to medical services was limited. Their knowledge, rooted in both African and local traditions, formed the foundation of maternal health care for many Gullah Geechee families.

Throughout the 20th century, Gullah Geechee communities in Jacksonville faced challenges from segregation, urban renewal, and disinvestment. Yet they remained strong. The Works Progress Administration (WPA) of the 1930s offered new opportunities for employment and introduced early documentation efforts around Black cultural heritage. Churches, schools, and community centers became anchors for organizing and protest. Resistance to discriminatory practices has a long legacy in Jacksonville.

This resistance connects to Gullah Geechee values of self-determination and collective care. The culture is grounded in family networks, mutual aid, and community pride. These values guided the historic development of the fraternal organizations, schools, and churches established in Jacksonville. Together, these institutions created systems of support that met community needs long before equal access to public resources was possible.

The bonds of community extended beyond formal institutions. Everyday life was marked by shared experience. Families gathered for meals that reflected both African and Southern influences.

Dishes like okra soup, rice, and seafood connect the coastal environment to lifetimes of culinary practice. In this sense, food serves as a form of cultural storytelling, a way of remembering who people were and where they came from.

Music, language, and faith provided other outlets for shared experience and carried those memories forward. Spirituals, gospel, and blues grew out of Gullah Geechee expressive traditions that blended African rhythms and call-and-response patterns with Christian beliefs. In Jacksonville, these forms of worship and artistry flourished, shaping the city's soundscape and contributing to broader movements in American music.

Cemeteries across Northeast Florida also speak to the enduring heritage of Gullah Geechee people. Burial practices include specific spiritual elements reflected in Western African traditions. These sacred spaces remain among the most powerful testaments to the Gullah Geechee presence in Jacksonville.

Today, many cultural heritage sites across the city help tell the ongoing story of the Gullah Geechee people in Jacksonville. The Masonic Temple in LaVilla, built in 1916, stands as a symbol of Black leadership and community organization. Stanton School reflects the long pursuit of education and equality. Churches, homes, and cemeteries across Jacksonville continue to share the lives and legacies of Gullah Geechee descendants. Visiting these places offers both a history lesson and a chance to connect with living culture.

Gullah Geechee heritage is not a relic of the past. It is an active, evolving way of life. The language, crafts, food, and faith of the Gullah Geechee people remain vital expressions of identity. In Jacksonville, these traditions appear in the gatherings that take place on porches and in church halls, at family reunions, and at community festivals. They live in the recipes passed down, the hymns sung, and the stories shared among generations.

Gullah Geechee heritage matters because it tells the story of resilience and creativity in the face of centuries of change. It offers lessons about community, sustainability, and belonging that remain relevant today. The Gullah Geechee experience shows how culture can adapt without losing its essence. Heritage can serve as both anchor and compass.

For Jacksonville, recognizing and celebrating this heritage deepens understanding of the city itself. Too many are quick to criticize Jacksonville for lacking an identity, but the reality is that the city has a wealth of identities and stories. Gullah Geechee culture is one of the most enduring and prominent identities of the city and deserves recognition as such.

Preserving Gullah Geechee culture in Jacksonville requires diligence, respect, and active participation. It means protecting historic sites and environmental resources, supporting cultural practitioners, and ensuring that descendants have the resources to tell their own stories. It also means listening to elders as experts, to the land and water itself, and to the echoes that move through the rivers and streets of Jacksonville. These stories remind us that the past is not gone. It lives in the ways people speak, cook, gather, and care for one another and the place we call home. By learning from the past, we honor those who came before and ensure that their stories, practices, and traditions continue to shape the future.

One

The People

Jacksonville, Florida, holds a unique place within the Gullah Geechee Cultural Heritage Corridor (GGCHC). The corridor is a national heritage area established by Congress in 2006 to honor a living culture that bridges African and American identities. Stretching from Wilmington, North Carolina, to St. Augustine, Florida, the GGCHC recognizes a nationally distinctive landscape shaped by natural, cultural, historical, and spiritual resources. The GGCHC centers not only on place but also on people whose language, traditions, and resilience continue to define the coastal South.

Gullah Geechee people are descendants of West and Central Africans who were enslaved and brought to work the rice, indigo, and cotton plantations of the south Atlantic coast. Over generations, the African people and their descendants developed a distinctive creole culture rooted in African worldviews and adapted to the Carolina, Georgia, and Florida Lowcountry environment. Their traditions, expressed through faith, language, foodways, architecture, and art, represent one of the most enduring African cultural legacies in the United States.

The Sea Islands, a chain of tidal and barrier islands from South Carolina to Florida, were central to the development of Gullah Geechee culture. Their relative isolation allowed African customs, language, and craftsmanship to persist long after emancipation. The GGCHC extends 35 miles inland to communities like Jacksonville, where migration, freedom, and faith continued to shape a vibrant Black cultural identity.

From early colonial settlements like Fort Caroline and Fort Mose to the tabby ruins of Kingsley Plantation, Jacksonville's landscape bears deep imprints of Gullah Geechee history. The city became a destination for freedom seekers, a center for African American education and worship, and, by the early 20th century, the largest urban center within the area today designated as the GGCHC.

Today, Gullah Geechee heritage remains alive in Jacksonville's churches, food, music, and neighborhoods. This legacy is a testament to a culture that has endured through enslavement, segregation, and urban change. This chapter invites readers to learn more about the Gullah Geechee people and their culture.

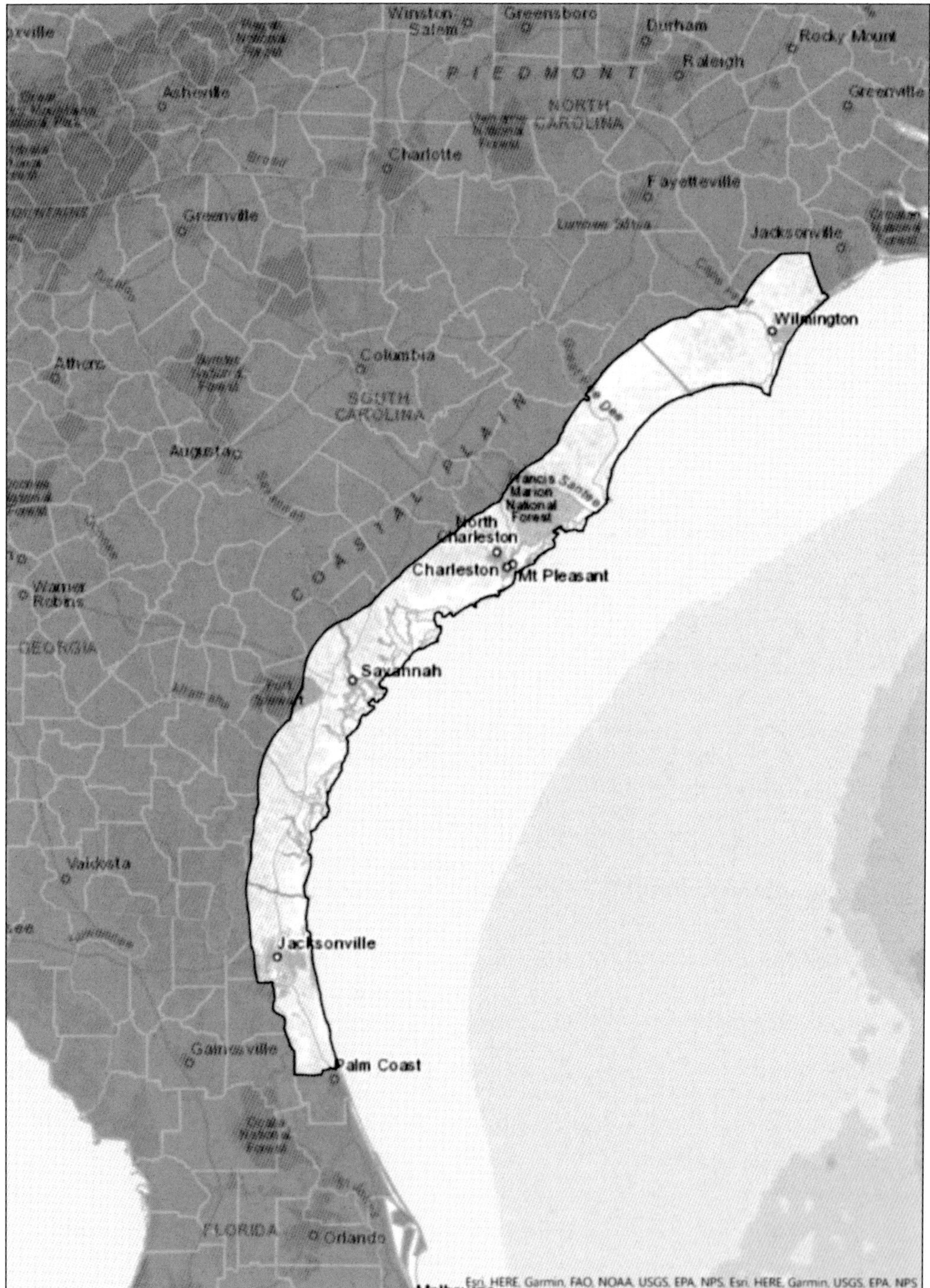

Jacksonville is the largest city within the Gullah Geechee Cultural Heritage Corridor, a national heritage area established by Congress in 2006. A national heritage area defines a geographically distinctive landscape shaped by natural, cultural, historical, and recreational resources. The GGCHC focuses on a group of people and a landscape as its subjects. (Gullah Geechee Cultural Heritage Corridor Commission.)

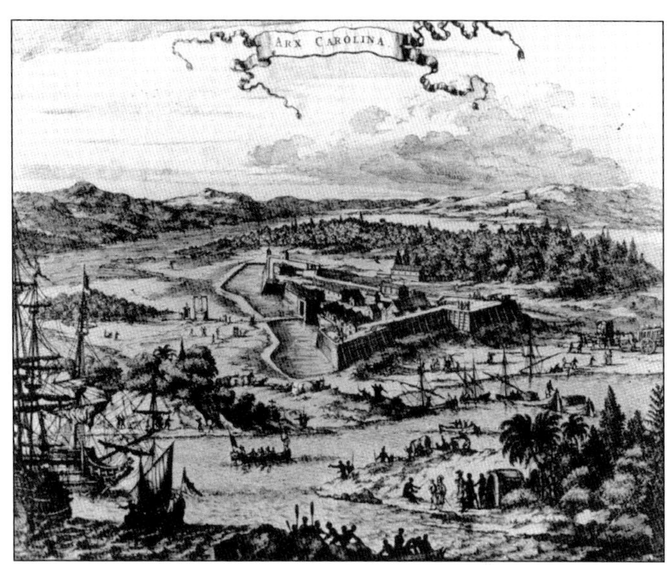

Pre-dating St. Augustine, the French settlement at Fort Caroline was established with nearly 200 settlers, including free Africans, in June 1564. It was located near the present-day St. Johns Bluff. It was destroyed in 1565 by Spanish conquistador Don Pedro Menéndez de Avilés, who had African crew members in his fleet and who founded St. Augustine. Northeast Florida represents some of the earliest stories of Black history for what would become the United States. (Library of Congress.)

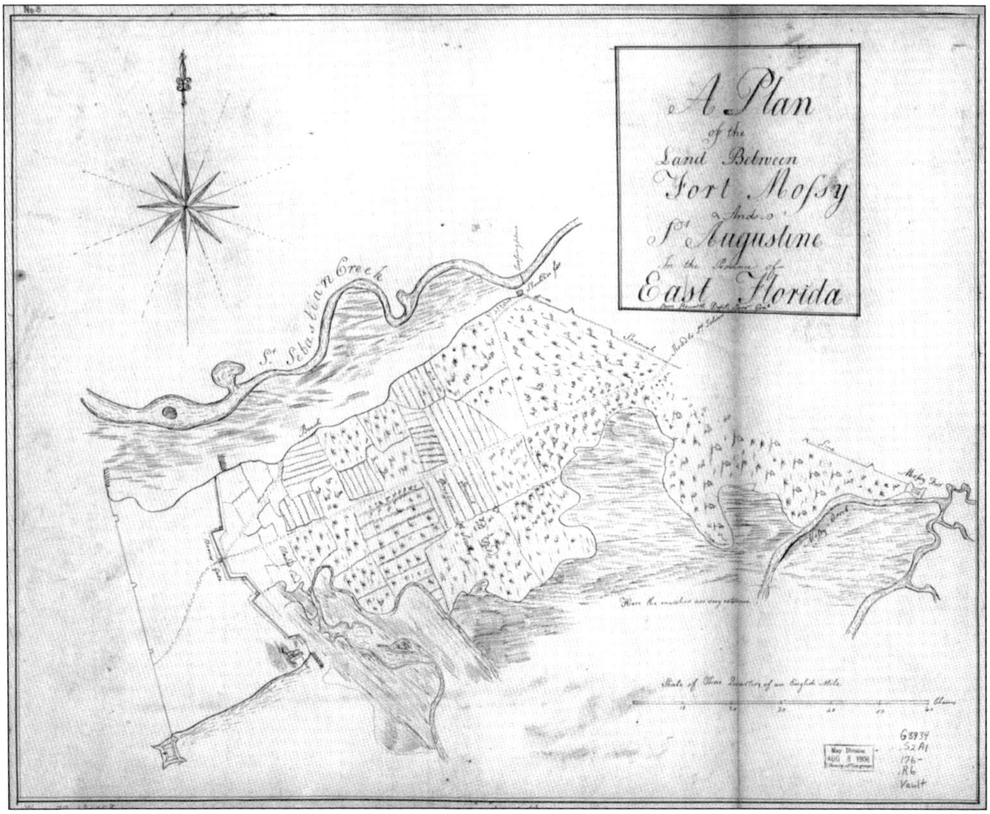

This 1760s map illustrates land between Fort Mose and St. Augustine in the Spanish province of East Florida, a destination for freedom seekers in Georgia and South Carolina. The first recorded fugitive enslaved from British Carolina escaped to St. Augustine by boat in October 1687. Fort Mose, the first legally sanctioned free Black settlement in what would become the territory of the United States, was established 38 miles south of present-day downtown Jacksonville in 1738. (Library of Congress.)

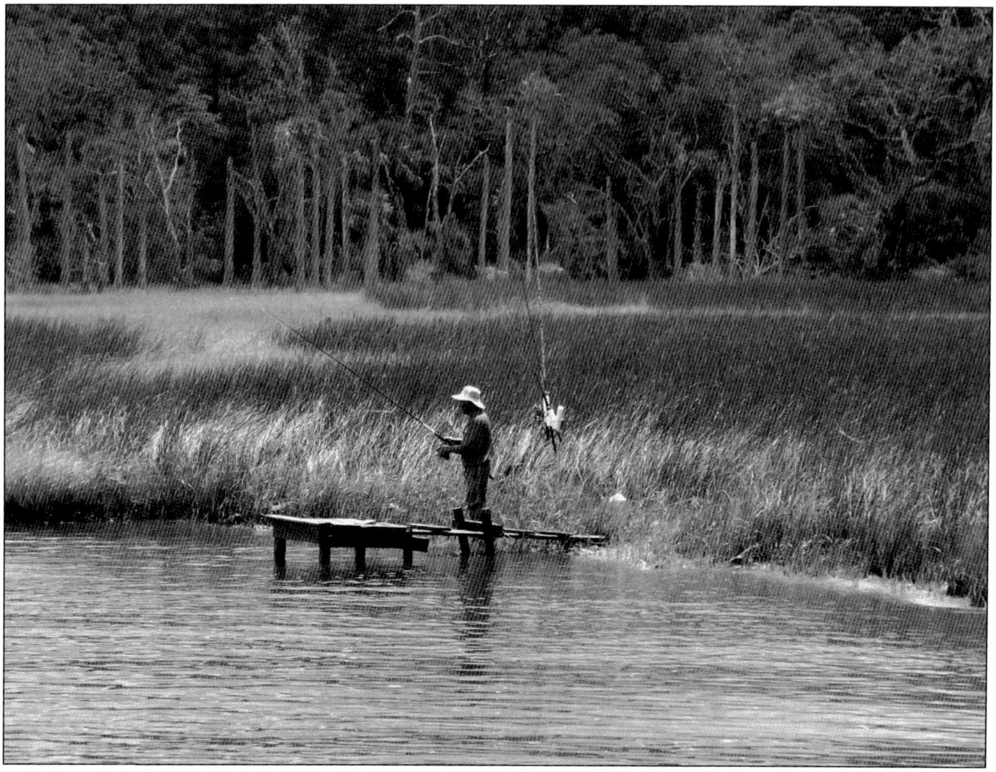

Associated with the Atlantic coastal region that stretches from Wilmington, North Carolina, to St. Augustine, Florida, the Gullah Geechee are descendants of Central and West African ancestors, many of whom arrived in America through the transatlantic slave trade. The mixing of these diverse African peoples created the creole Gullah Geechee culture, which has retained many African cultural expressions that can be experienced in Black Jacksonville's language, religious institutions, arts and crafts, architecture, music, and food. (Ennis Davis, AICP.)

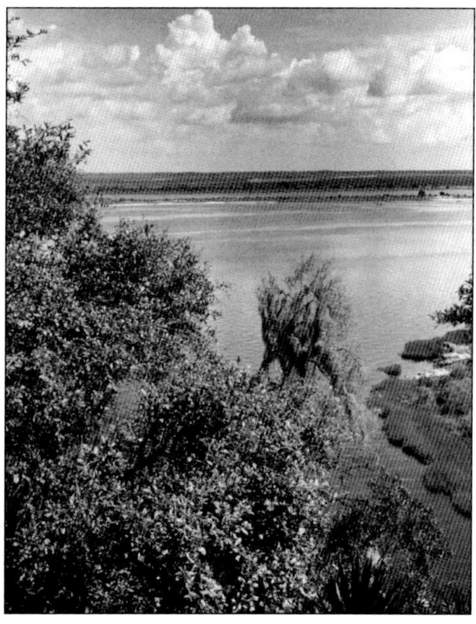

The Sea Islands are a chain of approximately 100 tidal and barrier islands stretching along the Atlantic coast from South Carolina to Florida. Following 16th-century European settlement, enslaved Africans were brought to labor on cotton, rice, and indigo plantations. From their resilience and shared traditions emerged the distinct Gullah culture and language that continue today. This is a view of Jacksonville's Sea Islands captured from the Fort Caroline National Memorial in 1959. (State Archives of Florida.)

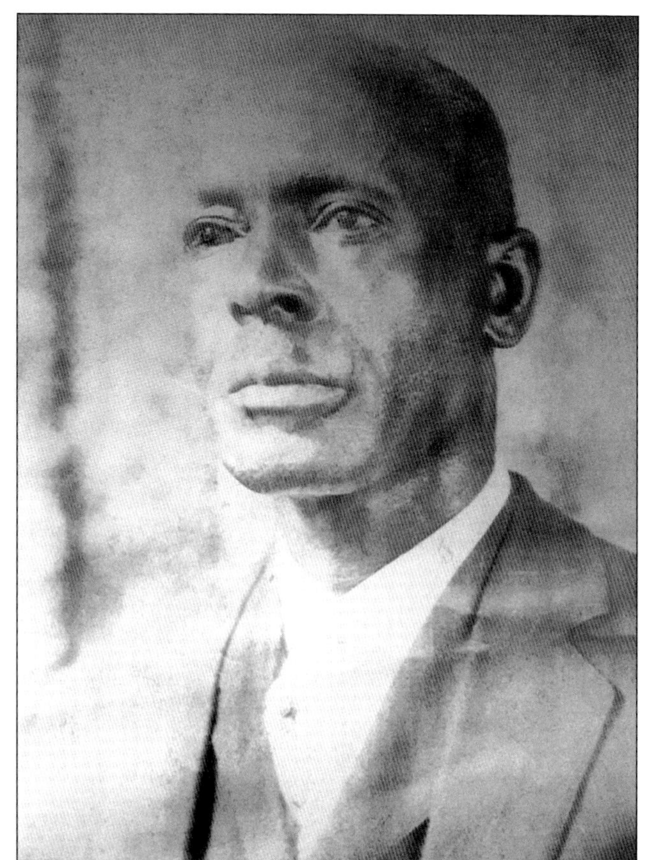

Raised in Wampee, South Carolina, Dr. Franklin Vereen (1872–1925), the maternal great-grandfather of author Ennis Davis, migrated to Florida following the Wilmington Insurrection of 1898. The term "Gullah" is believed to derive from "Angola," the homeland of many of the enslaved Africans brought through the port of Charleston. "Geechee" is linked to those near Georgia's Ogeechee River. Over time, these names merged, representing a shared yet regionally distinct culture. (Ennis Davis, AICP.)

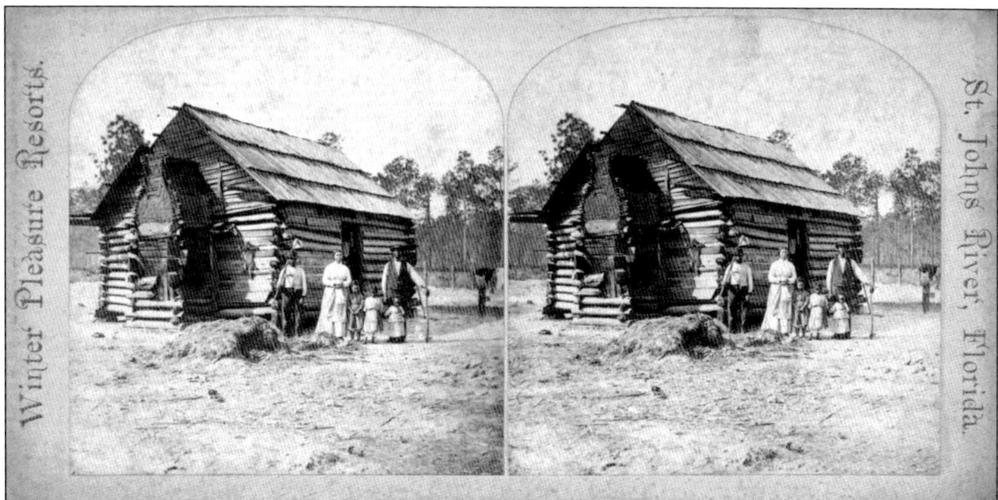

Gullah is an English-derived creole language spoken along the southeast US Atlantic coast. Linguistically, Gullah is largely traceable to English words. Sentence structure, intonation, and stress reveal more in common with languages on the west coast of Africa. Some sounds shift similarly to the Krio language in Sierra Leone. The Gullah language has influenced traditional Southern speech patterns and vocabulary and is recognized as an important linguistic contribution by Black people to America's heritage. (Jacksonville Public Library.)

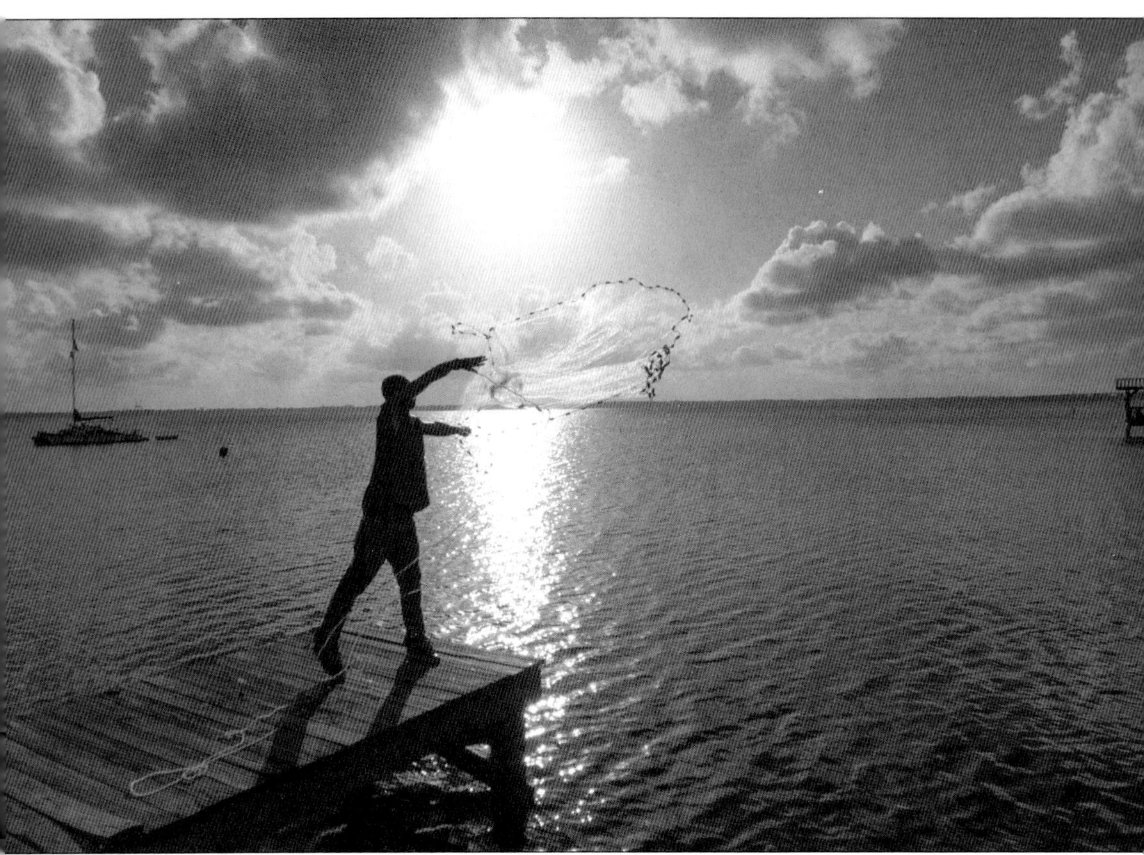

The ancestors of the Gullah Geechee people brought to America a rich legacy of African artistry, craftsmanship, and design. Their creations often blended beauty with practicality, textile arts for clothing and comfort, basket weaving for agriculture, and cast nets for fishing. This image of cast net fishing on the St. Johns River reflects that enduring tradition. Cast nets are particularly effective for catching shrimp, blue crabs, and fish used in traditional dishes like Lowcountry boils, fried shrimp, and fish. Net making remains a tangible link to the self-sufficiency and culture of Northeast Florida's Gullah Geechee community. Today, locals still cast their nets at popular spots along the St. Johns River, Heckscher Drive, the various bridges, and the Intracoastal Waterway. (City of Jacksonville.)

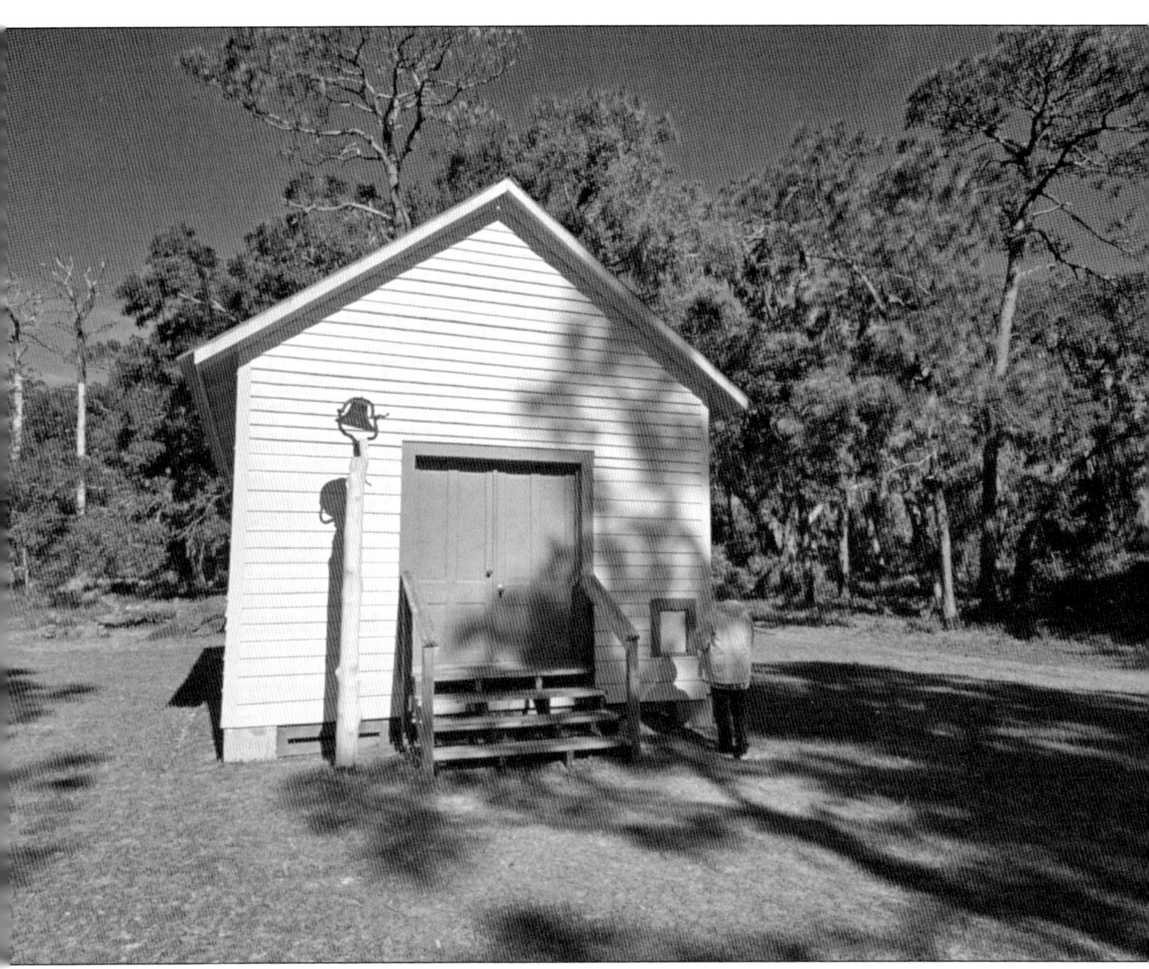

After the Civil War, Henry Leapheart journeyed from South Carolina to Jacksonville, bringing with him a remarkable talent for sculpting and designing building cornerstones, headstones, and other stonework. His craftsmanship became a family legacy, passed down to his three sons, George, Clarence, and Horace. Though all worked as Pullman porters on the railroad, they continued their artistry at home in Jacksonville's Eastside neighborhood, shaping enduring works of stone that spoke to skill and pride. The Leapheart family's craftsmanship remains visible today in historic cemeteries and churches throughout the Gullah Geechee Cultural Heritage Corridor. One notable example is the cornerstone of the First African Baptist Church at the Settlement on Cumberland Island, carved by George Leapheart in 1937. (*The Jaxson.*)

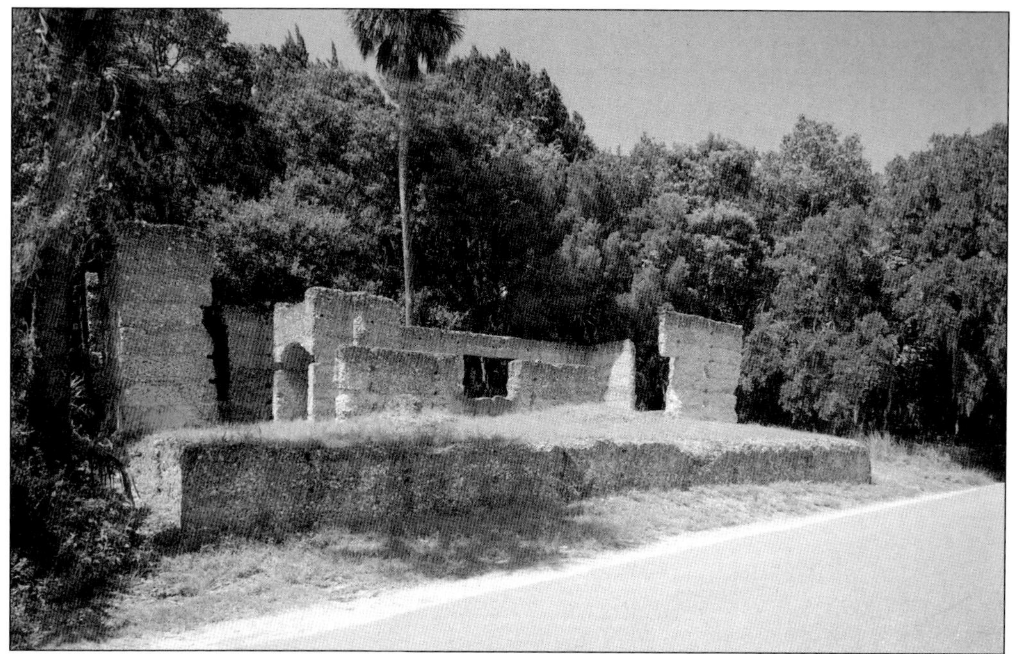

The ruins of the Charles R. Thomson House on Fort George Island, built in 1854, showcase tabby construction, an enduring symbol of Gullah Geechee heritage. Made from oyster shells, sand, lime, and water, tabby utilizes materials abundant along the Atlantic coast. Native American shell mounds or middens often provided shells, while enslaved African laborers brought and refined the techniques needed for construction. (Library of Congress.)

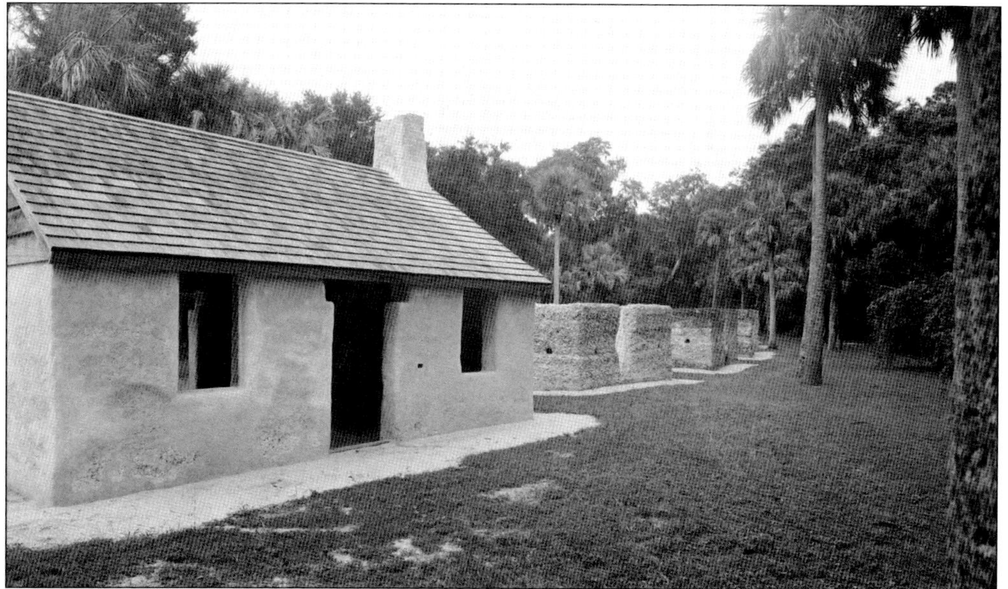

At Kingsley Plantation on Fort George Island, the enslaved quarters were arranged in a semicircle reflecting West African village patterns. Built from tabby, they housed 60 to 80 enslaved families. Enslaved laborers with specialized skills burned the shells to produce lime, then carefully mixed and poured the material in layers to form sturdy walls, structures that remain among the most significant traces of plantation life in Florida. (Library of Congress.)

Music in the Gullah community emerged from the realities of slavery and traditions carried to the Americas by enslaved Africans. Its rhythms, melodies, and call-and-response patterns laid the foundation for many American musical forms, influencing genres such as spirituals, gospel, ragtime, blues, jazz, soul, and hip hop. Shown here is an early-20th-century Jacksonville musician photographed with a banjo. The banjo originated from West African gourd-lute instruments brought to the Americas by enslaved Africans. (State Archives of Florida.)

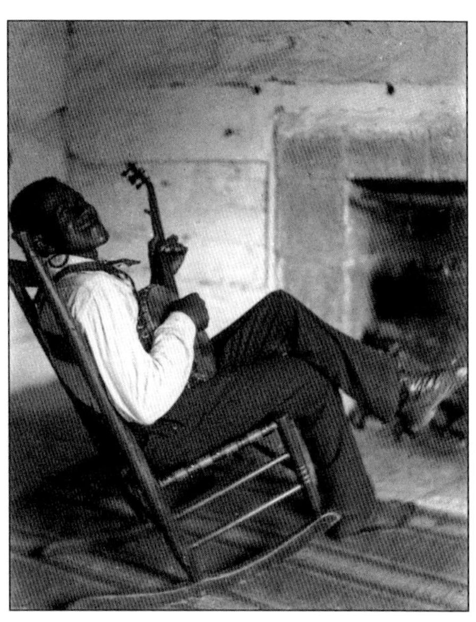

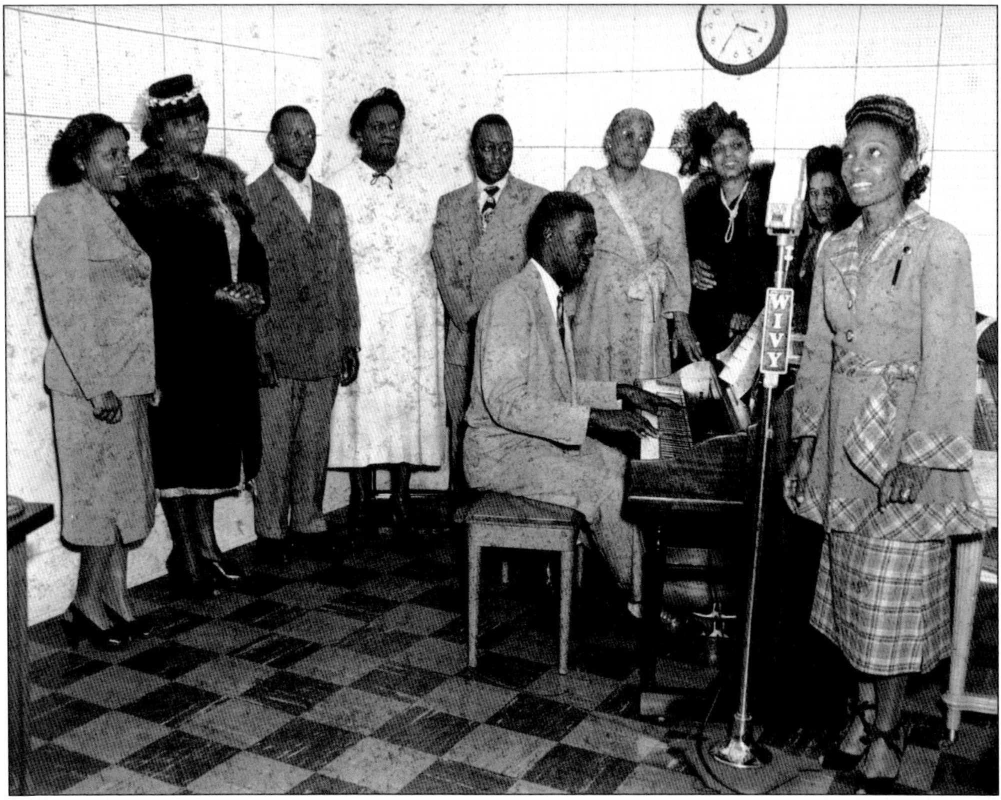

A powerful expression of Gullah Geechee culture is the call-and-response, or shout-form, musical tradition rooted in African heritage. This dynamic exchange between a leader's call and the congregation's response became central to Black religious services and influenced gospel, jazz, and blues, as illustrated in this Ethel Davenport gospel performance. In Jacksonville, with its many historic churches, call-and-response singing and rhythmic preaching continue to thrive, preserving a living link between African traditions and contemporary worship. (Ritz Theatre & Museum.)

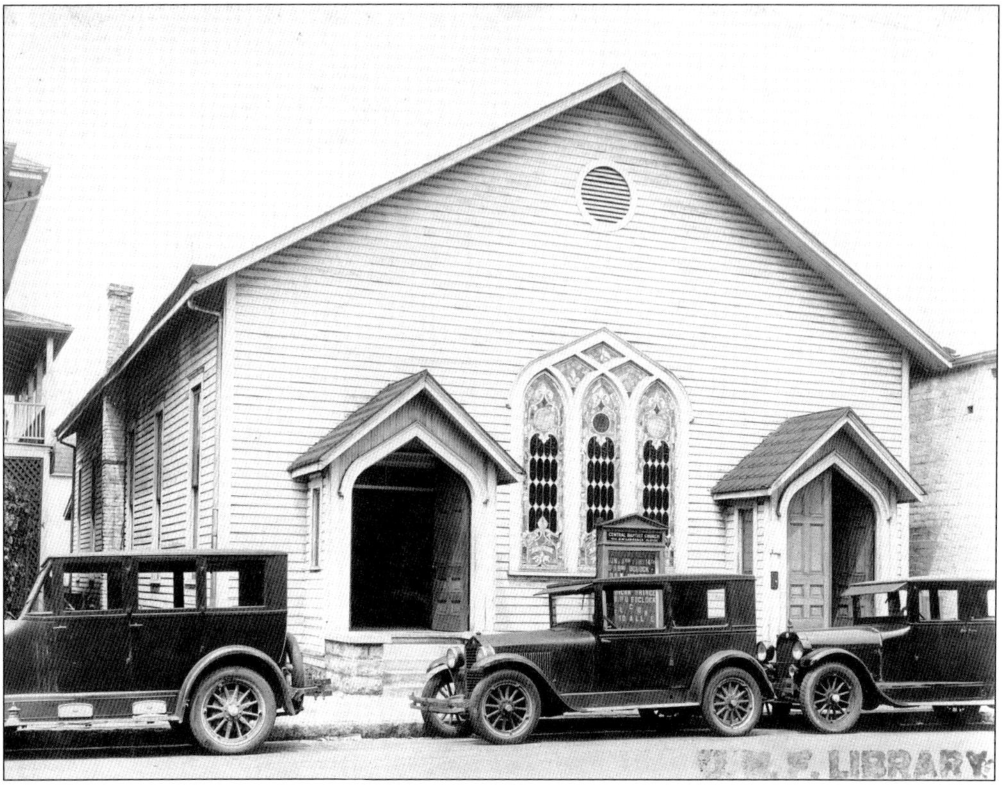

A photograph of the Central Baptist Church at 115 West State Street illustrates that religion and spirituality have long sustained Jacksonville's Gullah Geechee community. Enslaved Africans encountered Christianity, blending its teachings with African-rooted beliefs and traditions. Central to their faith is a deep reverence for God, community over individuality, respect for elders and ancestors, strong kinship bonds, and harmony with nature. (Special Collections, Thomas G. Carpenter Library, University of North Florida.)

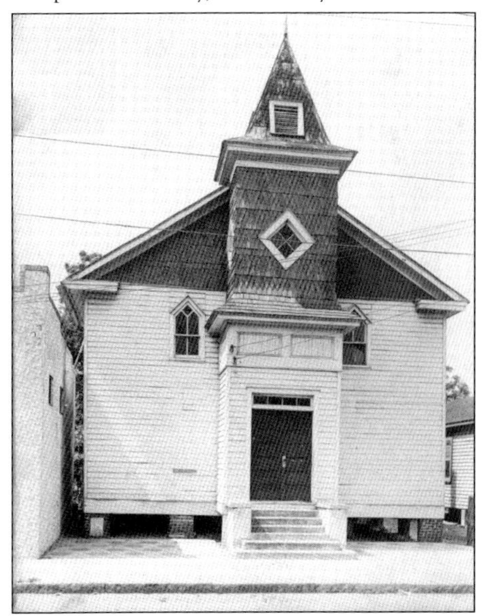

Praise houses and brush arbors were worship spaces that served as a place for Gullah Geechee people to gather and worship. Praise houses date to the plantation era, when enslaved people gathered in an elder's home or a specially designated building for religious services. The buildings were usually small, wood-framed structures, such as the St. Luke Baptist Church at 1440 East Church Street. These spaces evolved into the more elaborate churches of the 20th century. (Special Collections, Thomas G. Carpenter Library, University of North Florida.)

Gullah Geechee folk tales have served both to educate and entertain. Various stories tell of talking animals, mythical creatures, and people with supernatural powers. The stories could have been used to guide escape, explain the origin of the universe, provide instruction, or share delight. Culturally, many of the tales are connected to West African tales. Told over time, these folk tales created social and cultural continuity. An 1895 illustration of Br'er Rabbit is shown here. (A.B. Frost.)

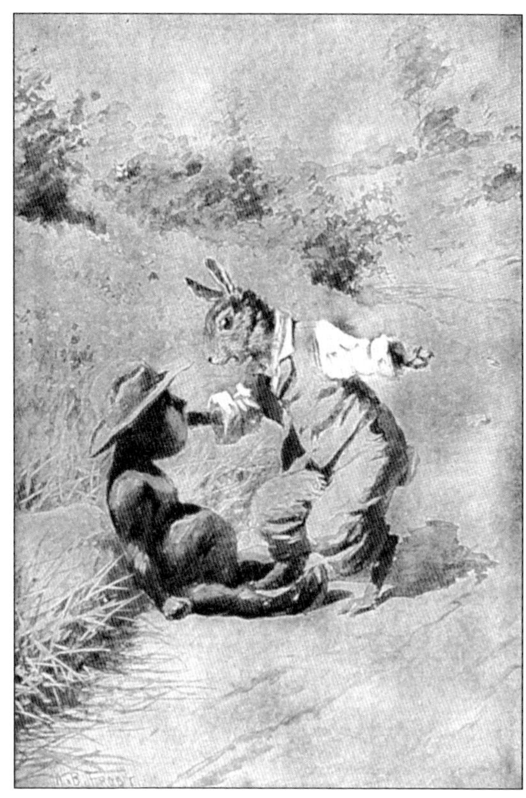

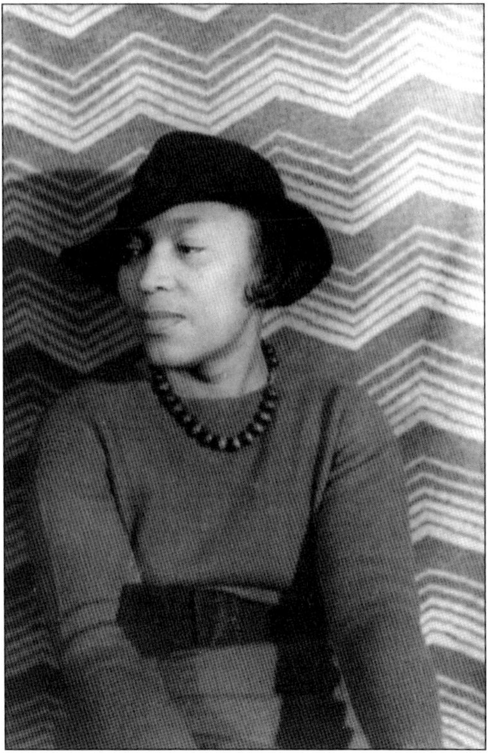

Raised in Eatonville, Florida, Zora Neale Hurston (1891–1960) became a celebrated writer, anthropologist, and folklorist of the Harlem Renaissance. After her mother's death, she moved to Jacksonville, where she lived, visited, worked, and found inspiration throughout her life. Hurston collected Gullah Geechee folk songs such as "Oh, the Buford Boat Done Come." Preserved at the Library of Congress, these recordings offer a glimpse into the musical and cultural traditions of the Gullah Geechee people. (Library of Congress.)

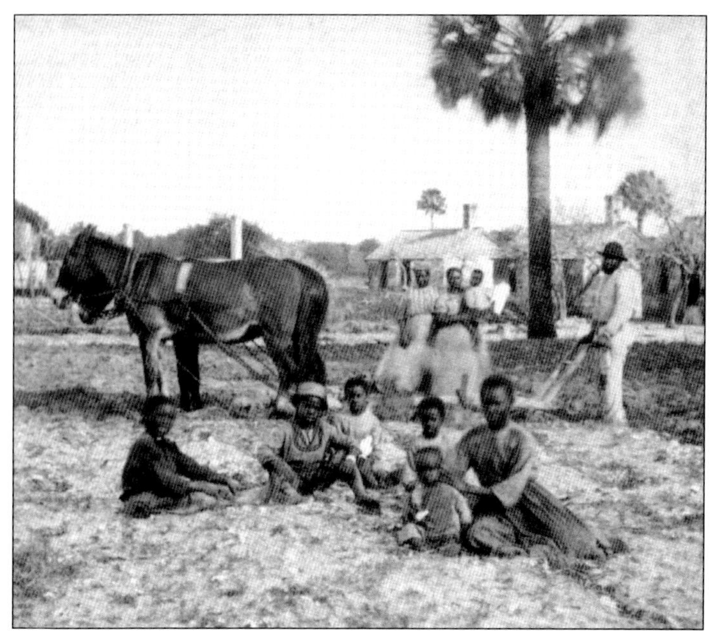

Kingsley Plantation was established in 1797. Born in Africa and enslaved by Zephaniah Kingsley in 1806, Gullah Jack was later sold South Carolinian Paul Pritchard. By 1821, he lived in Charleston and aided Denmark Vesey's revolt to free the enslaved and sail to Haiti. Described as a powerful sorcerer and root doctor, Gullah Jack was captured and executed in 1822. However, he remains revered for his spiritual power, resistance, and enduring African cultural legacy. (Ritz Theatre & Museum.)

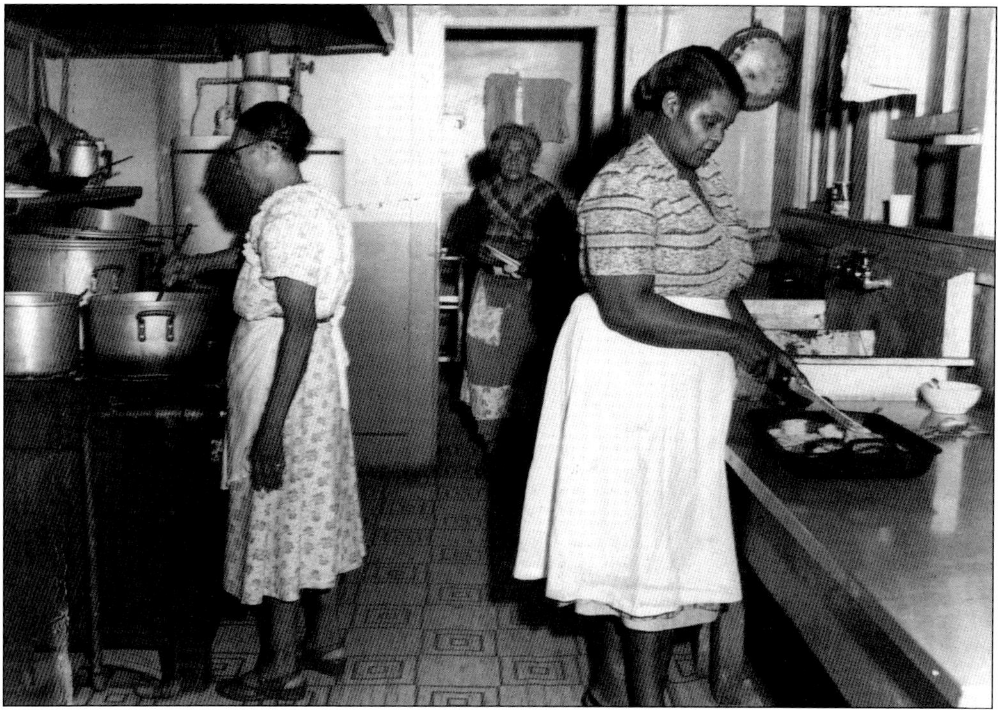

The Gullah Geechee diet included vegetables, fruits, game, seafood, and livestock, along with African crops like okra, rice, hot peppers, and yams and Native American staples like corn, berries, and tomatoes. African cooking methods, seasonings, and communal food traditions shaped daily life. Because the enslaved were plantation cooks, much of today's Southern cuisine originates from their creativity and culture. Here, Annie James, Jennie Hart, and Bertha Wilbert cook in the kitchen at Mercy Hospital. (Special Collections, Thomas G. Carpenter Library, University of North Florida.)

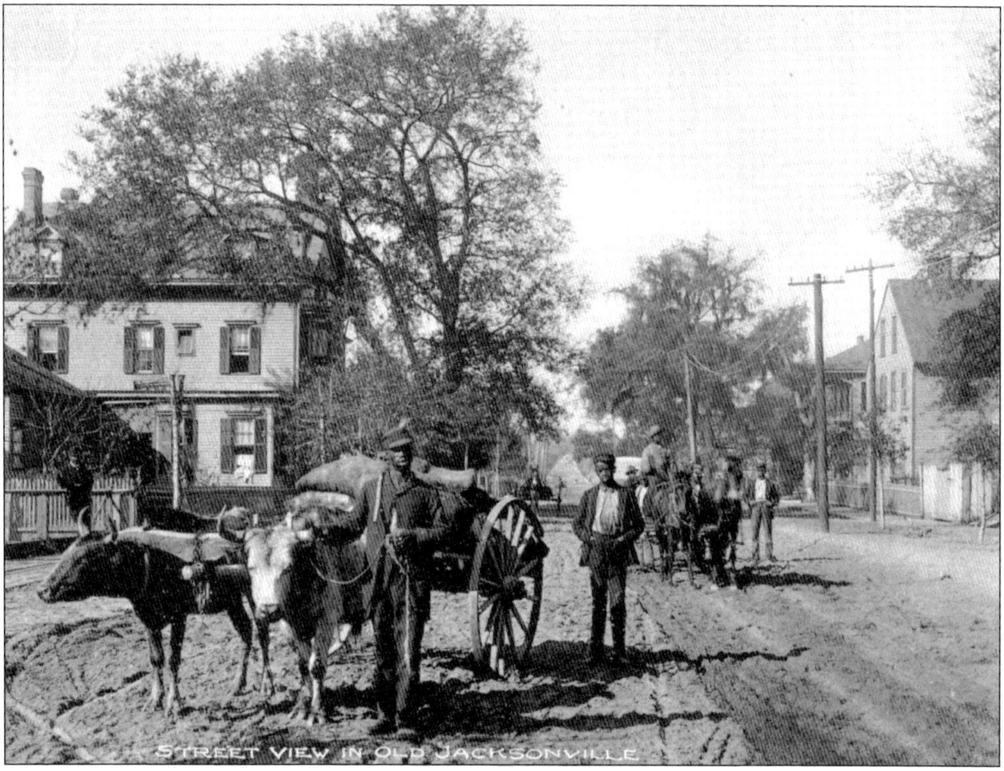

STREET VIEW IN OLD JACKSONVILLE

Jacksonville exemplifies a Gullah Geechee Cultural Heritage Corridor city that prospered after the Confederacy's defeat. Following the Civil War, it evolved into a regional railroad hub and Gilded Age resort destination. Experiencing swift growth, Jacksonville surpassed Wilmington in population by 1895 and overtook Savannah and Charleston in the early 1900s. By 1915, it was the largest city in the corridor, and by the time of this 1897 street scene, it was already the most populous city in Florida. (Library of Congress.)

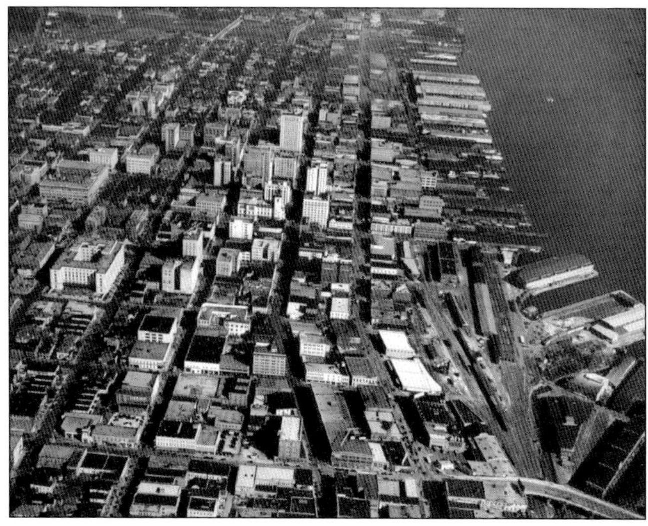

Known as the "Magic City" by Gullah Geechee descendants in Florida, Georgia, and South Carolina, Jacksonville grew rapidly, from 28,429 residents in 1900 to 129,549 by 1930. By July 2024, its population had reached 1,009,833. Though some traditions, like sweetgrass basket weaving, are rarer today, Gullah Geechee heritage continues to flourish in the local landscape, foodways, music, architecture, and faith communities, remaining central to the city's cultural identity. (University of Florida.)

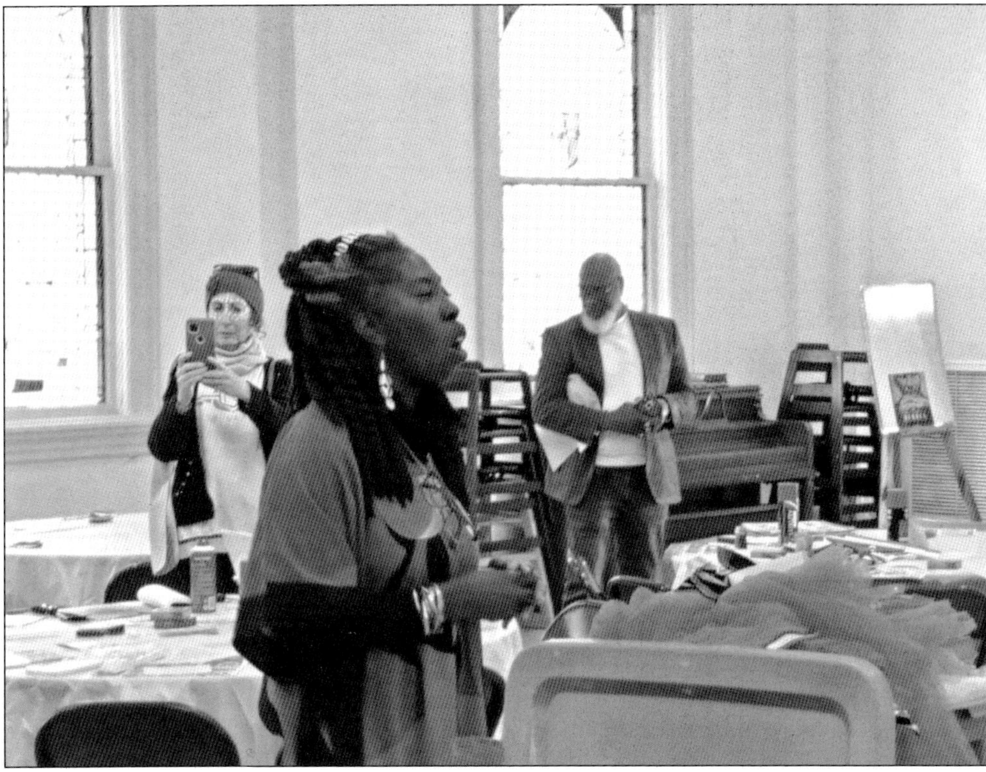

The Gullah Geechee Nation stretches from Jacksonville, North Carolina, to Jacksonville, Florida, encompassing the Sea Islands and lands reaching 30 miles inland to the St. Johns River. Long regarded as a "nation within a nation," the Gullah Geechee people declared their sovereignty in 2000, electing Queen Quet as their first chieftess and head of state. (Ennis Davis, AICP.)

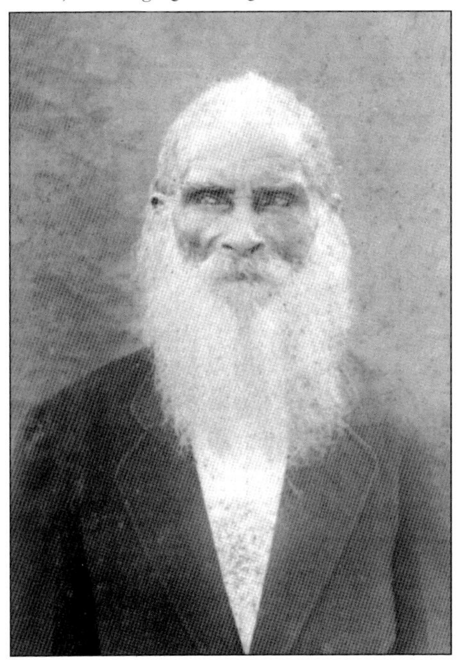

Rev. Henry Harrison (1803–1917), better known as Father Harrison, was once enslaved at the Harrison Plantation on Amelia Island. He came to Jacksonville when the area was known as Cowford. Born to an Indigenous mother, he spoke the native language and witnessed the Seminole Wars. It was said that he had a natural instinct for medicine and that he cured some of the most complicated diseases. He eventually moved to Greenland, south of Jacksonville, where he accumulated a large tract of land. (Special Collections, Thomas G. Carpenter Library, University of North Florida.)

Two

The Past

The story of Jacksonville's Gullah Geechee heritage begins long before the city itself. This heritage is rooted in the layered histories of Indigenous peoples and the shifting layers of European colonial rule. Northeast Florida occupies a unique place within the Gullah Geechee Cultural Heritage Corridor, shaped by cultural encounters that unfolded differently here than in the British-ruled Carolinas or Georgia. For example, free African Moors were present with the French at the establishment of Fort Caroline in 1564. The Spanish colonial system in Northeast Florida left distinct legacies. During the first Spanish period, slavery operated with some pathways toward freedom. Enslaved Africans could petition for manumission and marry within the church, and escapees from British Carolina and Georgia found refuge.

Many enslaved in Northeast Florida had been brought from South Carolina or Georgia, while others were directly from Africa and the Caribbean, sustaining cultural continuities. Florida's waterways and proximity to Seminole communities offered further possibilities for escape and autonomy. Maroon settlements took root in swamps and along rivers, where Gullah Geechee people blended African, Seminole, and Spanish traditions. The region was also tied to the "Saltwater Railroad," with maritime routes enabling movement and communication for freedom-seekers.

Urban slavery in Jacksonville looked different from plantation slavery. Enslaved people labored not only in fields and forests but also as pilots, stevedores, carpenters, masons, and mill hands, placing them at the heart of the city's growth. The Civil War transformed these dynamics. When federal troops occupied Jacksonville in 1862, hundreds of enslaved people fled to Union lines. More than a thousand men from Northeast Florida, enslaved and free, enlisted in the US Colored Troops.

These foundations carried into the Reconstruction era and early 20th century in Jacksonville: the rise of tourism in the 1870s–1890s, the devastation of the Great Fire of 1901, and the Great Migration. The Acosta and Mathews Bridges physically connected the growing city, even as migration networks linked Jacksonville's Gullah Geechee descendants to New York and beyond. This chapter explores these foundational stories that define Jacksonville's Gullah Geechee heritage.

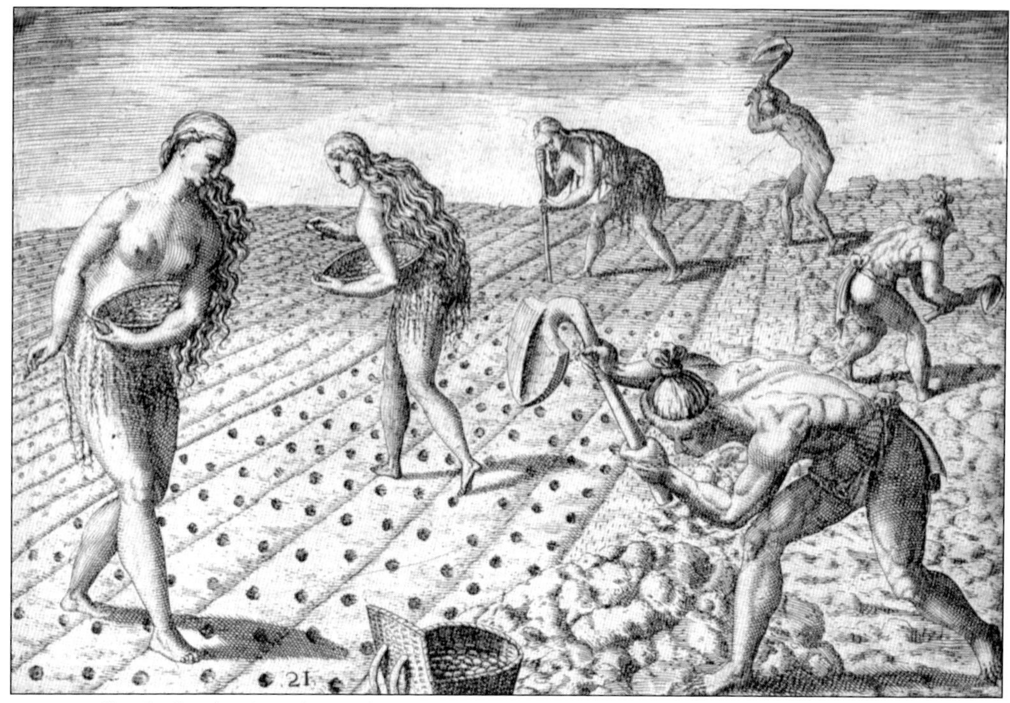

Historically, the land referred to today as Jacksonville, Florida, is on the traditional homelands and territories of the Timucua and their ancestors. The state of Florida today is home to the Seminole, Miccosukee, Muscogee, and Choctaw people and to individuals of many other Native groups. In Jacksonville, the Mocama people are a specific group of the Timucua people who lived here and spoke Mocama, which is a dialect of Timucua. *Mocama* means "the sea." (Library of Congress.)

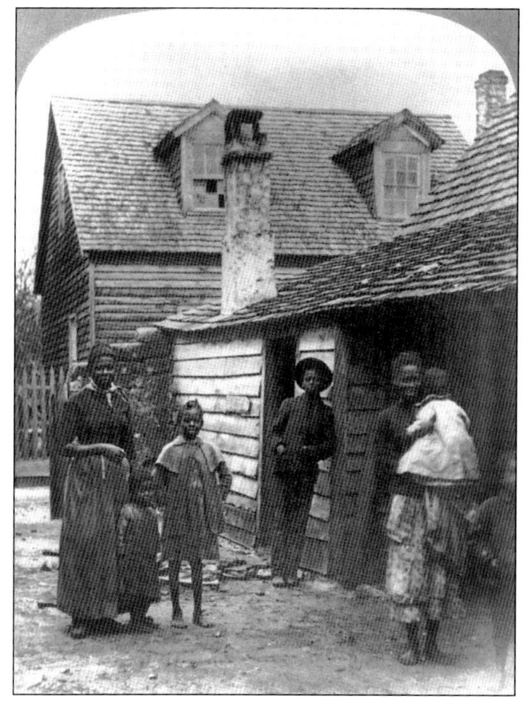

This 19th-century stereograph shows African Americans in St. Augustine. Northeast Florida experienced two Spanish colonial periods, from 1513 to 1763 and 1784 to 1821. Spanish laws were generally more flexible toward people of African descent. Enslaved Africans could purchase freedom, and free Black people held property and legal rights. During the first Spanish period, Florida was a refuge for freedom seekers from the British colonies. (Library of Congress.)

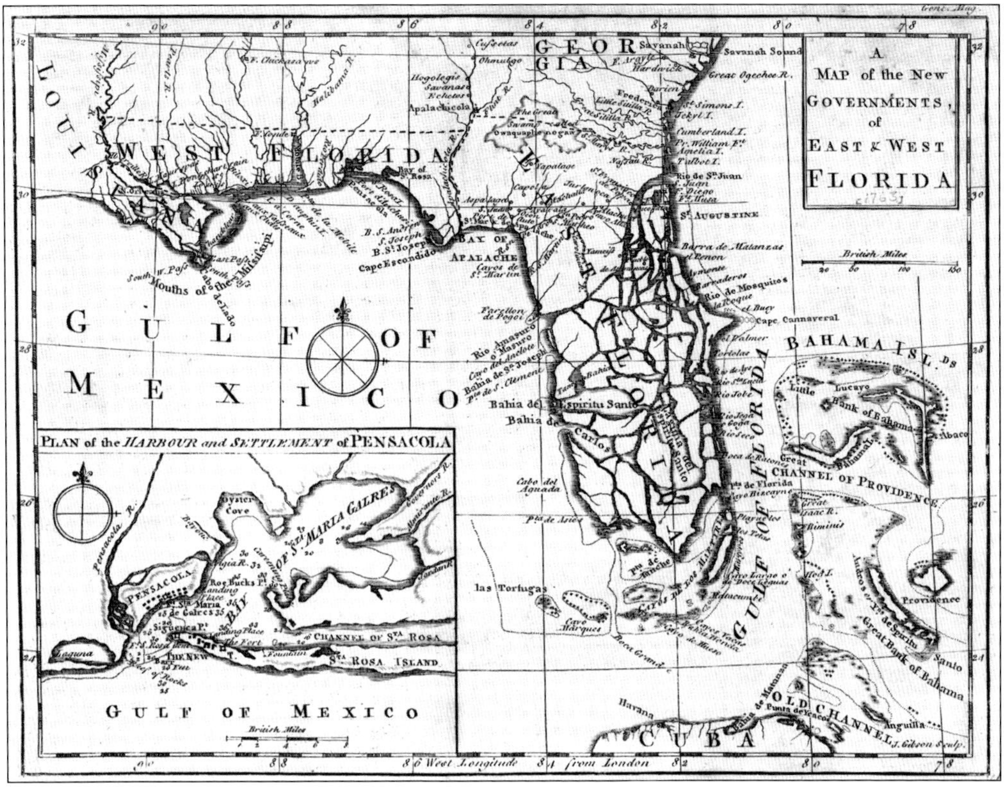

During the British period (1764–1783), Florida became a more restrictive environment for people of African descent. The British expanded plantation agriculture, increasing the demand for enslaved labor. Harsh slave codes modeled after those in South Carolina and Georgia replaced the more flexible Spanish rule. Freedom for Black people became rare, and those previously free under Spanish law often faced re-enslavement or were forced to flee the colony. This map depicts Florida in 1763. (State Archives of Florida.)

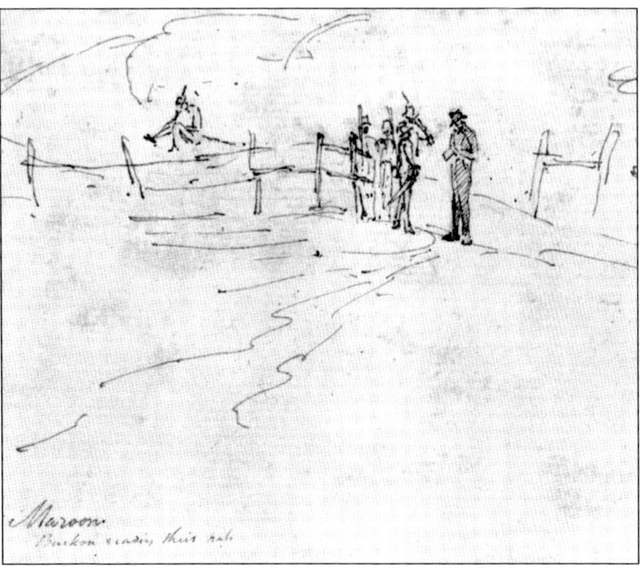

Enslaved people joined with Indigenous people in "maroon" settlements. After colonial rule ended, Florida became part of the United States. Andrew Jackson, who directed the forced removal of Indigenous people in Florida, is the namesake for Jacksonville. US military campaigns against the Seminoles sought to suppress Maroon communities of freedom seekers who lived independently or alongside the Seminoles. This 1808 drawing shows a White man (*buckra*) reading the freedom papers of Maroons on a road. (Library of Congress.)

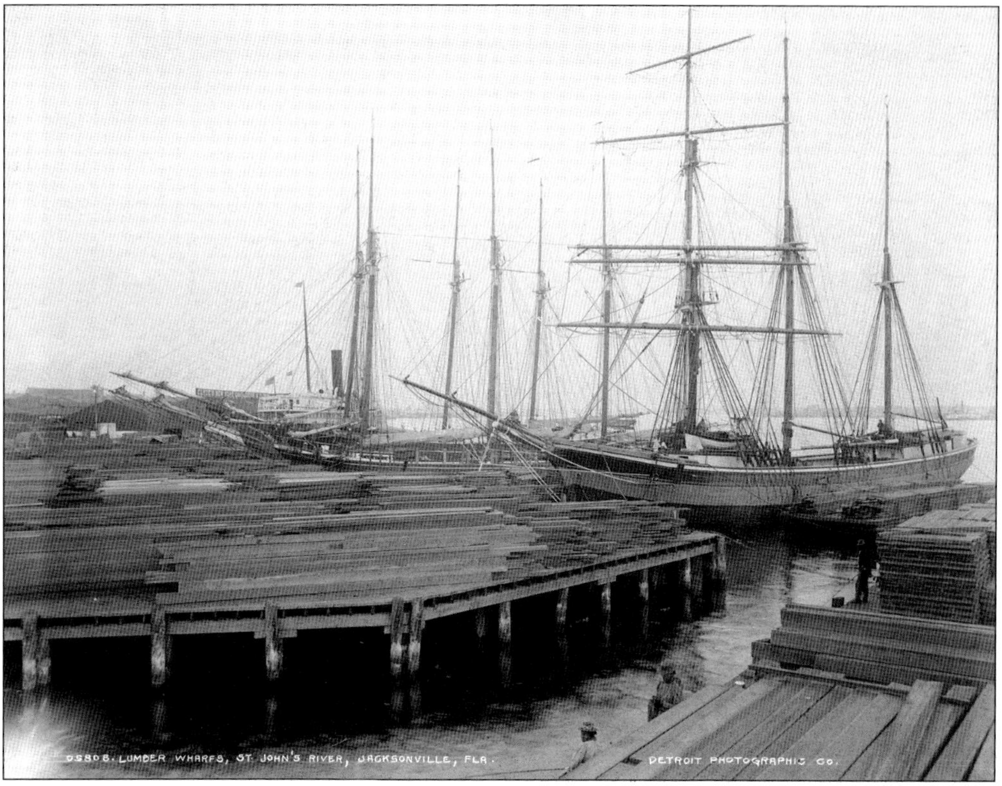

Founded in 1822, Jacksonville grew into a hub for shipping agricultural products from surrounding plantations to market. The lumber trade fueled Northeast Florida's growth, as vast forests and strong demand from the North and the Caribbean shaped the economy. By the 1850s, rafts, barges, and steamboats carried lumber to sawmills in Jacksonville. (Library of Congress.)

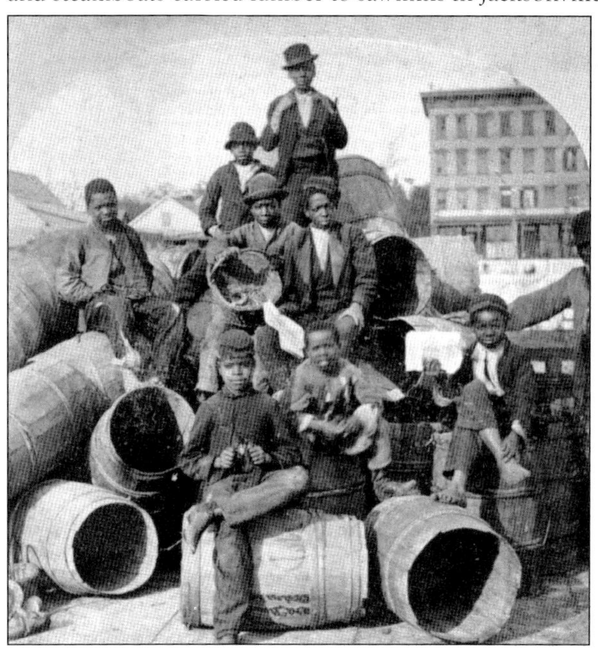

As a bustling river port, Jacksonville developed into a city shaped by enslaved laborers who worked as loggers, turpentine workers, river pilots, stevedores, carpenters, masons, and mill hands. From 1842 to 1860, its population expanded from 450 to more than 2,100, surpassing St. Augustine as Northeast Florida's leading center and port. (Ritz Theatre & Museum.)

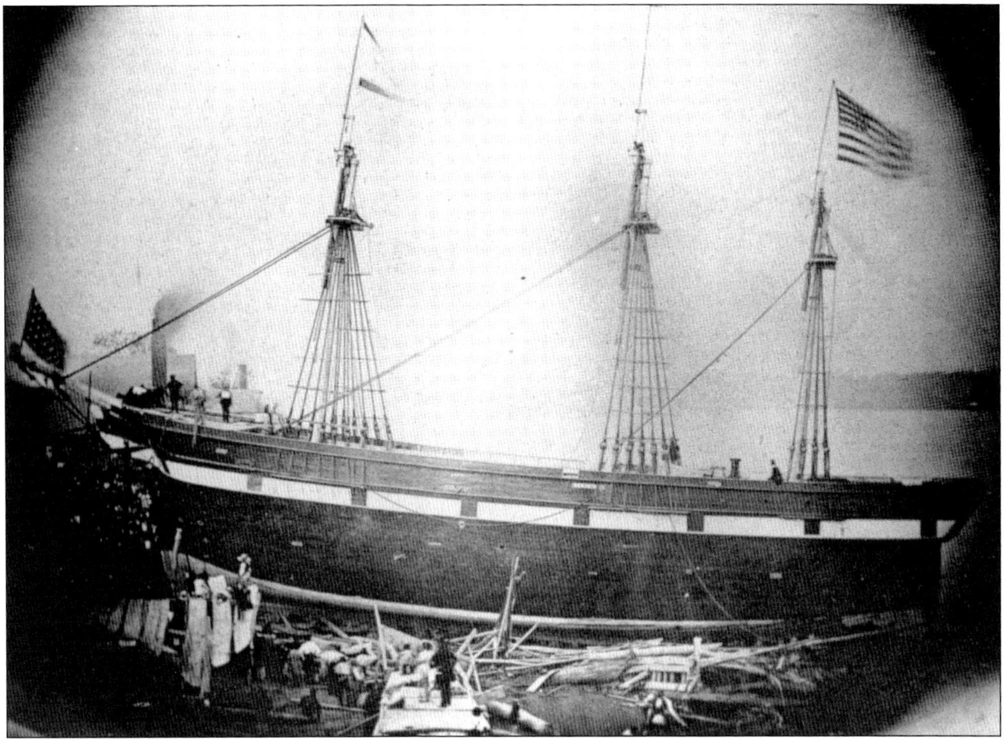

Enslaved people were sometimes permitted to hire themselves out. They may not have always acted as their enslavers had intended. Jacksonville's wharves welcomed self-hire enslaved, who sometimes seized opportunities to stow away on northern-bound vessels and escape. An enslaved man in the possession of merchant Thomas O. Holmes hired himself and worked as a stevedore before stowing away on the Boston schooner *Matilda in* 1855. (Missouri History Society.)

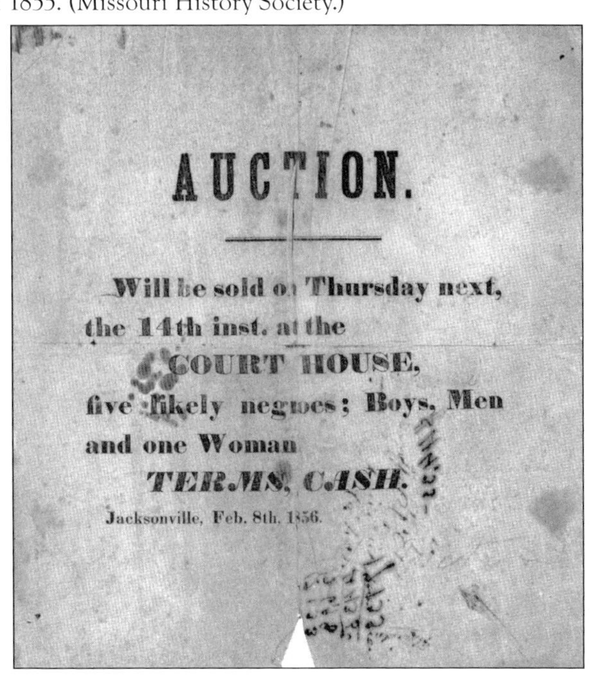

AUCTION.

Will be sold on Thursday next, the 14th inst. at the COURT HOUSE, five likely negroes; Boys, Men and one Woman

TERMS, CASH.

Jacksonville, Feb. 8th, 1856.

This 1856 auction notice advertised the sale of enslaved people at the Duval County Courthouse at Forsyth and Market Streets. Jacksonville's expanding economy depended heavily on enslaved labor. An 1856 assessment underscored this reality: the value of enslaved people in Jacksonville was $277,020, second to real estate assessed at $430,255. These figures reflect the scale of human bondage in Jacksonville and the central role slavery played in shaping the city's early economy. (State Archives of Florida.)

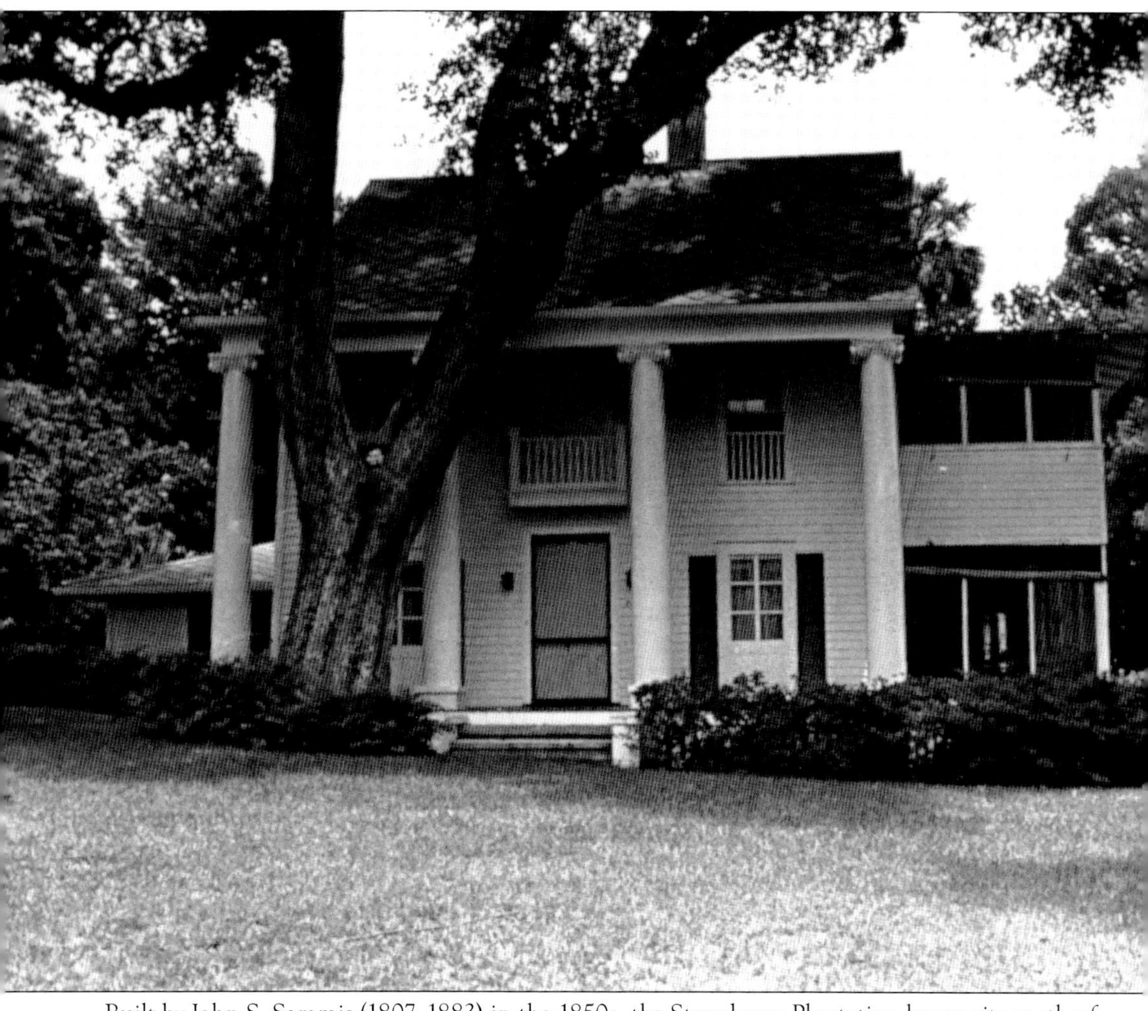

Built by John S. Sammis (1807–1883) in the 1850s, the Strawberry Plantation house sits south of the Mathews Bridge in Arlington. Sammis moved to Florida to work for Zephaniah Kingsley and Anta Madjiguène Ndiaye and married their daughter, Mary Kingsley. His 8,000-acre Strawberry Plantation along the St. Johns River and Pottsburg Creek produced cotton, rice, and other crops, and included a lumber mill, cotton gin, gristmill, and brickyard whose enslaved Africans made bricks used in downtown Jacksonville. Sammis later freed some of the enslaved and supported the Union during the Civil War. Later, a neighborhood was built around the house and family cemetery. It was listed on the National Register of Historic Places in 1979. (Florida Division of Historical Resources.)

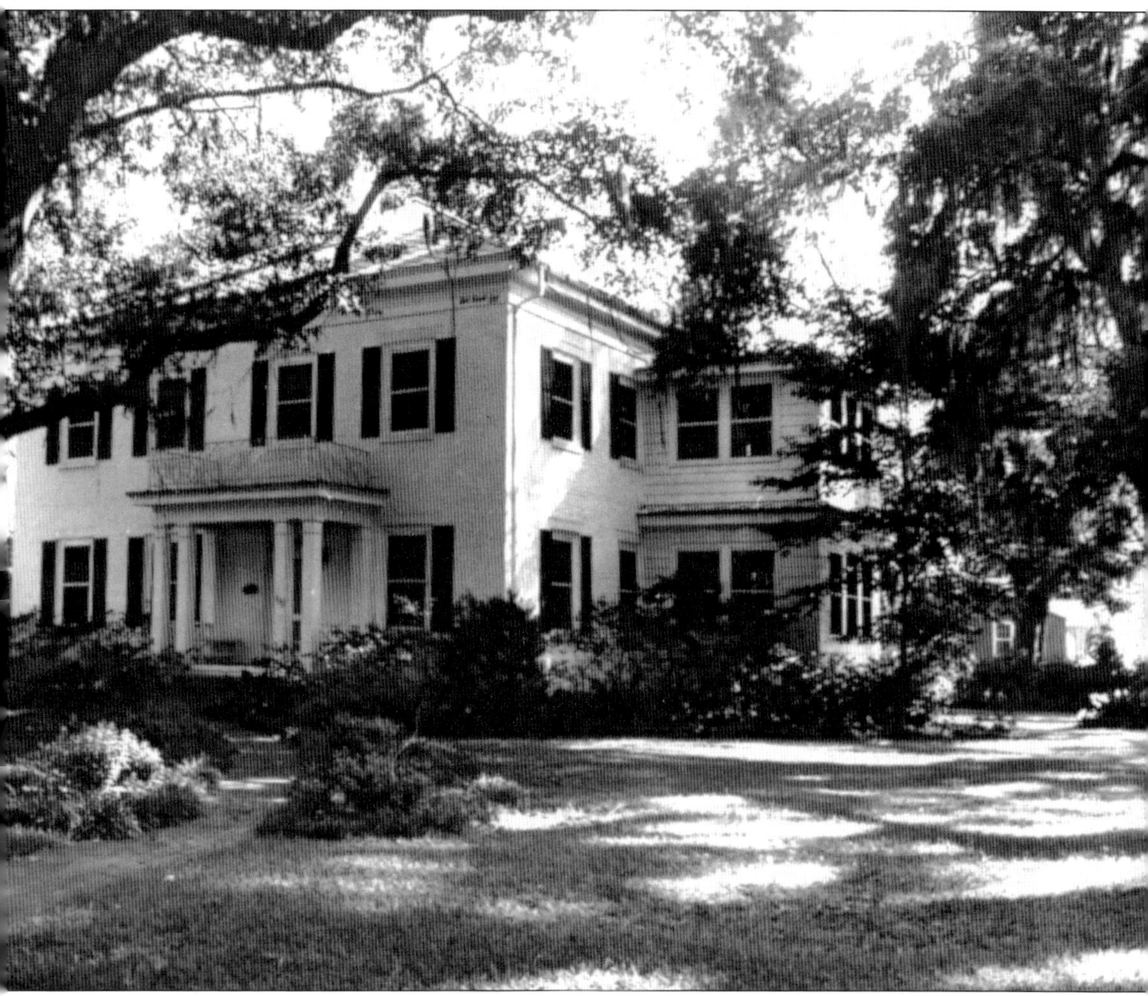

Nestled within the Colonial Manor subdivision, the former Red Bank Plantation house is Jacksonville's second-oldest continuously occupied residence. Built between 1854 and 1857 by planter and Duval County sheriff Albert Gallatin Philips, the home stands on what was once a 450-acre plantation dating to the late 18th century. Over the years, the property passed through several notable owners, including William Craig, Isaiah D. Hart (founder of Jacksonville), and Isaac Hendricks (namesake of Hendricks Avenue). Albert's son, Henry B. Philips, later lent his name to Philips Highway. Following the Civil War, the Philips family retained the house while the surrounding land was subdivided and developed, giving rise to the Colonial Manor neighborhood, which continues to surround this piece of Jacksonville's early history. (Florida Division of Historical Resources.)

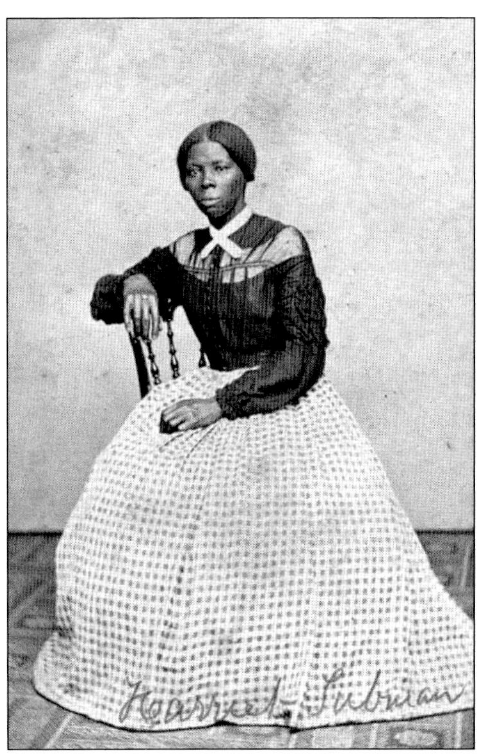

During the Civil War, Jacksonville came under Union control four times. The third occupation in March 1863 included two of the first Black regiments organized in the Union army, the 1st and 2nd South Carolina Colored Infantry. Shown in 1868, Harriet Tubman aided the Union's capture of the city. Nurse Susie King Taylor also served, teaching soldiers to read. These troops later became the 33rd and 34th US Colored Infantry, with veterans settling throughout Jacksonville after the war. (Library of Congress.)

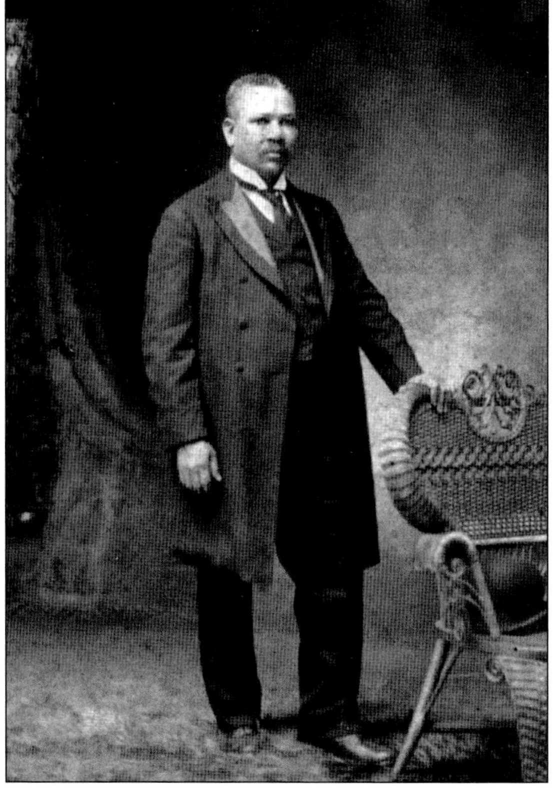

Albert Sammis served in the 1st South Carolina Volunteer Infantry, later reorganized as the 33rd US Colored Infantry Regiment. Sammis was the grandson of plantation owner Zephaniah Kingsley Jr. and his enslaved wife, Anta Madjiguène Ndiaye. Pension records show that at least 17 fellow soldiers throughout the Gullah Geechee Cultural Heritage Corridor knew Sammis before his enlistment. After the Civil War, Sammis maintained ties with fellow veterans, including Susie King Taylor, the pioneering Gullah Geechee nurse and educator from coastal Georgia. (Special Collections, Thomas G. Carpenter Library, University of North Florida.)

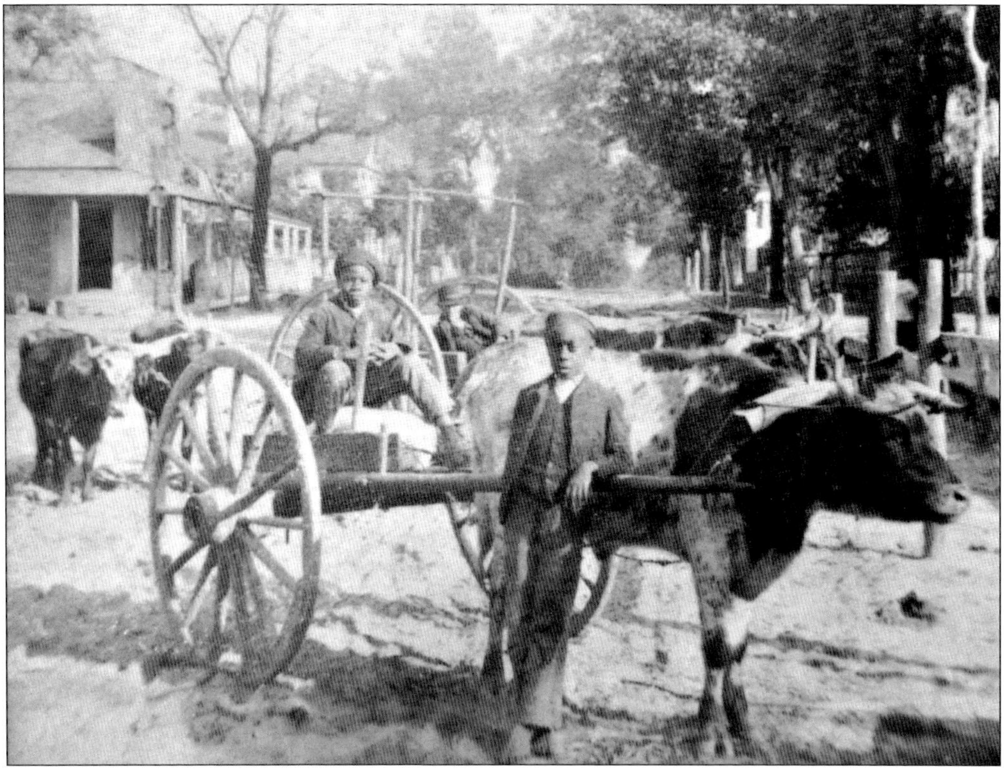

This picture captures a Jacksonville street scene in 1897. For Gullah Geechee descendants in Florida, Georgia, and South Carolina, Jacksonville was known as the "Magic City" during an era when Black Americans flocked to the city seeking economic opportunities. By 1900, Black Americans made up 57 percent of Jacksonville's population, setting it apart from the racial demographics of other Southern cities at the time. (Jacksonville Public Library.)

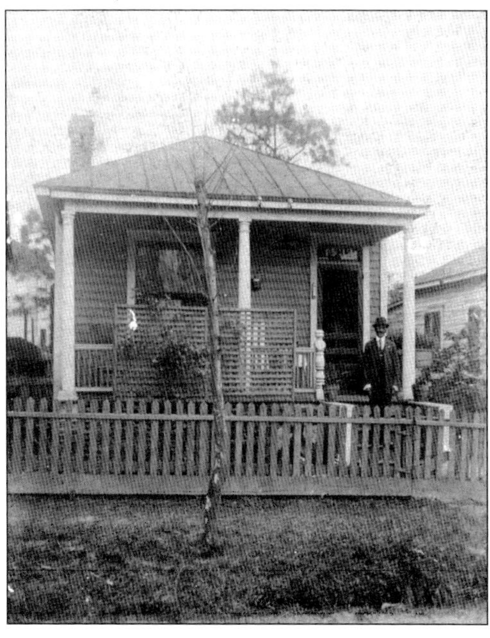

Shotgun homes, known for their long, narrow design, one room wide and several deep, originated in Haiti during the 1700s, blending West Indian and West African influences. After the Haitian Revolution, migrants brought the style to New Orleans, where it spread across the American South. Affordable and adaptable, these homes became staples of Jacksonville's working-class Gullah Geechee neighborhoods, often featuring decorative porches and trim that reflected evolving architectural trends. (Special Collections, Thomas G. Carpenter Library, University of North Florida.)

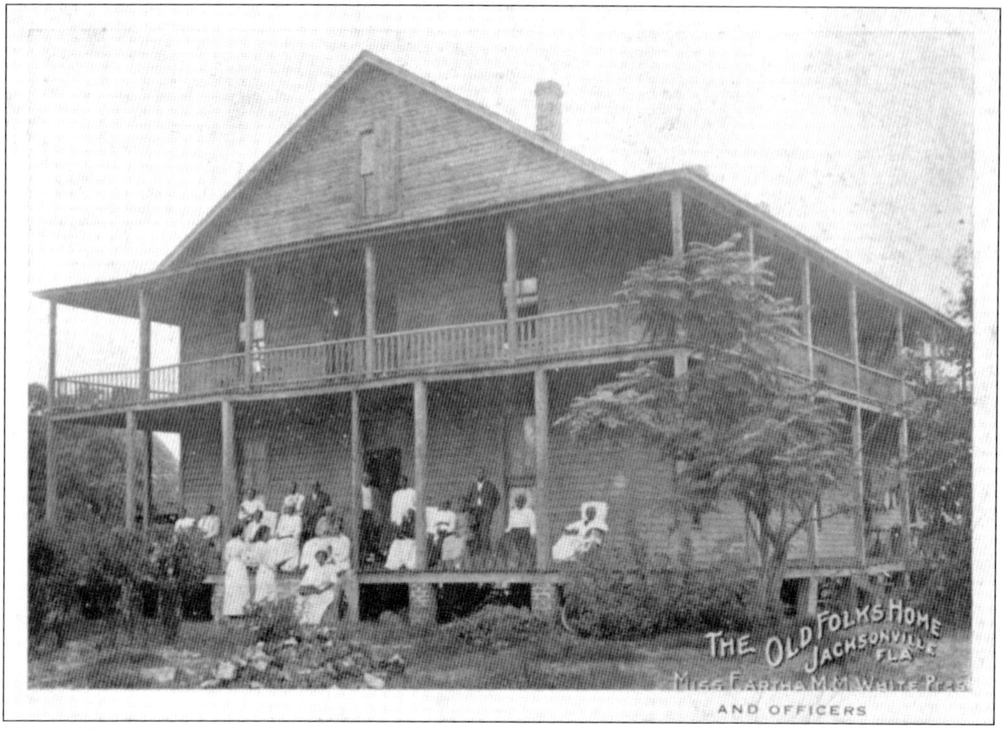

The modern front porch traces its origins to the Yoruba people of West Africa, whose architectural traditions carried through the transatlantic slave trade. In the American South, porches became vital spaces for community gathering, storytelling, and spiritual reflection, offering comfort and protection in the region's hot and humid climate. Here, residents pose for a photograph on the front porch of the Old Folks Home. (Special Collections, Thomas G. Carpenter Library, University of North Florida.)

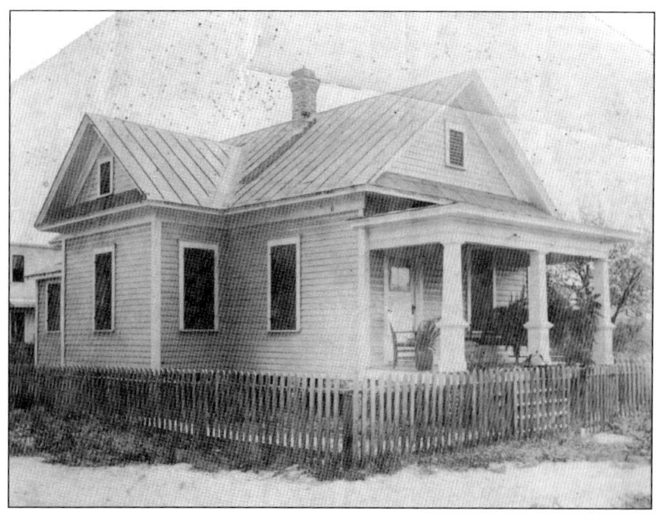

This early-20th-century shotgun house was built by Joseph Haygood Blodgett in Durkeeville. Born into slavery, Blodgett arrived in Jacksonville in the 1890s with just $1.10. After the Great Fire of 1901, he built 258 houses, keeping 199 as rentals, and became one of Florida's first Black millionaires. Today, Durkeeville holds the largest collection of surviving structures designed and built by Blodgett. (Thomas G. Carpenter Library, University of North Florida.)

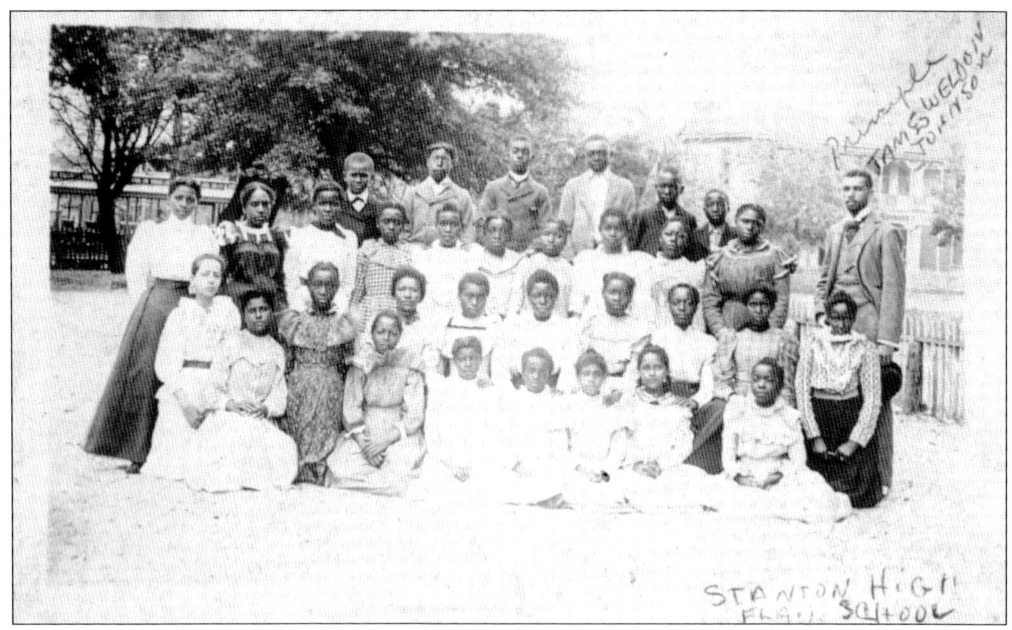

In 1900, James Weldon Johnson wrote "Lift Ev'ry Voice and Sing" in Jacksonville as a poem set to music by his brother, John Rosamond Johnson. First performed by 500 students at Jacksonville's Stanton Institute, it celebrates faith, freedom, and resilience. Named the "Negro National Anthem" by the NAACP in 1919, the song endures as a powerful symbol of Black pride. Here, Stanton principal James Weldon Johnson is photographed with his students. (Yale University.)

Jacksonville's Great Fire of 1901 destroyed 148 city blocks, killed seven people, and left 8,677 homeless. It is the third-largest urban fire in American history behind the 1906 San Francisco Earthquake and the Chicago Fire of 1871. It only took the city two years to rebuild, ushering in a new era of growth and opportunity for Gullah Geechee people in Northeast Florida and those who migrated to the city from Georgia and South Carolina. (Jacksonville Public Library.)

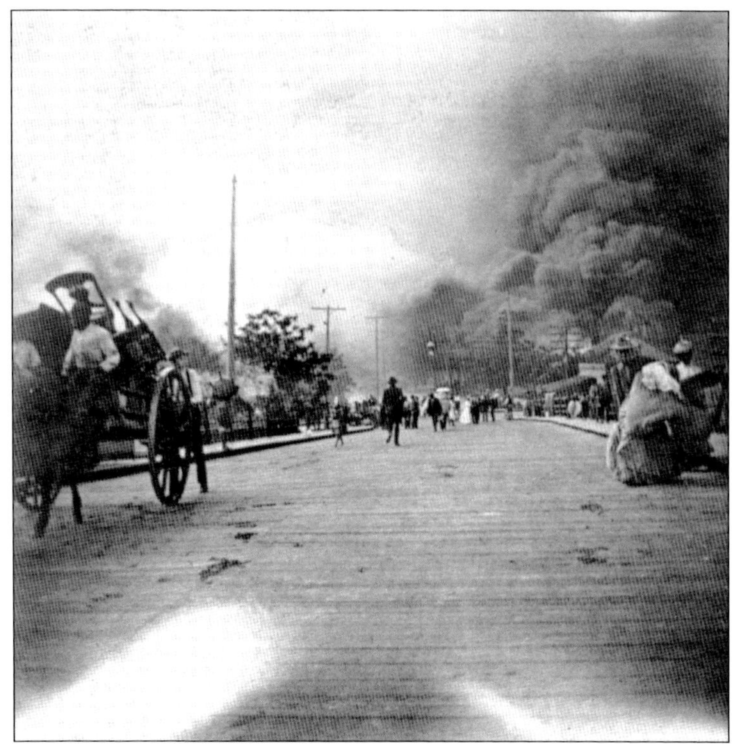

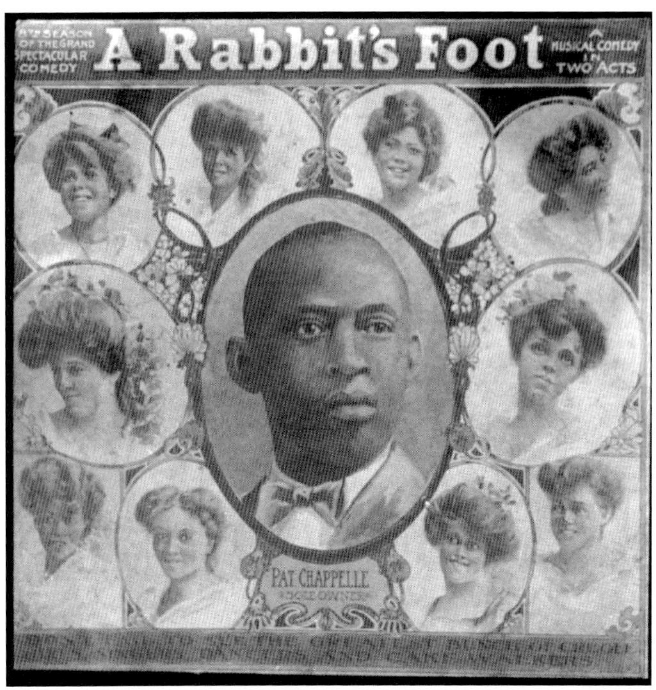

Born in Jacksonville's LaVilla neighborhood in 1869 to parents from South Carolina, Pat Chappelle rose from performing in saloons to founding the Rabbit's Foot Company in 1900, headquartered in LaVilla. This traveling vaudeville show made him known as "the Black P.T. Barnum" and one of the largest Black employers in entertainment. Launching stars like Ma Rainey and Bessie Smith, Chappelle also opened Jacksonville's Excelsior Hall in 1898, one of the South's first Black-owned theaters. (Special Collections, Thomas G. Carpenter Library, University of North Florida.)

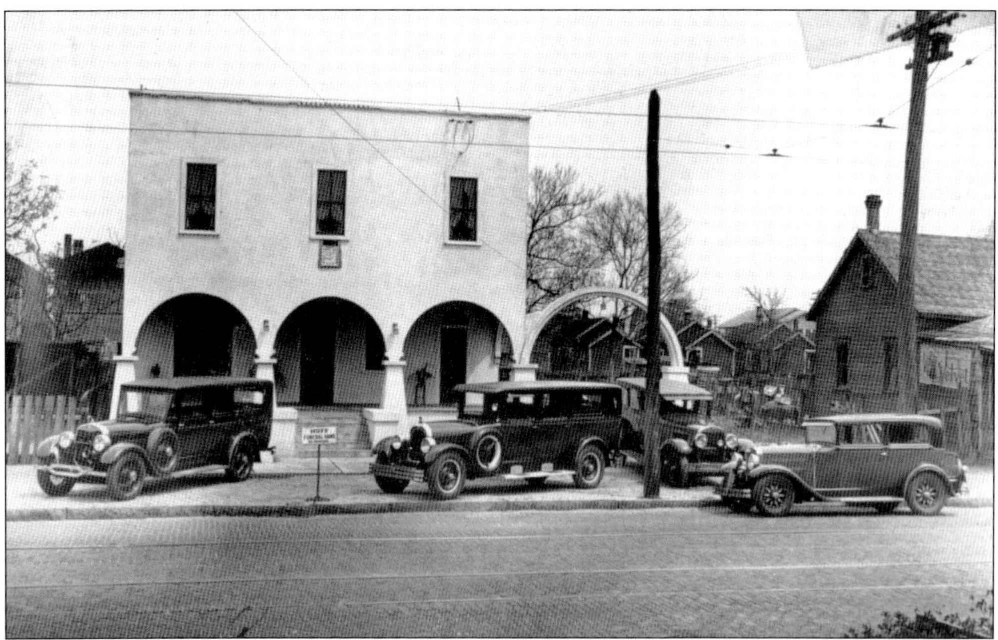

In 1903, the North Jacksonville Street Railway, Town & Improvement Company began serving the Black community. Founded by Black leaders, it was known as "the Colored Man's Railroad." Operated by Black conductors, the line remained vital to Black riders until it closed in 1936. Here, tracks can be seen on Davis Street near Huffs Funeral Home in Hansontown. The Davis Street line spurred the growth of neighborhoods that became the heart of Northwest Jacksonville. (Special Collections, Thomas G. Carpenter Library, University of North Florida.)

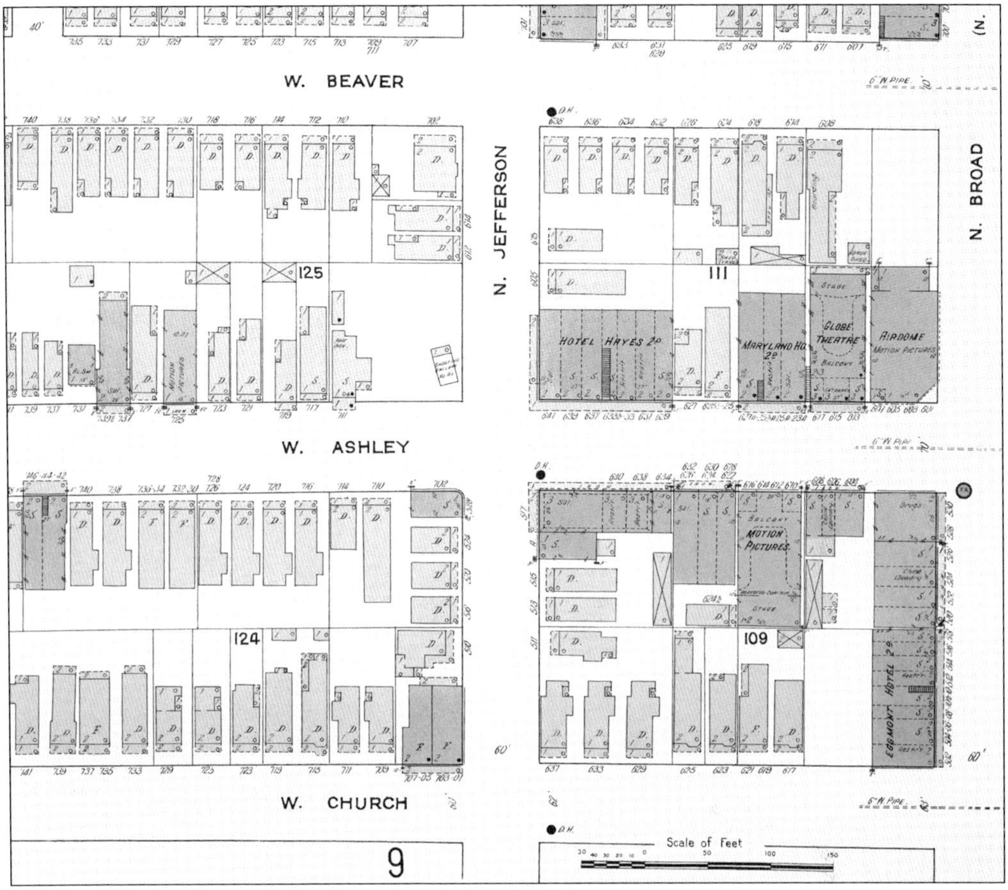

Opened in 1909 on Ashley Street and shown in this 1913 Sanborn fire insurance map, the Colored Airdome was celebrated as the South's largest theater for African Americans. In 1910, it hosted the world's first documented public blues performance. The venue also popularized the "Jacksonville Rounder's Dance," later known as the Black Bottom Dance, which became America's top social dance after its Broadway debut in 1926. (University of Florida.)

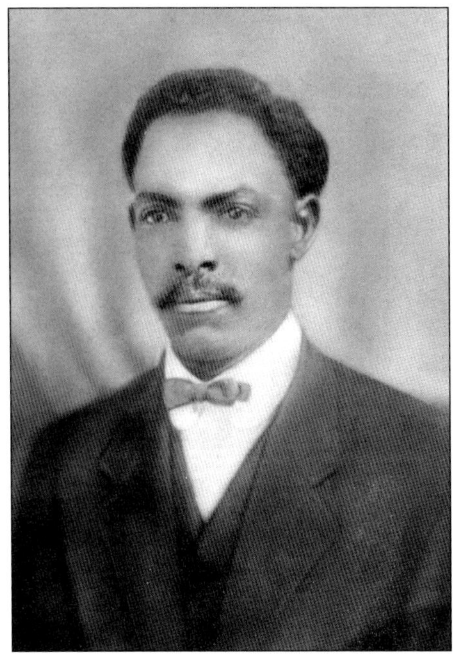

In 1916, Jacksonville's Eastside resident Matthew Ward published his poem "Bound for the Promised Land" in the *Chicago Defender*, urging Black Southerners to escape racism and seek new opportunities in the North. As thousands left Jacksonville, the city's economy faltered, unable to stop the exodus. This Great Migration moved six million Black Americans nationwide, reshaping the country's social and economic fabric and standing as a landmark act of collective resistance. (Ritz Theatre & Museum.)

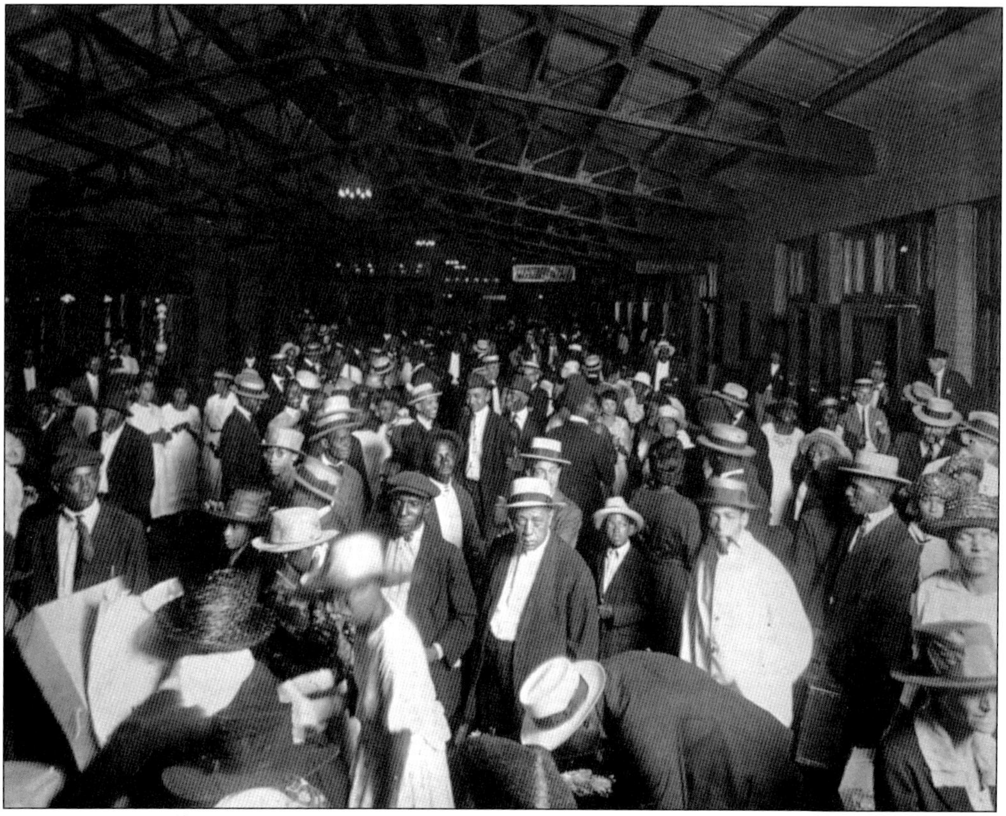

This 1921 photograph of the Jacksonville Terminal's concourse reflects the city's role as a major hub of the Great Migration. Between 1916 and 1920, more than 6,000 of Jacksonville's 35,000 Black residents left the city, joined by 14,000 others from nearby rural areas. Studies show that Jacksonville, along with West Florida and Tampa, saw the South's largest proportional outmigration of African Americans seeking economic opportunity and an escape from racial oppression. (State Archives of Florida.)

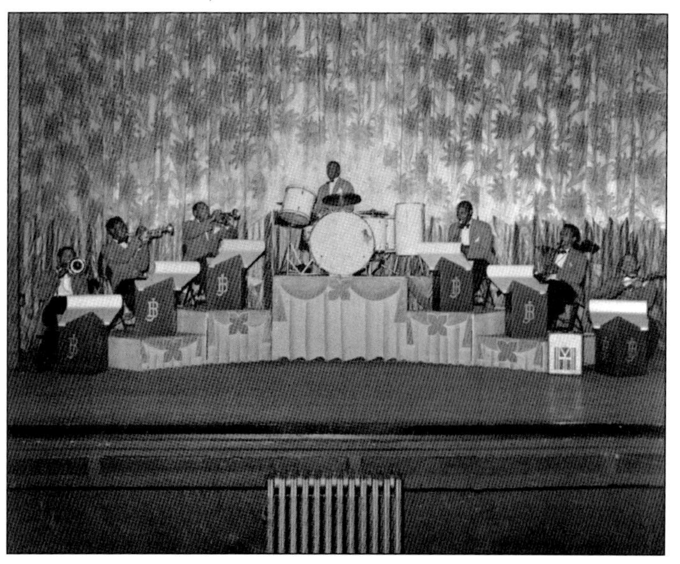

During the early years of vaudeville, ragtime, jazz, and blues, LaVilla became Florida's leading destination on the famed Chitlin' Circuit, a network of Black-owned nightclubs, theaters, and juke joints that provided safe stages for African American performers during segregation. Renowned Jacksonville venues on the circuit included the Strand Theatre, Manuel's Tap Room, Hi-Hat Club, Knights of Pythias, and the Lenape Bar. (Ritz Theatre & Museum.)

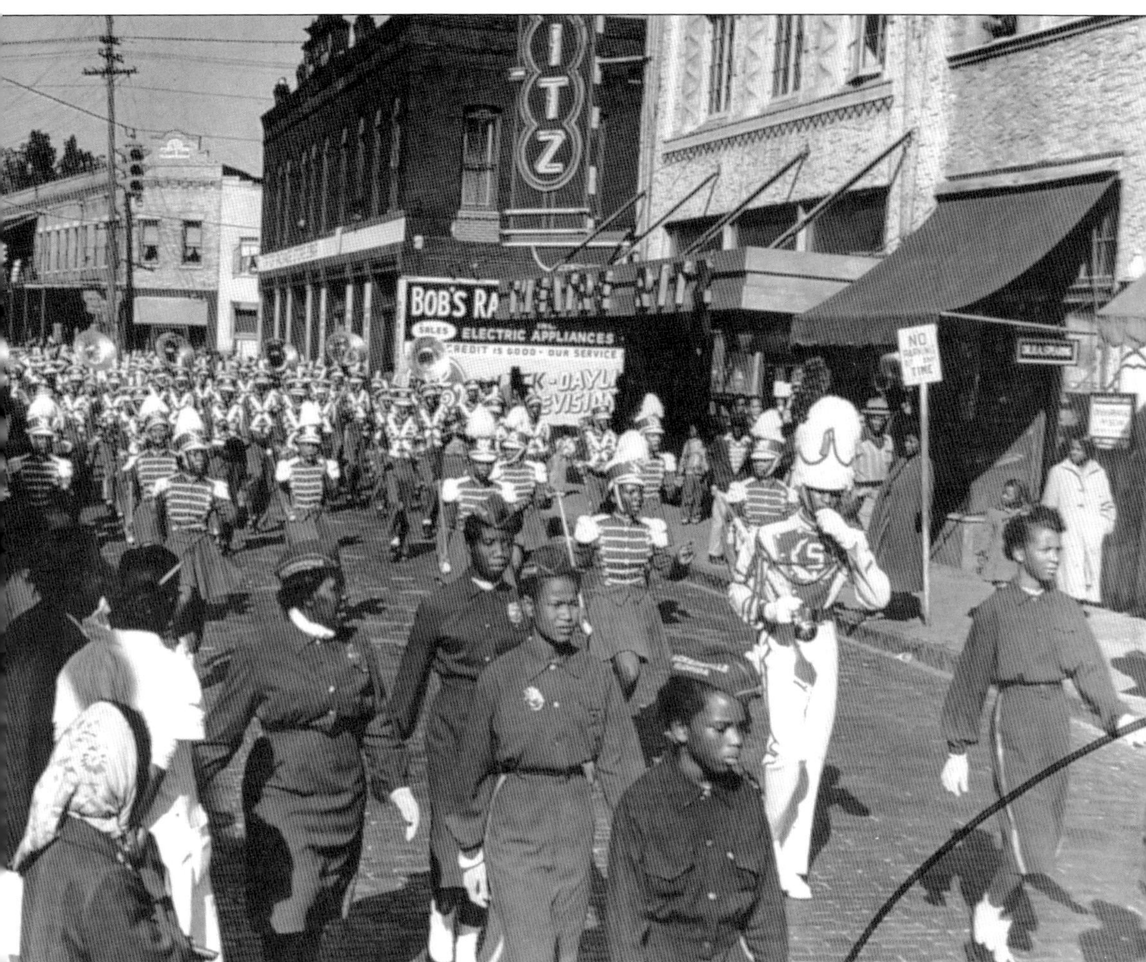

Once called Second Street, Davis Street flourished after Jacksonville's Great Fire of 1901 as a bustling corridor of hotels, restaurants, theaters, and shops in LaVilla. Landmarks such as Nick's Pool Parlor, the Flagler Hotel, Boston Chop House, Ritz Theatre, and the Cookman Institute anchored the district's vitality. Davis Street's decline began after 1950 as urban renewal projects and the construction of Interstate 95 erased much of its historic landscape. (Ritz Theatre & Museum.)

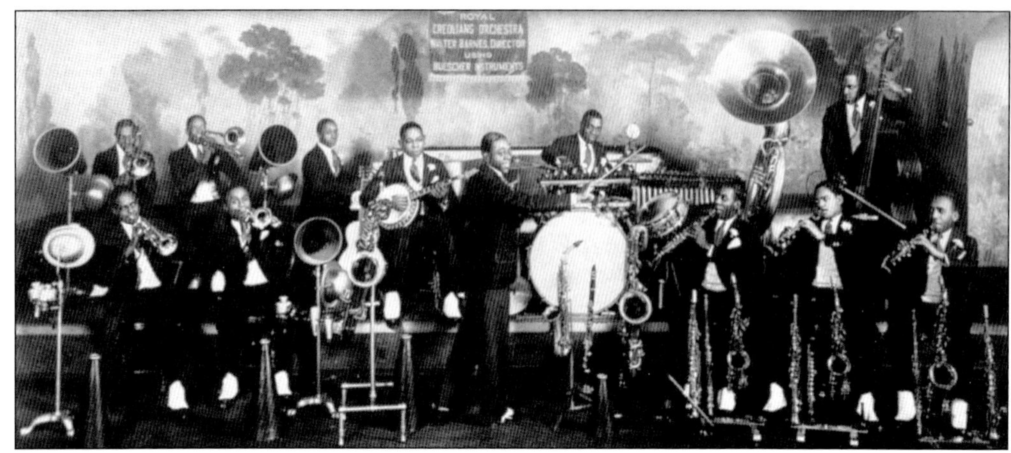

Standing at center, Walter Barnes performs with his Royal Creolians Orchestra in 1928. Barnes is credited with pioneering the Chitlin' Circuit. After the fall of the Theatre Owners Booking Association, he organized a network of safe, successful venues for Black entertainers across the South in the 1930s. Operating from his winter base in Jacksonville, Barnes's routes, publicized through the *Chicago Defender*, became the famed Chitlin' Circuit, inspiring countless performers even after his death in 1940. (Walter Barnes Recording Orchestra.)

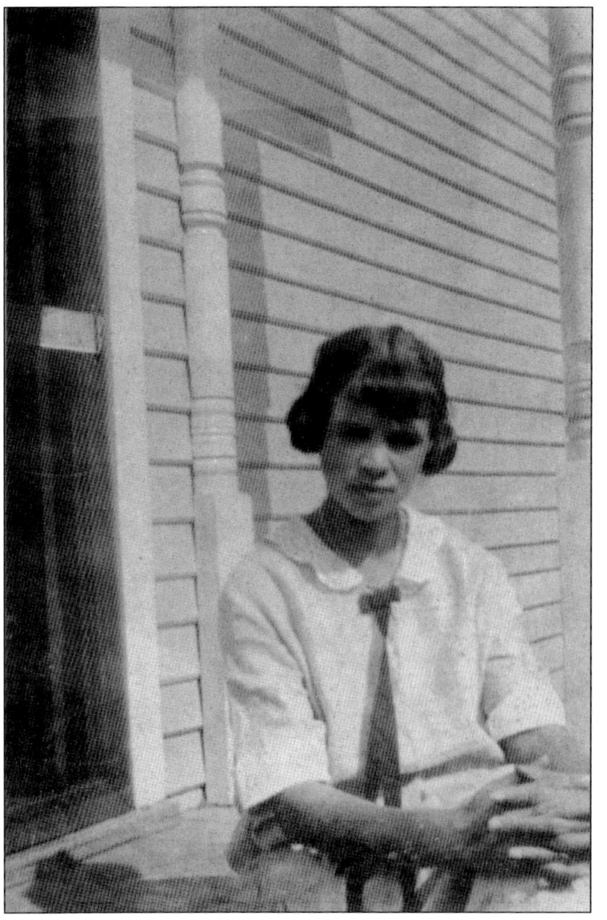

During the 1930s, Jacksonville ethnographer Viola B. Muse worked for the Negro Writers Unit of the Florida Federal Writers' Project, part of the WPA. The WPA employed Black residents across Northeast Florida in public works, education, and cultural documentation. Muse interviewed formerly enslaved people and community elders, preserving invaluable stories of Black life, labor, and culture. Her work ensured that Florida's Black American history remains a vital part of the national record. (Special Collections, Thomas G. Carpenter Library, University of North Florida.)

During World War II, the US Navy transformed Jacksonville's economy, building three naval bases while the Marine Corps established Blount Island Command. By 1944, shipbuilding operations in the Eastside employed thousands of Gullah Geechee residents among its 20,000 workers. Today, shipbuilding continues to play a vital role in the Eastside's maritime economy and community identity. (National Archives.)

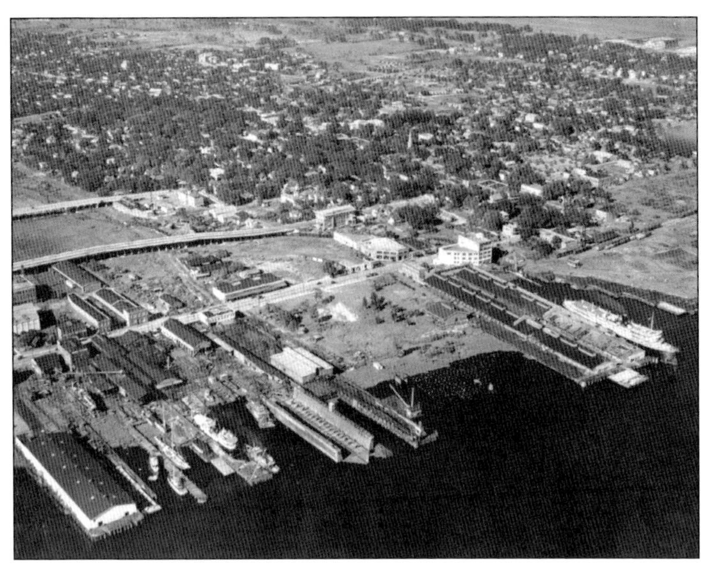

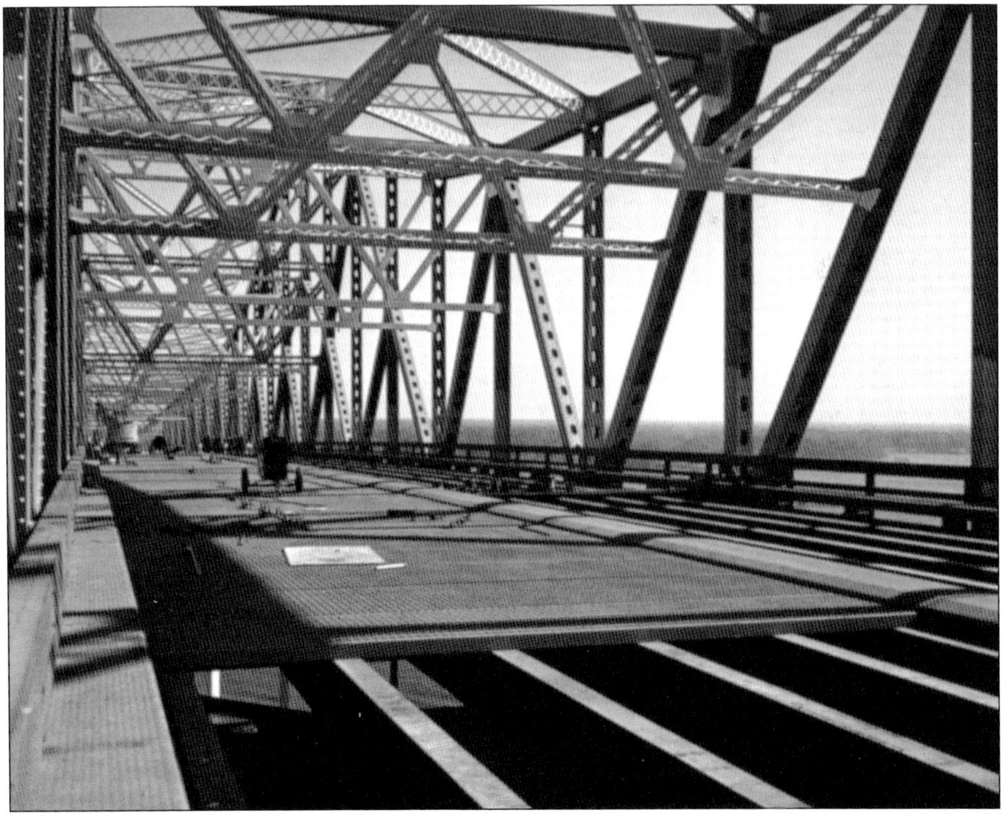

Named after the state legislator who helped gather its funding, John E. Mathews, this bridge opened in 1953 over the St. Johns River, connecting Jacksonville and Arlington. The opening of the bridge was a key factor in the population boom in Arlington. Once rural and isolated Gullah Geechee settlements, such as Cosmo, Fulton, Lone Star, and Chaseville, began to be engulfed by rapid mid-century and postwar suburban development. (State Archives of Florida.)

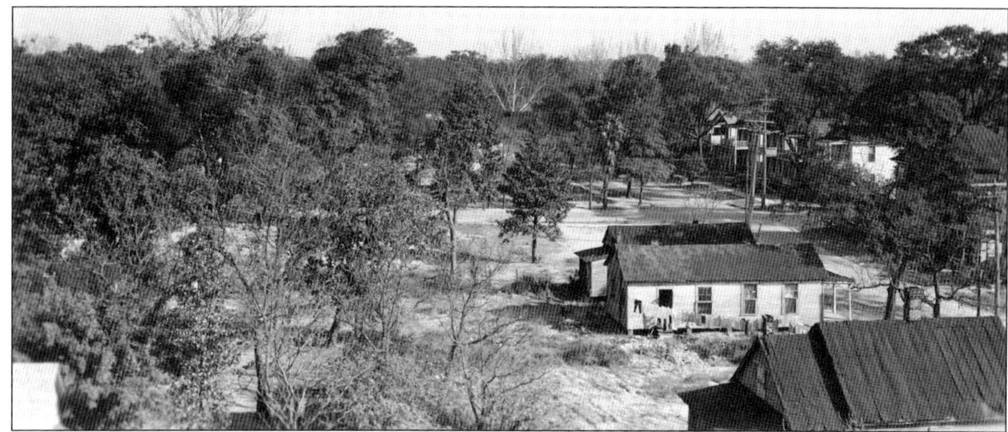

Throughout the 20th century, Jacksonville's Gullah Geechee neighborhoods have been negatively impacted through redlining, urban renewal, and discriminatory public infrastructure investments and policy. During the 1950s, several hundred Eastside residences and businesses were lost due to the construction of the Mathews Bridge and Union Street and Haines Street Expressways. When this aerial photograph was captured in 1952, land clearing efforts were underway for the construction of the Union Street Expressway. (National Archives.)

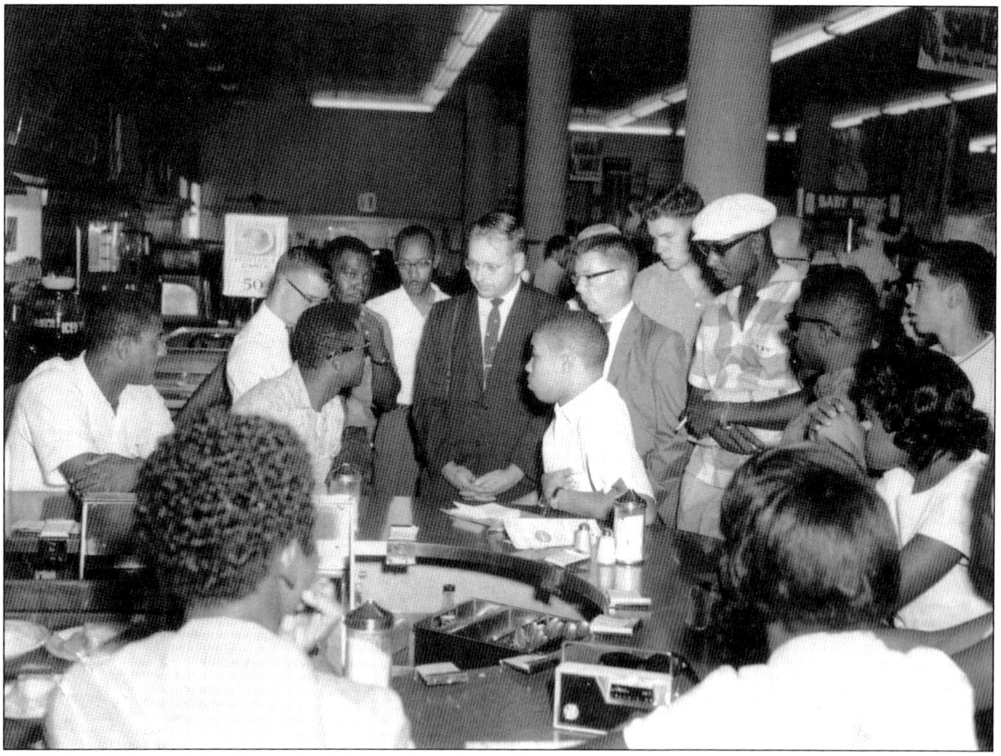

In 1960, led by Rodney Hurst, Alton Yates, and Marjorie Meeks, the Jacksonville Youth Council NAACP held sit-ins to protest segregated lunch counters under adviser Rutledge Pearson. After two weeks, on August 27, more than 200 white men brutally attacked the peaceful demonstrators with ax handles and bats. The violence, later known as "Ax Handle Saturday," led to negotiations that integrated downtown lunch counters in 1961. (Rodney Lawrence Hurst Sr. Papers, Thomas G. Carpenter Library, University of North Florida.)

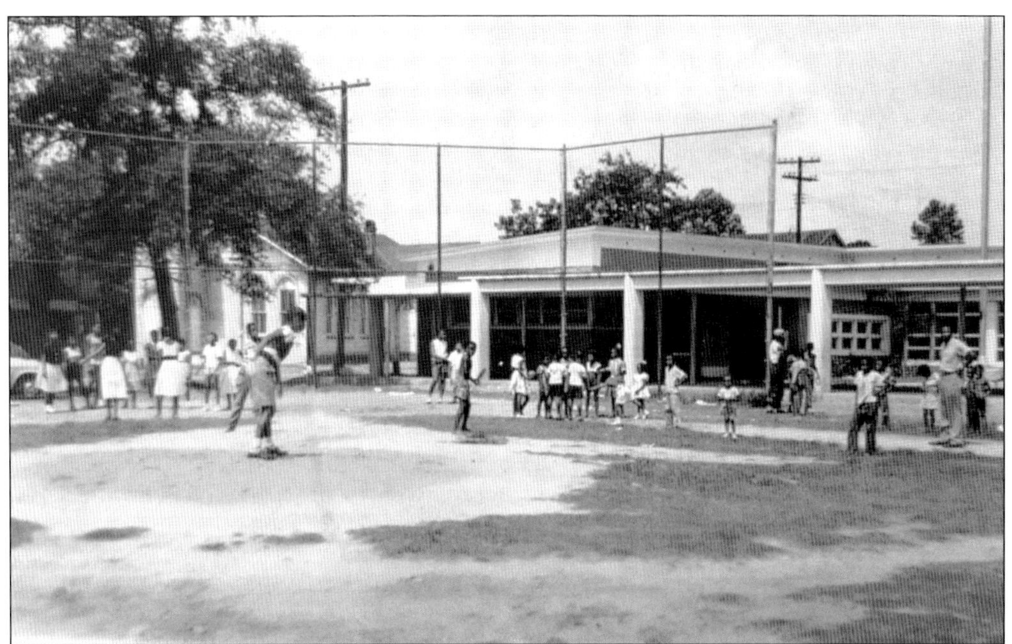

Forest Park Elementary opened in 1954 as a replacement for the older West Lewisville Elementary School. Built at the intersection of Forest and Goodwin Streets, the school had an enrollment of 744 elementary students in 1955. Forest Park became one of eight all-Back urban schools in Jacksonville to close in 1971 after US district judge Gerald Tjoflat ordered massive crosstown busing in Duval County as part of school integration. (Jacksonville Public Library Special Collections Department.)

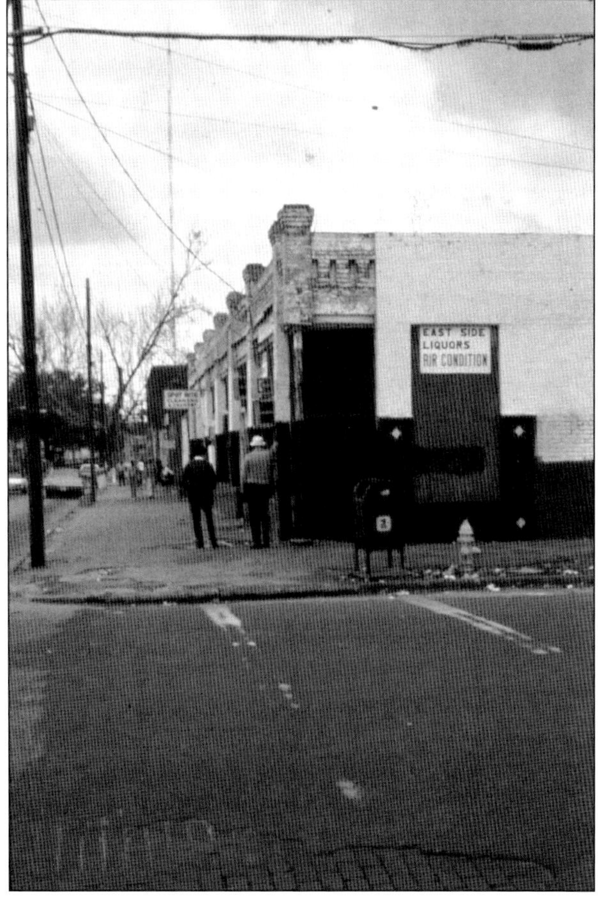

On October 31, 1969, a White salesman shot a Black 20-year-old, Buck Riley, on Florida Avenue, sparking chaos that devastated the once-thriving corridor. As crowds reacted, buildings burned, businesses were looted, and vehicles were destroyed. Though rain eventually ended the unrest, the damage was lasting. With shops closed and owners fleeing, Florida Avenue, once a vibrant hub of Eastside Black commerce, never fully recovered. (Florida State College at Jacksonville.)

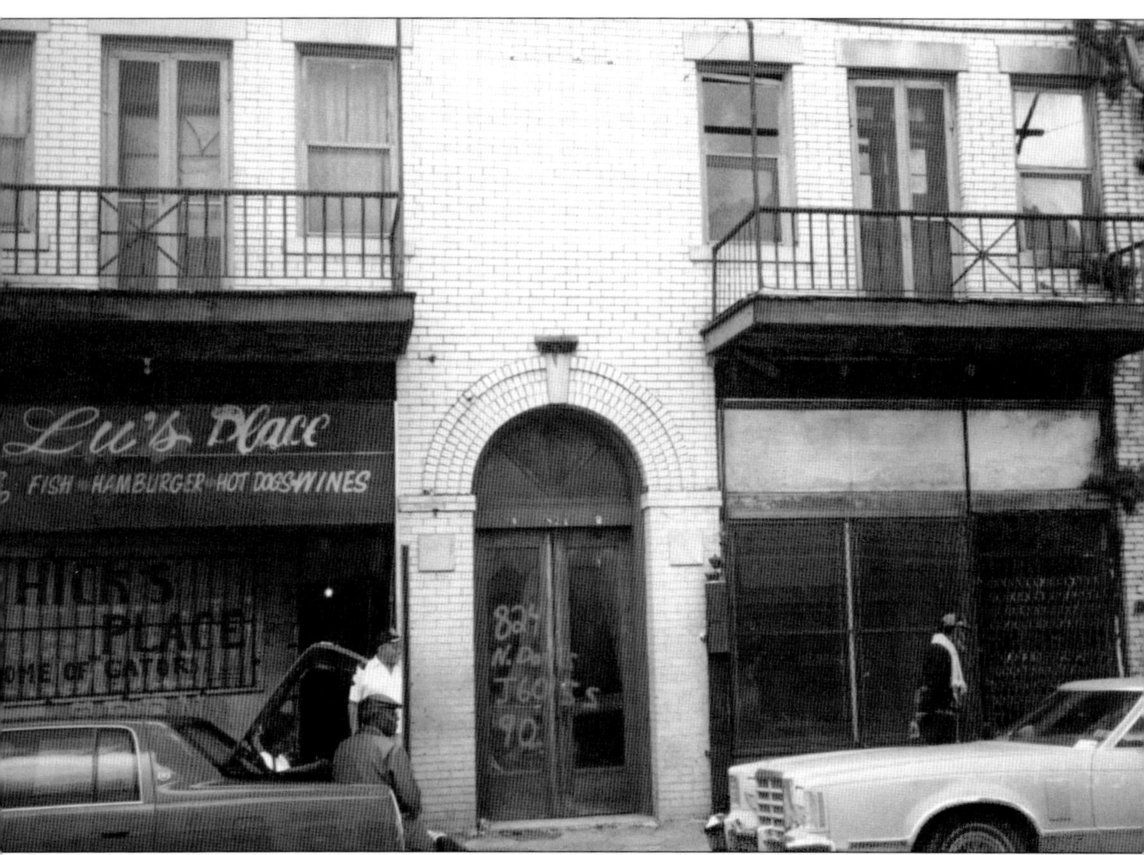

In this photograph, the 800 block of Davis Street awaits demolition due to the $235-million River City Renaissance initiative, launched by Mayor Ed Austin in 1993. Aimed at revitalizing LaVilla, Jacksonville's oldest Gullah Geechee neighborhood, the program instead erased large portions of this historic, multicultural community, displacing residents and dismantling one of the city's most vibrant centers of Black culture and heritage. (Ritz Theatre & Museum.)

Three

The Place

Jacksonville's Gullah Geechee neighborhoods demonstrate culture and self-determination. Rooted in the labor of enslaved Africans who cultivated the region's cotton, rice, citrus, lumber, and naval stores, these communities evolved after emancipation into settlements where freedom took physical and spiritual form. Across Duval County, Gullah Geechee descendants built new lives on familiar land. They transformed former plantation lands into places of worship, work, and kinship.

Neighborhoods such as Pine Forest, Cosmo, and Greenland emerged directly from the landscape of plantation enslavement, with residents fishing, farming, and forming churches that still anchor community life today. Within Jacksonville's expanding urban core, LaVilla, Hansontown, Sugar Hill, and Durkeeville became symbols of cultural achievement and enterprise. These urban Gullah Geechee neighborhoods became centers of music, education, and Black professional life. Brooklyn, Eastside, and West Lewisville reflect the city's rapid industrialization and the ways Black families secured homeownership and built community amid segregation and exclusionary zoning policies.

The Gullah Geechee experience in Jacksonville is also a story of loss and erasure. Urban renewal, interstate construction, and suburban expansion destroyed or displaced many of these neighborhoods, including Campbell Hill, Lone Star, and Chaseville. Yet their memories persist through churches, cemeteries, and family lineages that continue to tell the story of self-reliance and adaptation in the face of systemic injustice.

Collectively, these neighborhoods form a living archive of Jacksonville's Gullah Geechee legacy. Names like Sweetwater, Philips, Moncrief, and Edisto evoke both memory and geography and tie Jacksonville to the broader Lowcountry traditions of faith, craftsmanship, music, and connection to the land. This chapter explores how Gullah Geechee people created and shaped Jacksonville's neighborhoods.

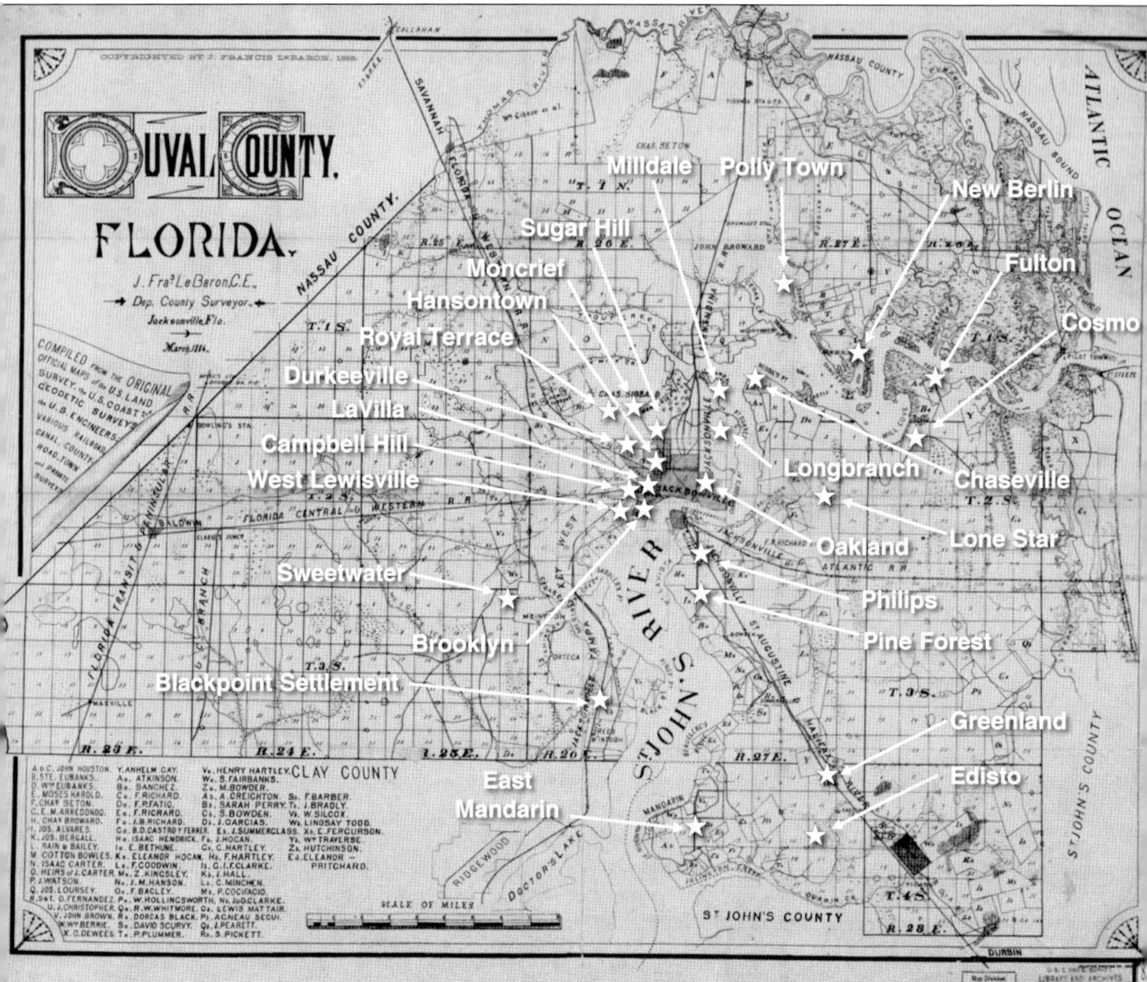

After the Civil War, formerly enslaved people left plantations, purchased land, and built self-sustaining communities throughout Duval County. Many other settlers migrated to Jacksonville from coastal Georgia and South Carolina seeking new economic opportunities and reconnection with lost family members. Between 1866 and 1916, most of these Gullah Geechee "settlement communities" were established along the St. Johns River and its many tributaries, where access to the water supported farming, fishing, and trade. Over time, some communities were lost to urban renewal and suburban expansion during the 20th century. Today, Jacksonville's historic Gullah Geechee communities face growing threats of development and displacement. Yet many remain cultural treasures, still inhabited by descendants of the original settlers who preserve their ancestors' land, heritage, and settlement patterns. (Ennis Davis, AICP.)

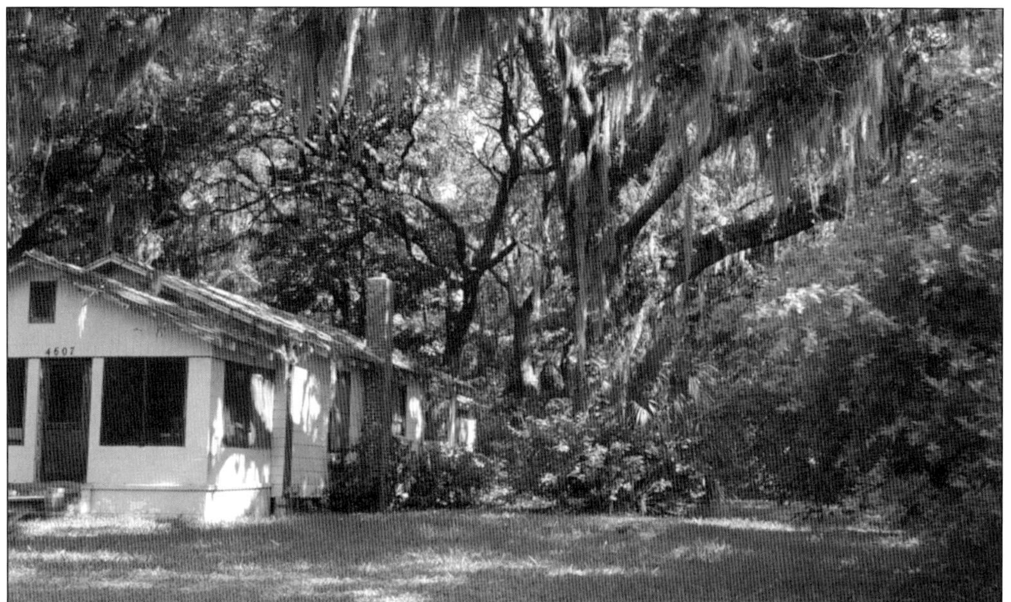

Before the Civil War ended, Mulberry Grove Plantation owner Arthur M. Reed sold part of his land to formerly enslaved people, who established the Blackpoint Settlement. This community later grew into the town of Yukon. In 1939, the US government acquired much of the land for Naval Air Station Jacksonville. Declared a flight and safety hazard, most of Yukon was closed by the Navy in 1963, erasing the once-thriving settlement. (Ennis Davis, AICP.)

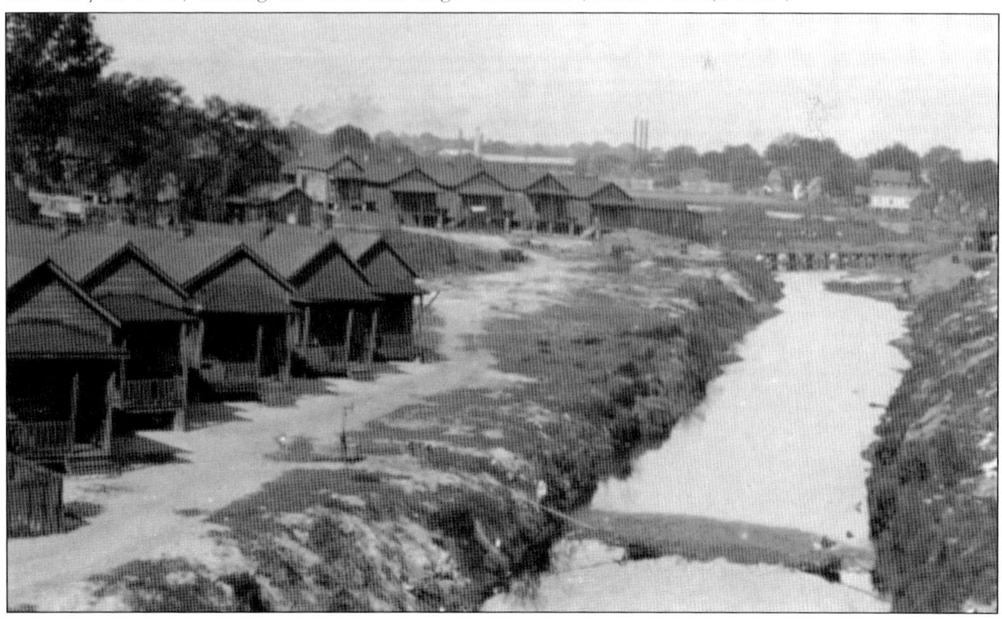

Brooklyn emerged on the former Dell's Bluff Plantation, where enslaved Africans cultivated cotton. During the Civil War, the site served as a camp for US Colored Troops. In 1868, Confederate veteran Miles Price acquired the land, and he platted Brooklyn in 1869. Adjacent to multiple rail lines, Brooklyn quickly became a destination for freedmen, women, and their descendants. The neighborhood grew to 6,000 residents by 1950, but urban renewal displaced much of its population. (Jacksonville Public Library.)

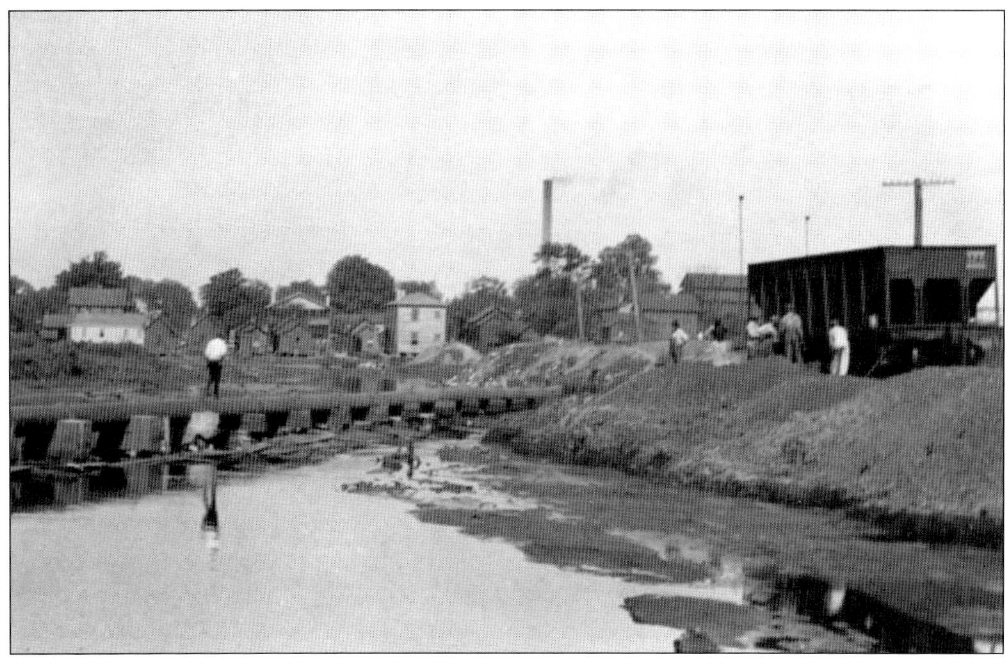

Campbell Hill, established in the early 1880s, straddled Myrtle Avenue between LaVilla's rail yards and McCoys Creek. Many residents were employed as railroad laborers. It was named after developer Alex B. Campbell. Campbell, who also owned a music store, published the first works of the famed composer Frederick Theodore Albert Delius in 1885. Campbell Hill was destroyed by the construction of Interstate 95's Myrtle Avenue Overpass in 1957. (Jacksonville Public Library.)

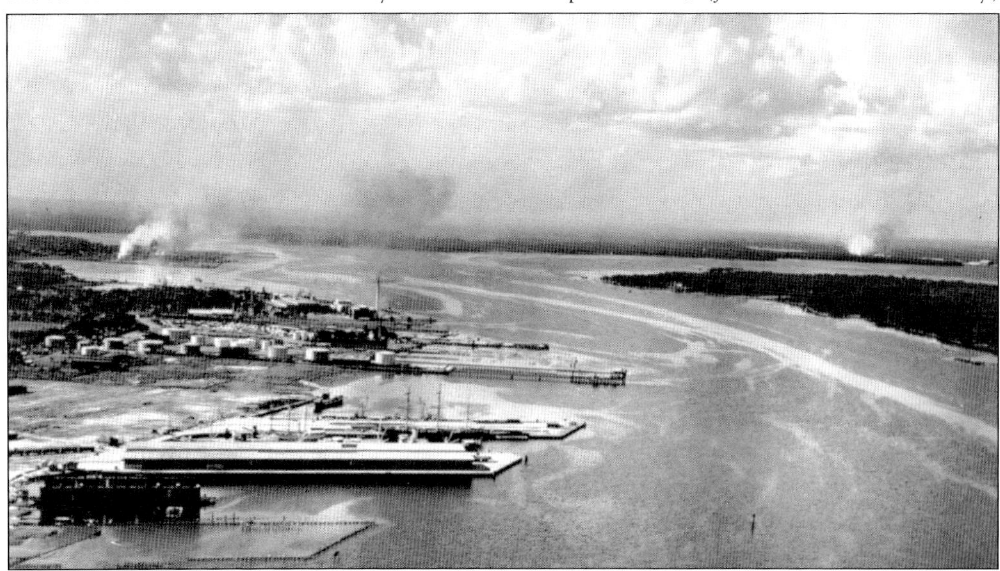

Chaseville emerged after shipyard owner Samuel Chase hired formerly enslaved men and US Colored Troops at Reddy Point. By 1880, it featured churches, schools, cemeteries, and a post office. This rural Gullah Geechee community was eventually erased by suburban growth after the 1953 Mathews Bridge opening. Following the opening of the University Park subdivision and Jacksonville University on January 5, 1959, Chaseville Road was renamed University Boulevard. (National Archives.)

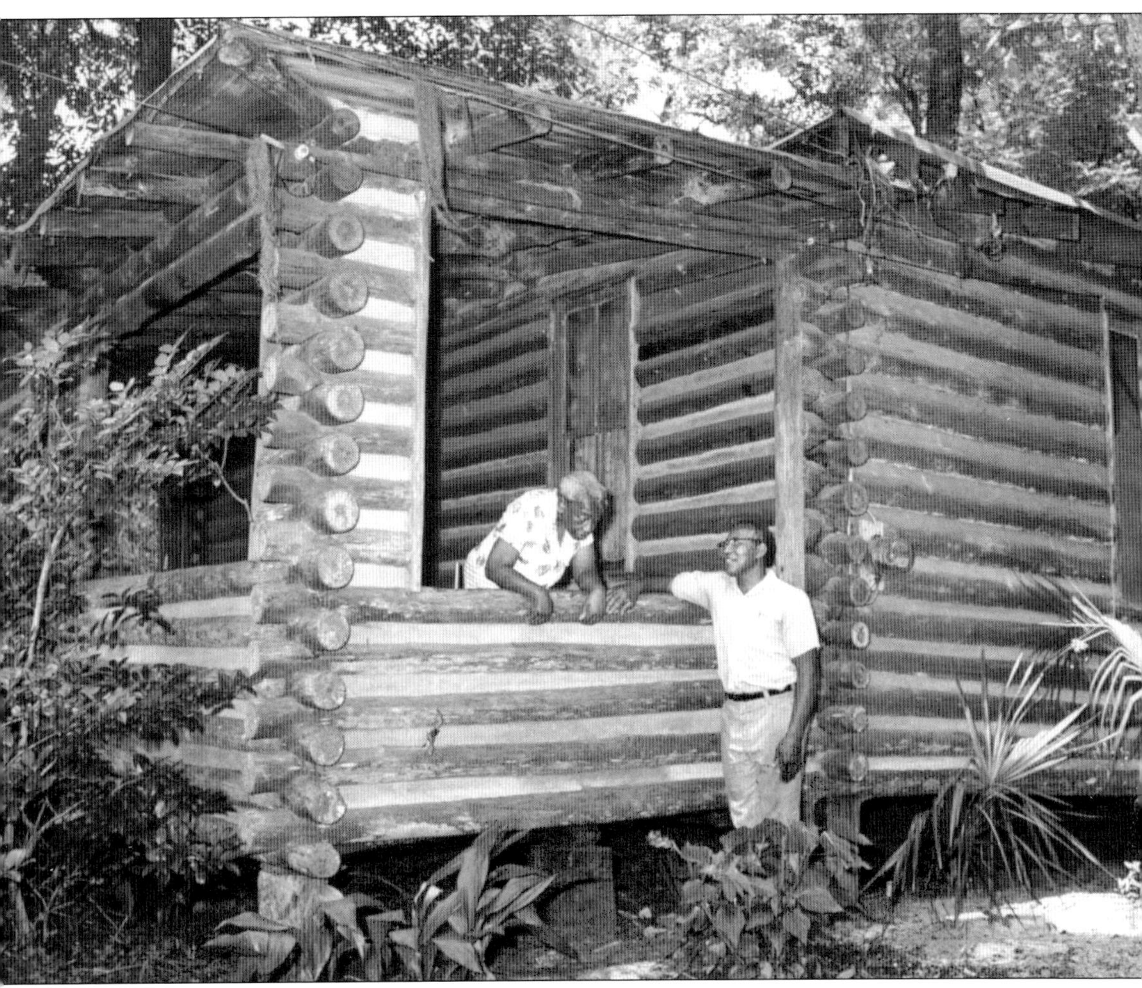

The settlement of Cosmo was established after the Civil War by newly freed Gullah Geechee families from coastal Florida, Georgia, and South Carolina. James and Polly Bartley purchased 40 acres of land in 1877 and are recognized as the first landowners in Cosmo. Cosmo residents made a living from hunting, farming, mullet fishing, crabbing, shrimping, and harvesting oysters at Mill Cove. The community had a post office and school. Cosmo remained in isolation until the construction of the Mathews Bridge. Subsequently, river dredging harmed Mill Cove's marine life, and suburban development encroached upon the community. Yet Cosmo survives. Historic sites in Cosmo include Palm Springs Cemetery, Alexander Memorial Methodist Church, and dwellings scattered in heavily wooded areas tucked between modern subdivisions. (Jacksonville Public Library.)

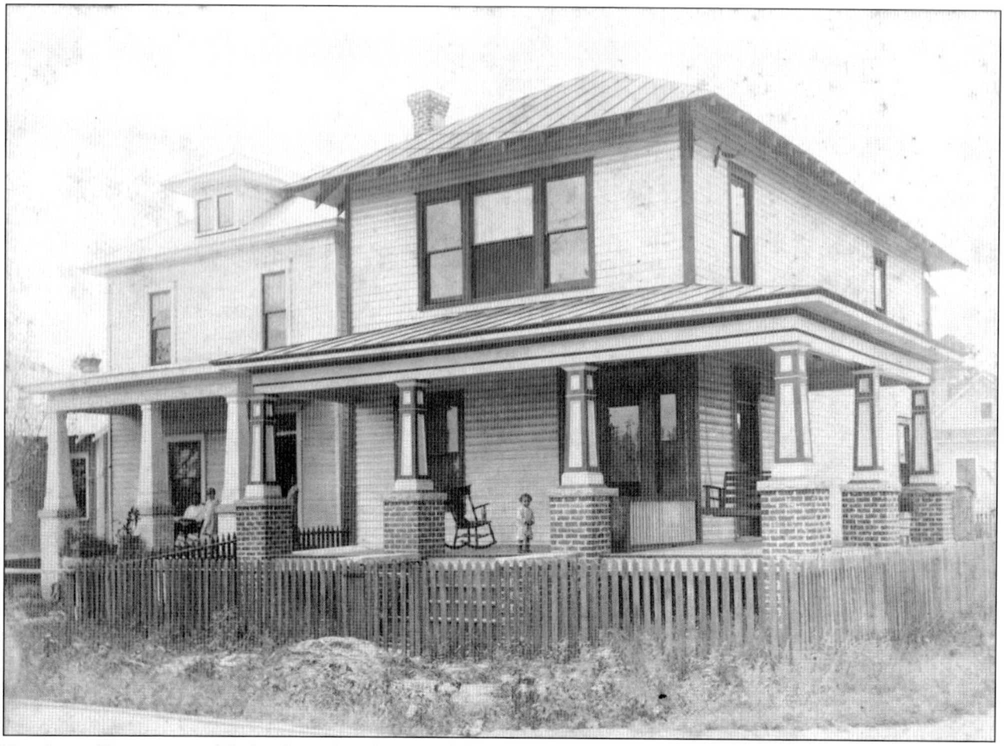

Durkeeville was established on land owned by Dr. Jay H. Durkee, son of Union officer Joseph Harvey Durkee. Originally from New York, Durkee settled in Jacksonville after the Civil War and became a leading real estate developer. The neighborhood became a desired early-20th-century address for Black professionals who were unable to live in affluent White neighborhoods. (Special Collections, Thomas G. Carpenter Library, University of North Florida.)

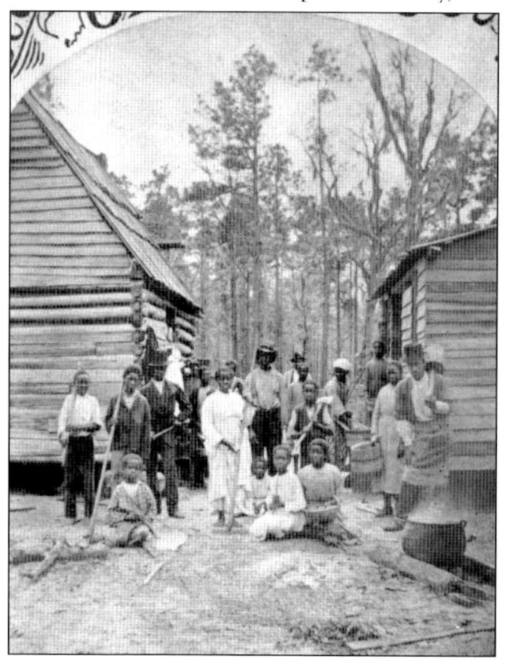

Mandarin was settled as St. Anthony in 1765 during the British period, with plantations worked by enslaved Gullah Geechee people. The community was renamed in 1830 for the mandarin orange and was incorporated in 1841. During the Civil War, Union troops liberated the enslaved. During Reconstruction, it became home to Gullah Geechee families and White farmers. Harriet Beecher Stowe wintered here, founding a church and an integrated school. Mandarin remained rural until suburban growth in the 1960s. (State Archives of Florida.)

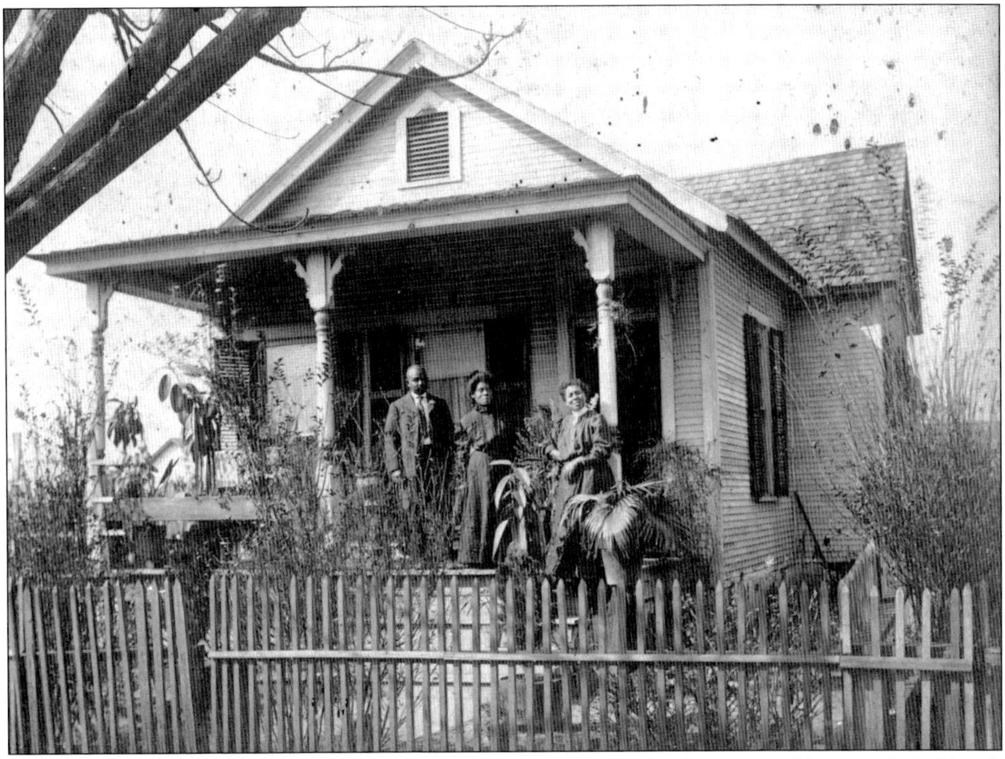

The Eastside is a collection of Gullah Geechee communities also known as "OutEast." Oakland, platted in 1869 by Jesse D. Cole and the oldest, attracted freedmen seeking housing and jobs at nearby docks and sawmills. Post–World War II events, including construction of the Mathews Bridge and new expressways, the 1969 Eastside Riot, and urban renewal, reshaped the neighborhood's landscape. Today, residents pursue "withintrification" strategies to preserve community identity while resisting gentrification and displacement. (Thomas G. Carpenter Library, University of North Florida.)

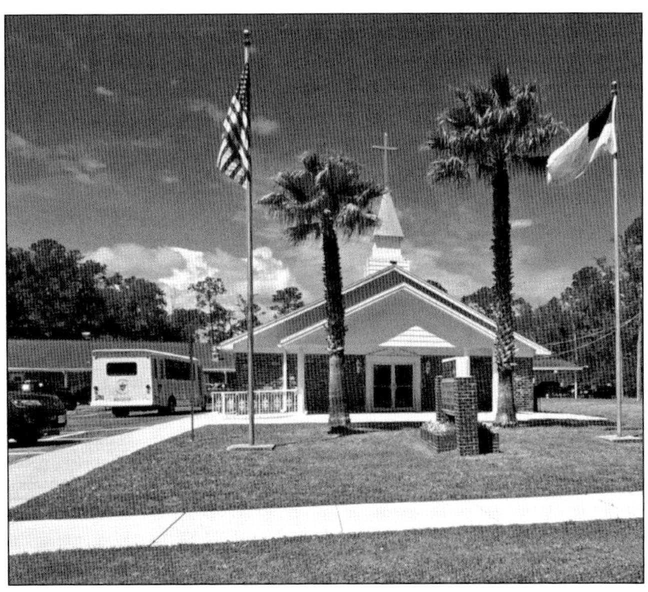

Dating to the 1870s, the Julington Creek Baptist Church was established by Gullah Geechee settlers from Edisto Island, South Carolina, who migrated to Duval County after the Civil War. They settled near Loretto and eventually established a small farming community named Edisto. During the second half of the 20th century, suburban sprawl eventually engulfed and erased this once rural settlement from existence. However, this Baptist congregation, named after the creek that flowed nearby, lives on. (Ennis Davis, AICP.)

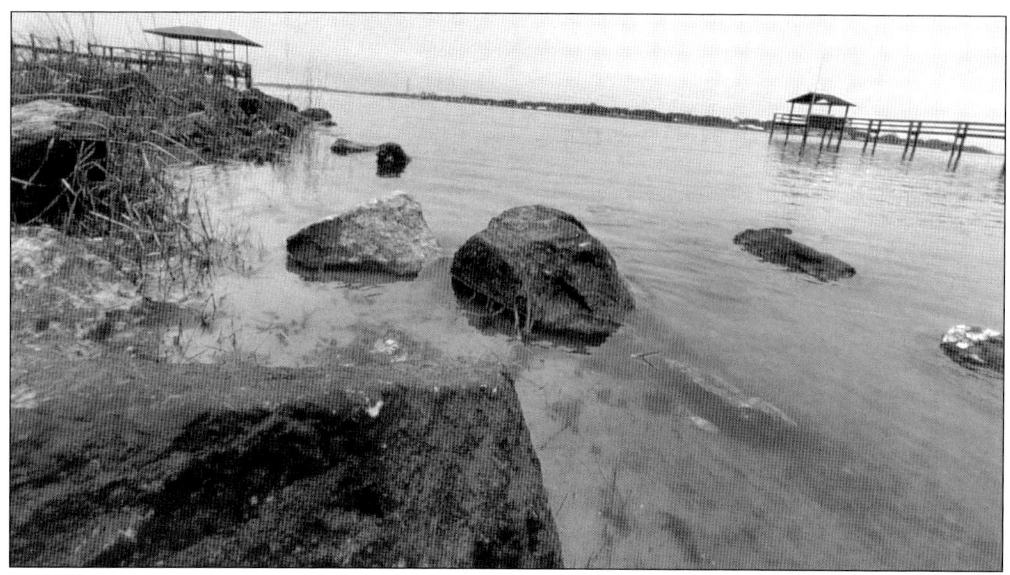

In 1883, Robert Fulton Cutting acquired 475 acres south of the St. Johns River. Envisioned as a settlement for freedmen, Fulton briefly thrived with a mission, post office, and farms before freezes and industry decline. Later sustained by fishing and Harry E. Olcott's Fulton Fish Company, the Gullah Geechee community was razed in the 1960s for modern subdivisions. Today, Fulton Landing at the St. Johns River is all that remains. (Ennis Davis, AICP.)

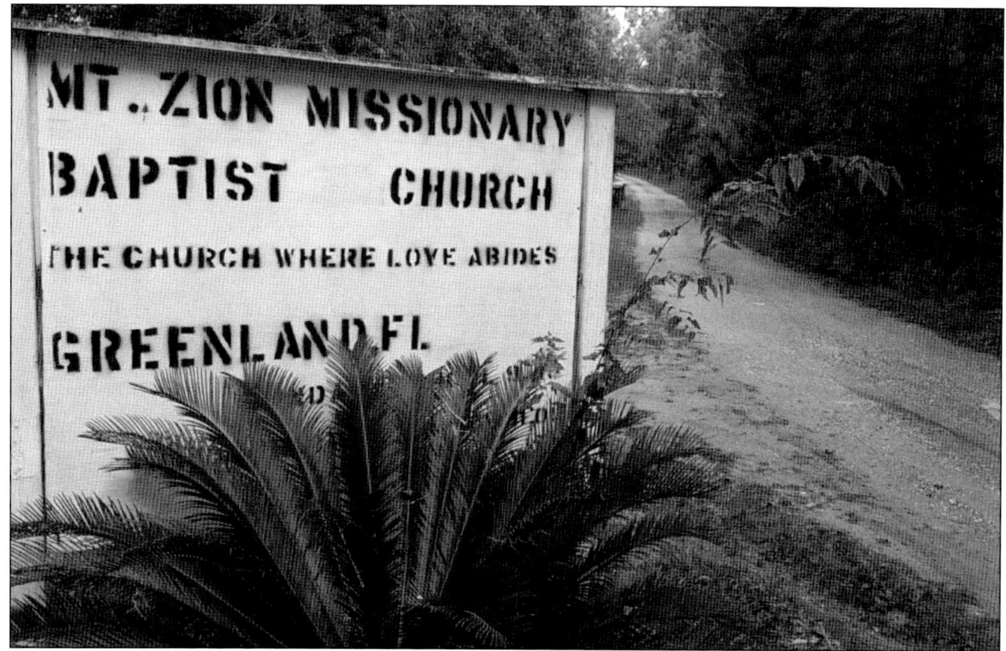

Greenland developed around Mount Zion Missionary Baptist Church, founded by freedmen in 1867. Centered on the turpentine and resin industry, the rural south Duval County community drew residents from Florida, Georgia, and South Carolina after emancipation. At its peak, Greenland supported a post office, school, and general store. Located north of Sweetwater Creek, Greenland's dirt streets still contain names after various trees, including Cedar, Pine, Elm, Magnolia, and Ash. (Ennis Davis, AICP.)

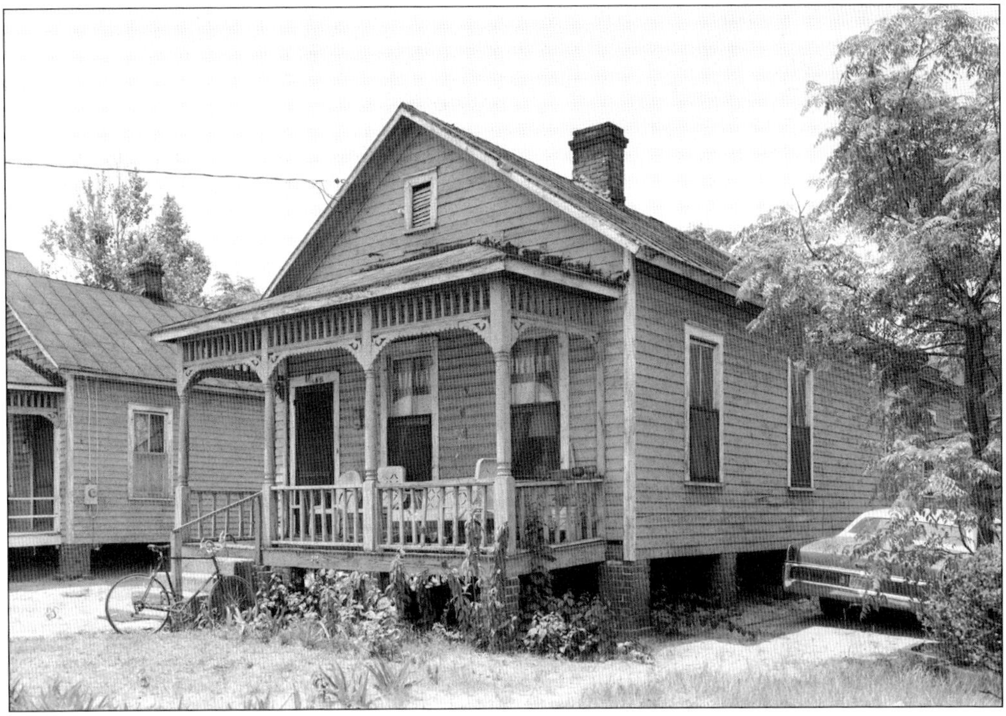

Founded in 1866 by Dr. Daniel Dustin Hanson, a surgeon with the 34th Regiment, US Colored Infantry, Hansontown was envisioned as a farming community for Black veterans and freedmen. The neighborhood, defined by shotgun houses and narrow unpaved streets, grew into a vibrant enclave. Urban renewal erased much of it. Blodgett Homes replaced its west side in 1942, and by 1977, the rest was razed for Florida State College of Jacksonville's downtown campus. (Jacksonville Public Library.)

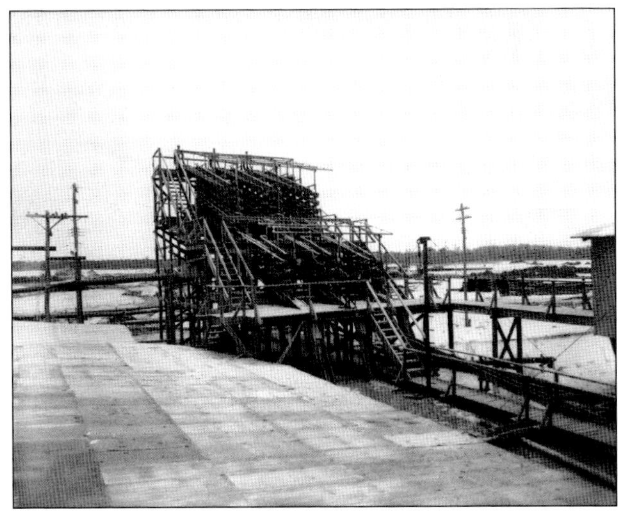

Founded along Strawberry Creek on former plantation land, Lone Star emerged by the 1860s around Mount Zion Methodist Church and the White Family Cemetery. Residents built a self-sufficient community sustained by nearby waterways and ties to neighboring Gullah Geechee settlements. Seen here some time from 1944 to 1961, the Humphreys Gold Mining Company produced titanium. Postwar suburban expansion erased much of Lone Star, leaving only the church and cemetery. (State Archives of Florida.)

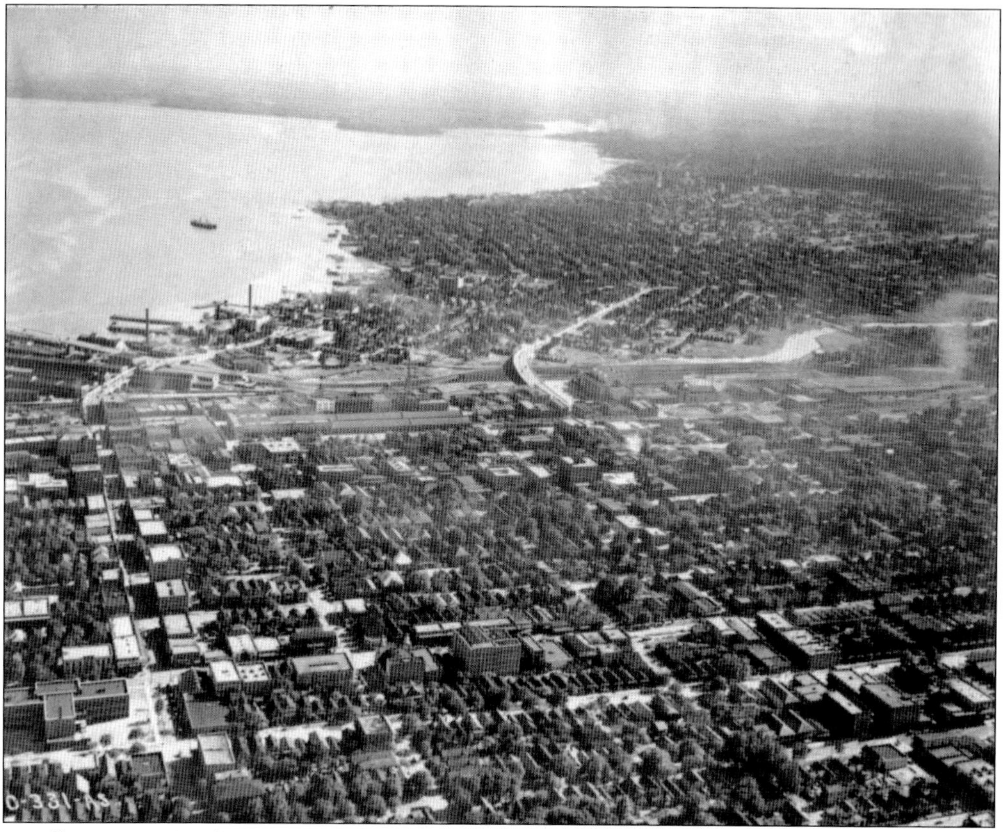

LaVilla is one of Jacksonville's oldest Gullah Geechee communities. Named after the LaVilla Plantation, LaVilla was established as a town in 1866 by Francis F. L'Engle, who served as the first mayor. LaVilla's population was 3,000 when it was annexed into Jacksonville in 1887. The neighborhood was anchored by Henry Flagler's Jacksonville Terminal railroad station. LaVilla became a cultural exchange partner with New Orleans and emerged as a major epicenter for ragtime, jazz, and blues during the early 20th century. LaVilla's people and culture influenced the Harlem Renaissance. A large portion of LaVilla was destroyed by major urban renewal projects, including the construction of Interstate 95 during the 1950s and the City of Jacksonville's 1990s River City Renaissance plan. (National Archives.)

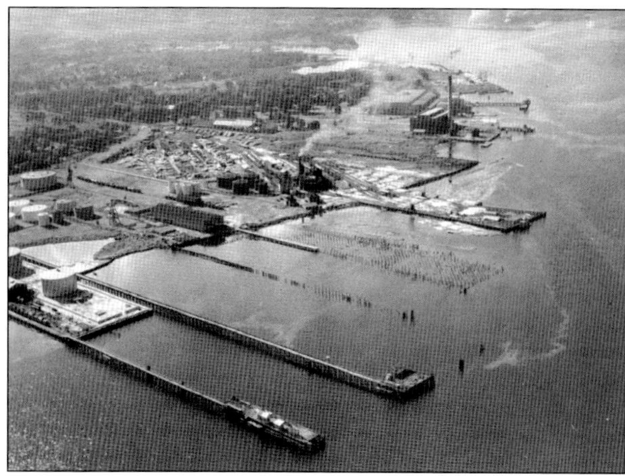

Affectionately known as "OutEast 21st," Longbranch was platted during the mid-1880s by James Jaquelin Daniel. Longbranch was named after the creek that forms its northern border with Evergreen Cemetery. Col. J.J. Daniel was the first president of the cemetery. Adjacent to JAXPORT's Talleyrand Marine Terminal and surrounded by railroads, early-20th-century industrial development led to the neighborhood being a destination for the area's Black labor force. (National Archives.)

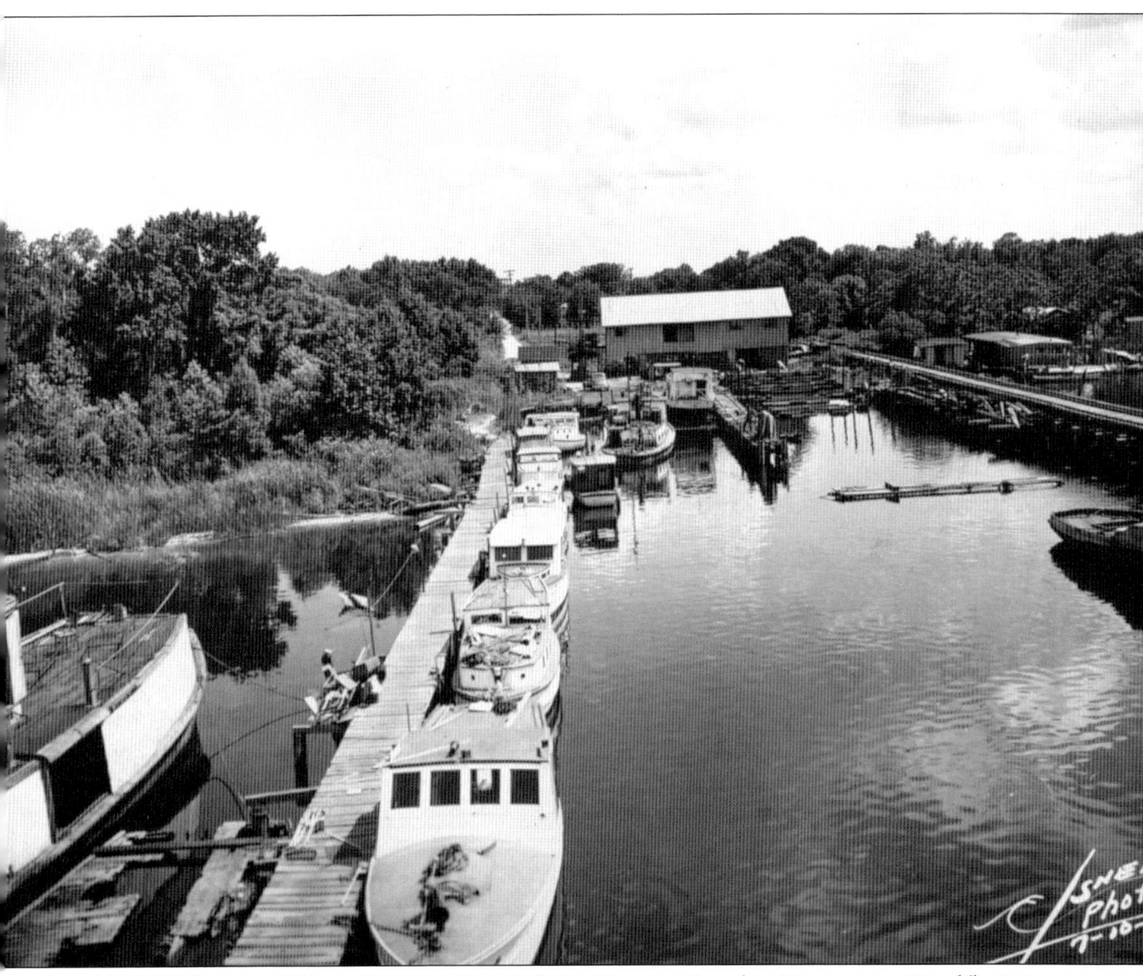

In 1896, Wellington Wilson Cummer founded the Cummer Lumber Company at Sandfly Point, capitalizing on Florida's vast cypress and timber resources. The sawmill soon became Jacksonville's largest employer. To accommodate Black workers, Charles E. Bell developed Bell's Subdivision along Evergreen Avenue, and by the early 20th century, the area was known as Milldale. Although the mill is long gone, the community endures today as part of Jacksonville's Panama Park neighborhood. (Ritz Theatre & Museum.)

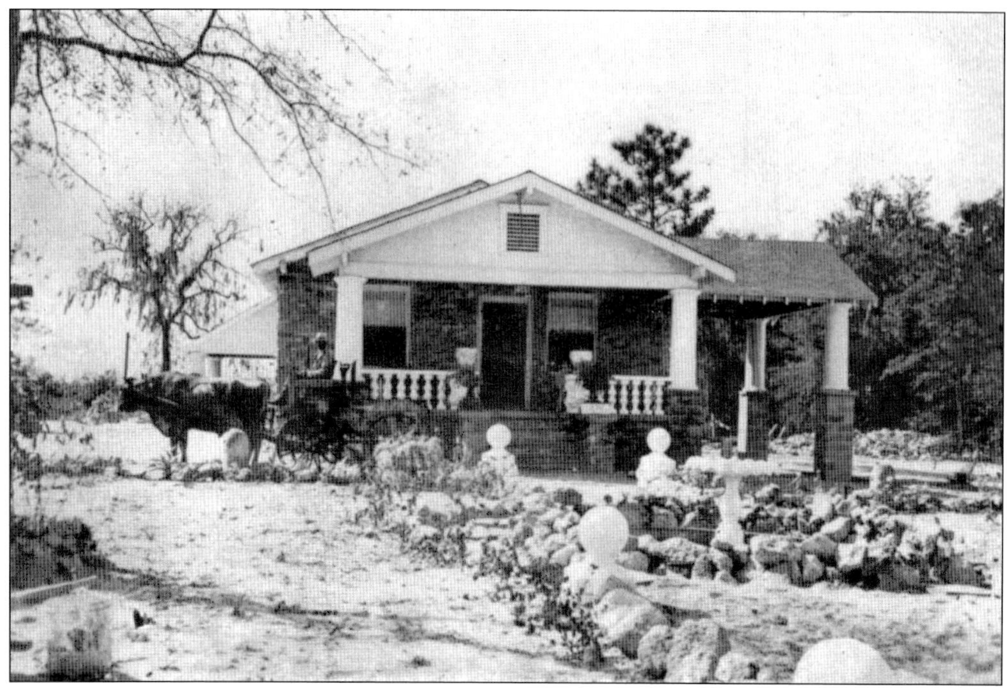

Developed in the 1870s around Moncrief Spring, Moncrief Park became a popular tourist attraction along one of Jacksonville's earliest paved roads. In 1903, the Black-owned "Colored Man's Railroad" extended streetcar service to the park, increasing its popularity. A horse racing track, known as the "Belmont of the South," opened in 1909, drawing crowds of up to 10,000. After racetrack gambling was outlawed in 1911, the site was sold and redeveloped in 1914 into the Black residential streetcar suburb of Moncrief. Before desegregation, the intersection of Myrtle Avenue, Moncrief Road, and West Twenty-Fifth and Twenty-Sixth Streets flourished as a thriving Black business district known as "the Point," serving as the social and economic heart of the community. (Special Collections, Thomas G. Carpenter Library, University of North Florida.)

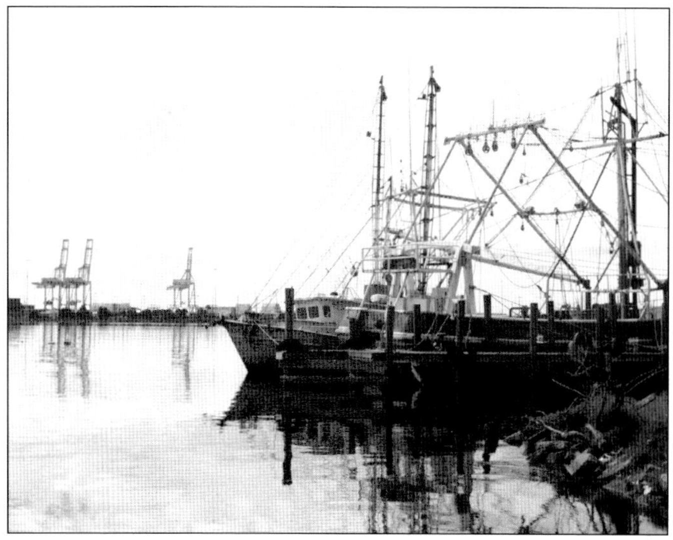

New Berlin was founded in 1860 when Dr. Henry Von Balsan acquired 50 acres at Yellow Bluff and renamed it after his German hometown. After the Civil War, New Berlin became a small fishing and shipbuilding village along the St. Johns River between downtown Jacksonville and Mayport. Shown here, the foot of Frederick Street was the location of Christopher's Pier, a Black-owned fish camp that was known for beer, wine, and fish. (Ennis Davis, AICP.)

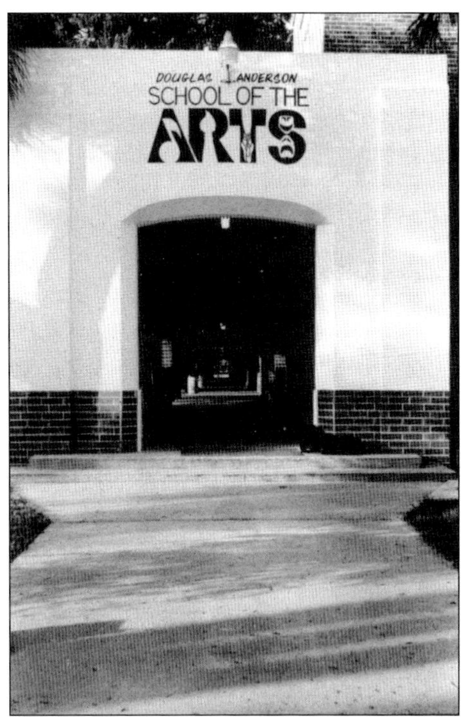

The Philips community, established by formerly enslaved people near Red Bank Plantation after emancipation, grew at the crossroads of Old Kings and St. Augustine Roads. Anchored by century-old churches and cemeteries, it is home to Douglas Anderson School of the Arts, shown here, which began as South Jacksonville's only high school for Black children during segregation. (Duval County Public Schools.)

Pine Forest dates to the 1770s, when the Orange Bluff and Jericho Plantations were established. More than 120 enslaved Africans cultivated various crops. It became the Red Bank Plantation in 1793. Following the Civil War, freedmen and women settled and established Pine Forest. By 1868, the Mount Zion African Methodist Episcopal (AME) Church was organized. Straddling St. Augustine Road between Emerson Street and University Boulevard, the neighborhood retains much of its character despite being surrounded by suburban sprawl. (State Archives of Florida.)

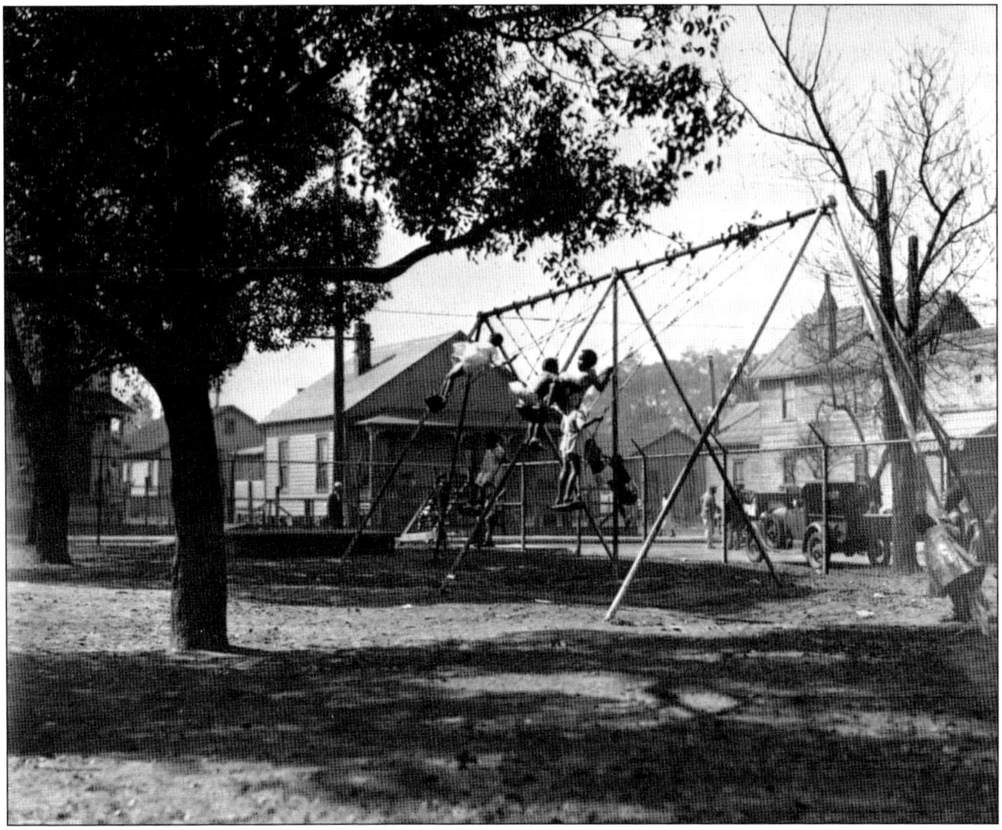

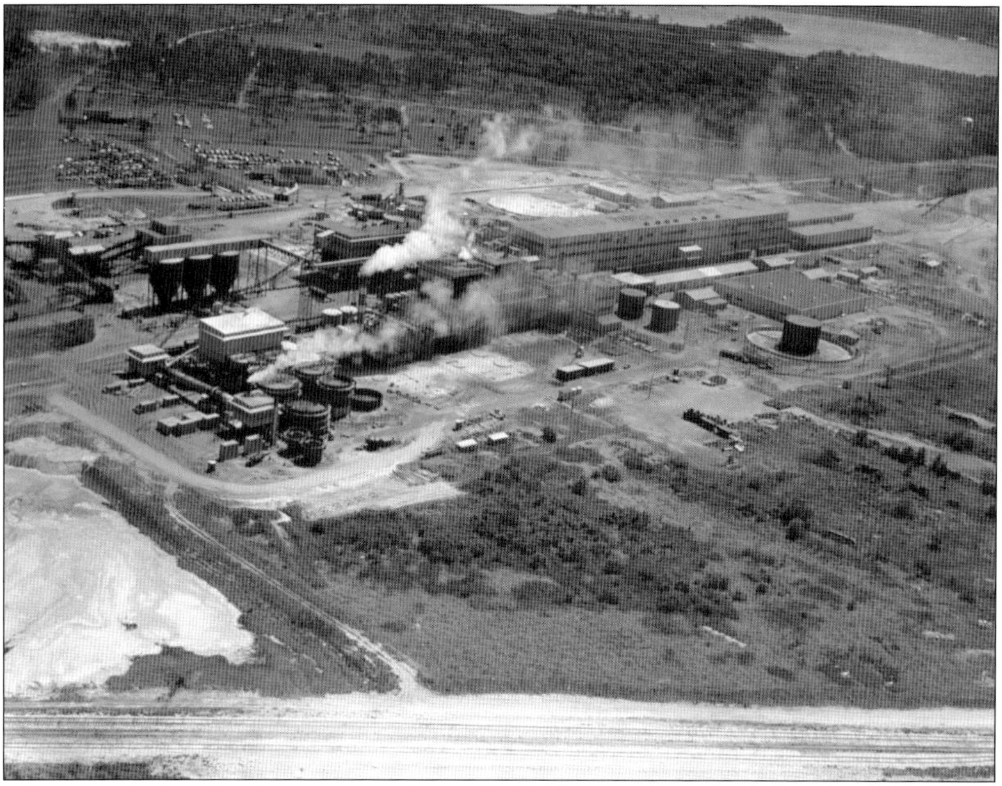

Polly Town developed on former Broward family land between Eastport Road and Dunn Creek. The Browards arrived from South Carolina in 1800 with enslaved people. In 1913, the Carpenter-O'Brien Lumber Company built a sawmill, which was later sold to Brooks-Scanlon, which added mill quarters for Black employees. Wesley Chapel AME Zion Church anchored the community. Photographed in 1953, the Smurfit Westrock Seminole paper mill opened there. The last Black families left in the 1970s. Remnants include a cemetery and tree-named streets. (State Archives of Florida.)

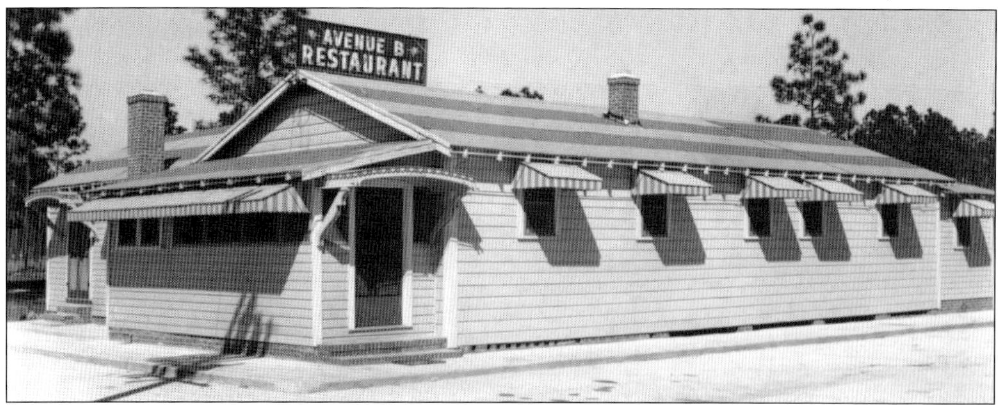

The Avenue B Restaurant was one of many Black-owned businesses near Royal Terrace. Bounded by Avenue B, Edgewood Avenue West, Moncrief Road, and West Forty-Fifth Street, Royal Terrace was known for its Chitlin' Circuit–era nightclubs and juke joints. Originally on the outskirts of northwest Jacksonville's urbanized Black neighborhoods, Royal Terrace's streets are named in honor of historically Black colleges and universities. A few examples include Tuskegee Road, Morehouse Road, Spellman Road, Benedict Road, and Xavier Road. (Ritz Theatre & Museum.)

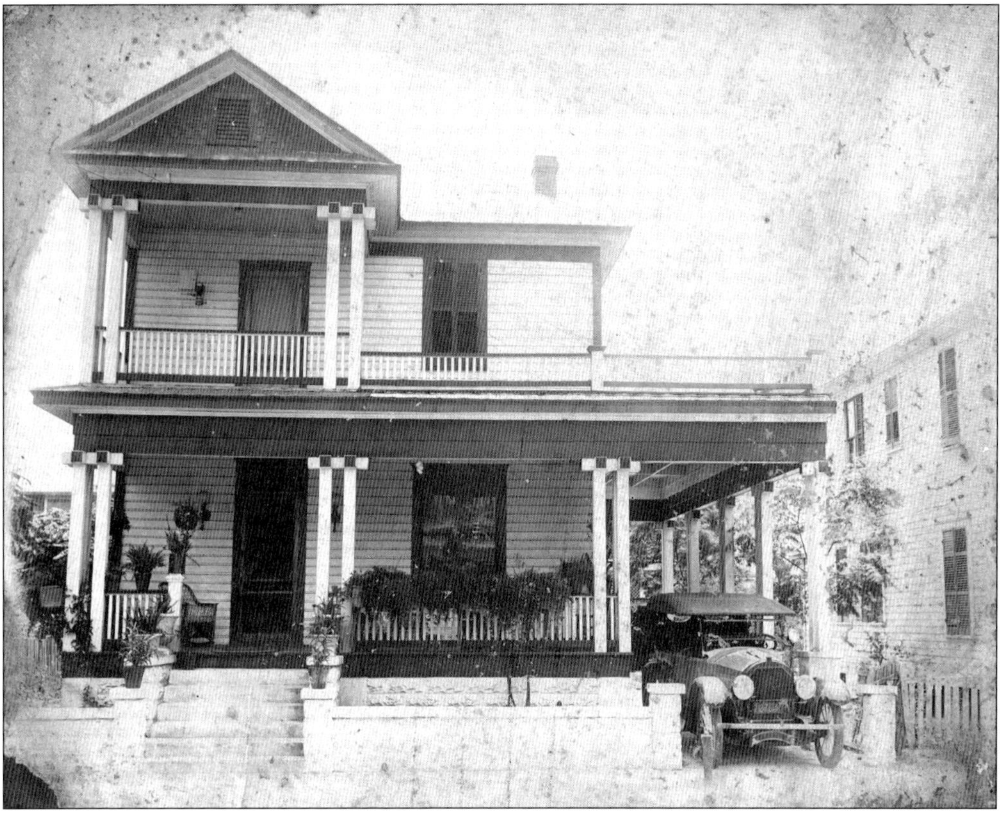

Sugar Hill, an upper-class African American neighborhood west of Hogans Creek, flourished after the 1901 Great Fire with the arrival of a Black-owned streetcar linking LaVilla to Moncrief Park. Anchored by the Cookman Institute, hospitals, and elegant, large homes, it was the neighborhood for Jacksonville's wealthy Black professionals. Redlined in the 1930s, Sugar Hill was later targeted for urban renewal. By the 1960s–1970s, most of Sugar Hill was razed for Interstate 95 and University of Florida Health Jacksonville. (Thomas G. Carpenter Library, University of North Florida.)

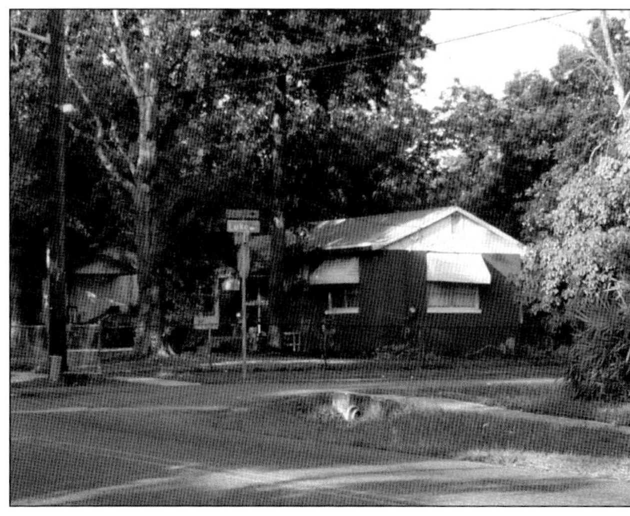

Sweetwater was settled by formerly enslaved Gullah Geechee people after the Civil War. Local folklore says its name came when a barrel of syrup spilled into a nearby stream, sweetening the water. Located in southwest Jacksonville, Sweetwater developed into a close-knit community with streets named for biblical figures, including Matthew, Mark, Luke, John, Esther, and Moses, reflecting the spiritual values and resilience of its residents as they built new lives in freedom. (Ennis Davis, AICP.)

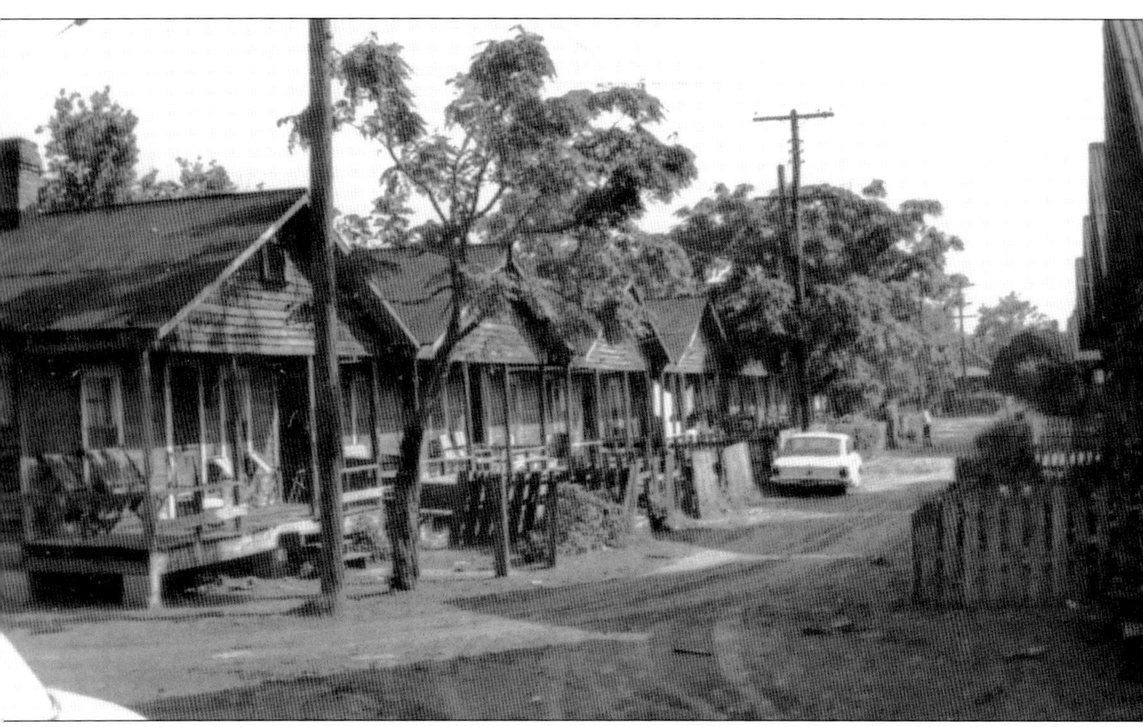

Also known as Mixontown, West Lewisville lies west of Brooklyn. The neighborhood was developed by Miles Price in 1875 as a response to neighboring Brooklyn's rapid growth. Originally isolated and rural, West Lewisville urbanized as a result of housing demand for the Black community following the Great Fire of 1901. Due to discriminatory zoning practices and redlining, by 1950, its rows of frame shotgun dwellings were adjacent to a slaughterhouse, poultry plant, and waste incinerator. (Jacksonville Public Library.)

Four

The Plate

Food has always been at the heart of Gullah Geechee life. This is certainly true in Jacksonville, where foodways are a bridge between land, water, ancestry, and memory. Drawing from West and Central African, Native American, European, and Caribbean traditions, the region's cuisine tells a story of creativity born from limited resources and of community sustained through flavor. Gullah Geechee food traditions remain an expression of identity in Jacksonville.

In the earliest days, one-pot meals of rice, shellfish, and vegetables (ancestors of today's perloo or pilau) fed families who worked the river or the fields. These dishes reflect the ingenuity of cooks who transformed humble ingredients into nourishment. Fishing, crabbing, and shrimping connected coastal communities like Cosmo and Mayport to centuries of maritime tradition. The harvest of Mayport shrimp continues to anchor local menus today.

Barbecue also carries deep ancestral roots. Its open-fire origins blend the techniques of Indigenous Floridians, the Taino people of the Caribbean, African pit-roasting traditions, and Spanish pork, all eventually evolving into the smokehouse flavors that define Jacksonville's barbecue style. Jacksonville's unique mustard-based barbecue sauce has connections to French and German plantation owners. Barbecue became both sustenance and a cultural and social institution.

Family-run restaurants such as Holley's Bar-B-Q and Nesbit Restaurant were built on these Gullah Geechee culinary traditions, passing recipes down through generations. Modern establishments like Celestia's Coastal Cuisine and Soul Food Bistro also carry those flavors forward.

Gullah Geechee foodways in Jacksonville are more than meals. They are living archives of survival, celebration, and community care. This chapter demonstrates that each dish, from garlic crabs to fried fish and grits, connects the past to the present. The story of Jacksonville can be tasted as much as it can be told.

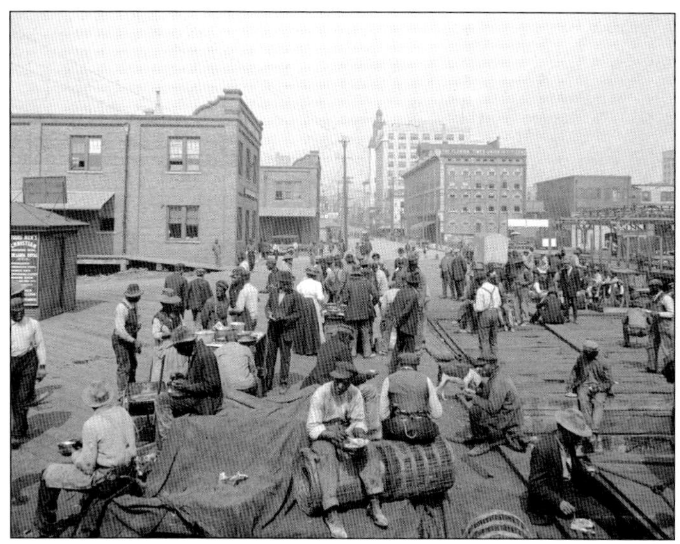

Gullah Geechee foodways are an important part of Jacksonville's culture. Many classic Southern dishes served locally are derived from Gullah Geechee culture. One-pot dishes and other recipes featuring shellfish and locally cultivated rice and fresh vegetables, forming a hodgepodge of flavors, are a cultural foundation of Gullah Geechee cuisine. Here, a one-pot dish was served for dinner at the downtown docks in 1910. (Library of Congress.)

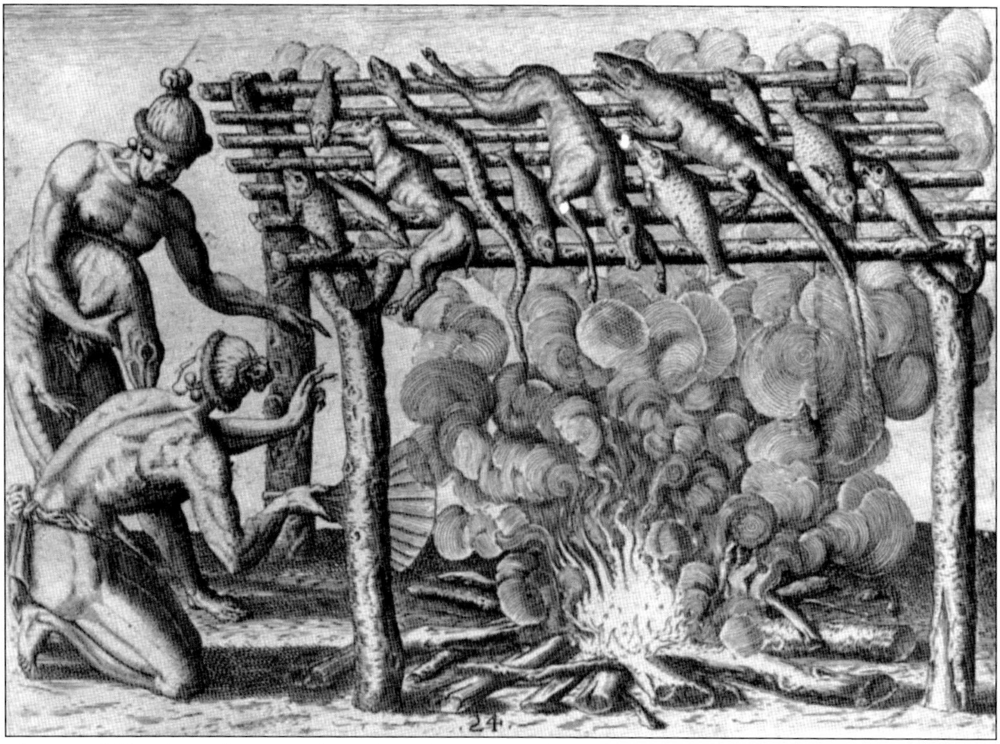

The word "barbecue" comes from *barbakoa*, an Indigenous Taino term for open-fire grilling. Indigenous Floridians and West and Central Africans also practiced open-pit cooking, roasting meat and fish over flames. Enslaved Africans blended these traditions, shaping the regional barbecue styles known today. In the 1560s, local Mocama people, part of the larger Timucua population along Florida's coast, were recorded smoking meat and fish over open fires, a reflection of these enduring culinary roots. (State Archives of Florida.)

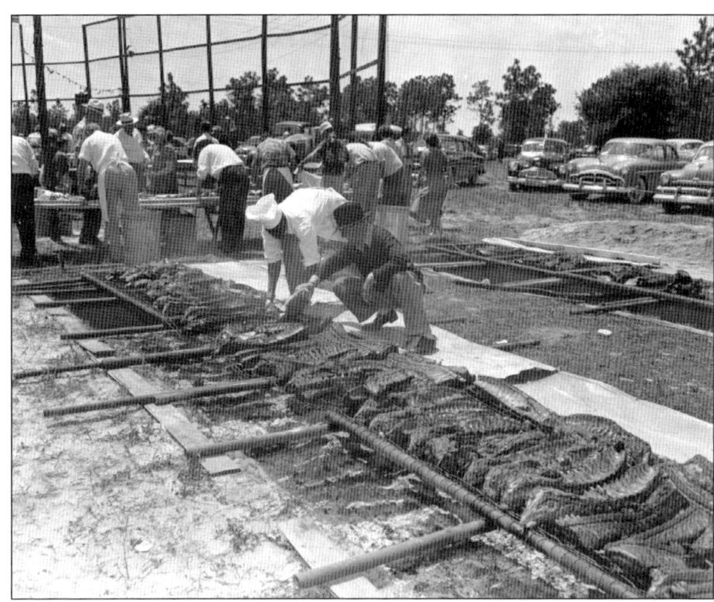

The grand opening of the Mathews Bridge on April 15, 1953, featured an open-pit barbecue, a fitting tribute to one of Jacksonville's celebrated cultural traditions. Rooted in the contributions of Gullah Geechee cooks, the art of slow-cooking meat over pits or indirect heat became more than a meal; it was a communal ritual that brought people together to share food, fellowship, and celebration. (State Archives of Florida.)

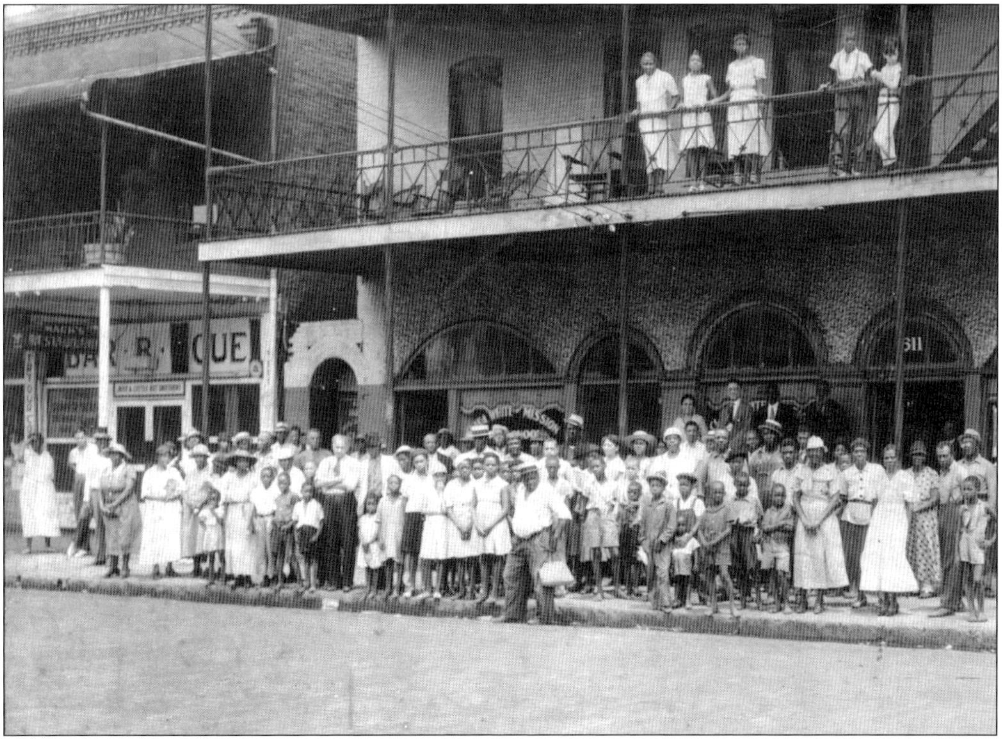

Mack's Restaurant specialized in barbecue with the slogan "Just a Little Bit Different." Near railroad yards, naval stores yards, sawmills, and riverfront wharves, Jacksonville's Black neighborhoods were known throughout the South for their nightlife, entertainment, music, and barbecue scene. By 1955, barbecue restaurants on or near LaVilla's West Ashley Street, the heart of Black commerce in Jacksonville, included A Brown Bar & Bar-B-Q, Bill's Bar-B-Que, Duck's, Ivory's Barbecue & Chili Parlor, and Singleton's Superior Bar-B-Q. (Eartha M.M. White Collection, Thomas G. Carpenter Library Special Collections and University Archives, University of North Florida.)

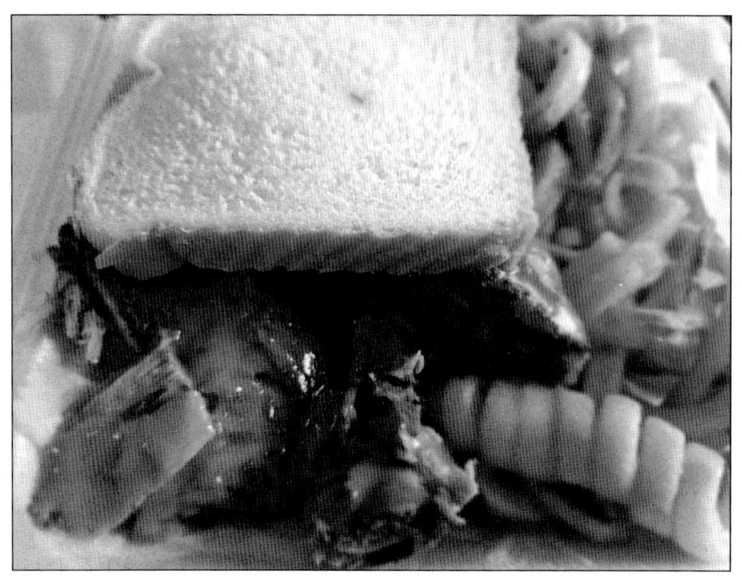

After World War II, the rib sandwich or plate became a local favorite. The sandwich consisted of three or four ribs served between slices of bread with mustard-based barbecue sauce. Eaten by hand, it remains a signature dish at Holley's Bar B Q, the city's oldest restaurant. Established by Jack Holley in 1937, Holley's is also credited as the birthplace of curly fries. (Ennis Davis, AICP.)

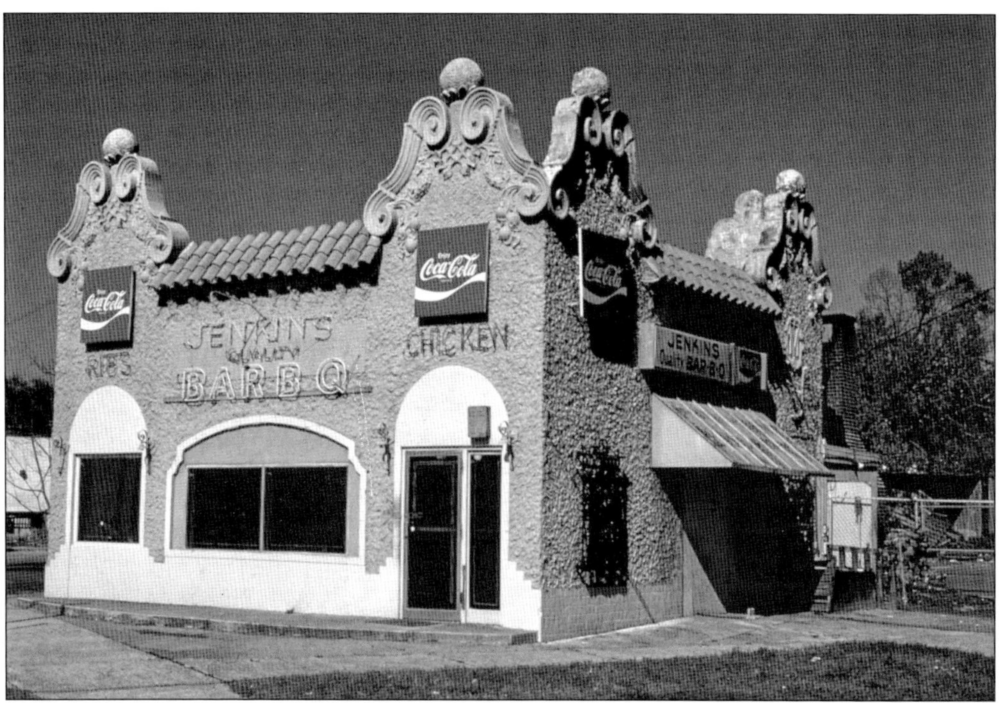

Jenkins Quality Bar-B-Q began in 1957, established by Melton and Willie Mae Jenkins Jr. Jenkins had a secret family barbecue sauce recipe handed down from his father. He used this to open up his first restaurant on Kings Road with a menu that strictly featured ribs and chicken. Advertising in those days was done by word of mouth. The family closed the restaurant's three locations on September 30, 2025, after 68 years of business. (Library of Congress.)

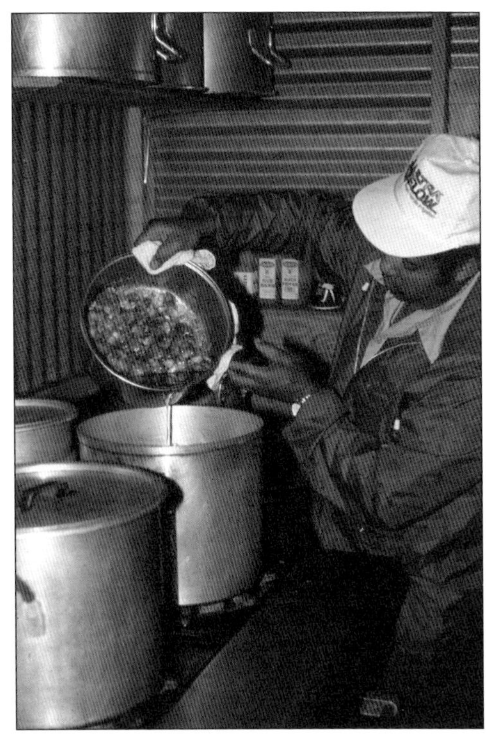

Sometimes spelled "purloo," "pilau," or "pirlou," perloo is a traditional one-pot rice dish with West African origins that is central to the cuisine in Jacksonville's Gullah Geechee community. Photographed in March 1988, Hiram Jenkins cooks chicken stock for a perloo dish at his barbecue stand in Mandarin. Hiram's BBQ was also known for its ribs and collard greens. (State Archives of Florida.)

Fishing holds deep cultural and historical importance within Jacksonville's Gullah Geechee community, serving as both a means of livelihood and a link to ancestral traditions. Using cast nets, crab traps, and shrimping techniques passed down through generations, community members fish for sustenance and commerce alike. This enduring practice sustains not only families but also the Gullah Geechee heritage, shaping local cuisine, identity, and the strong bonds that unite the community. (Ritz Theatre & Museum.)

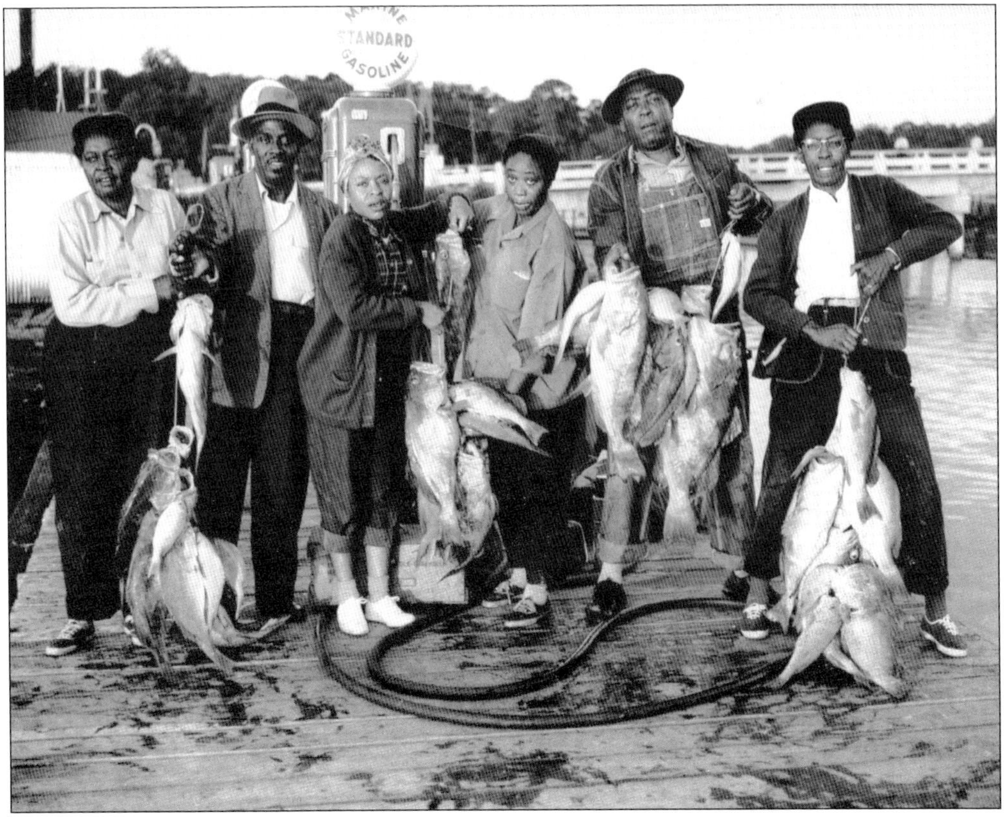

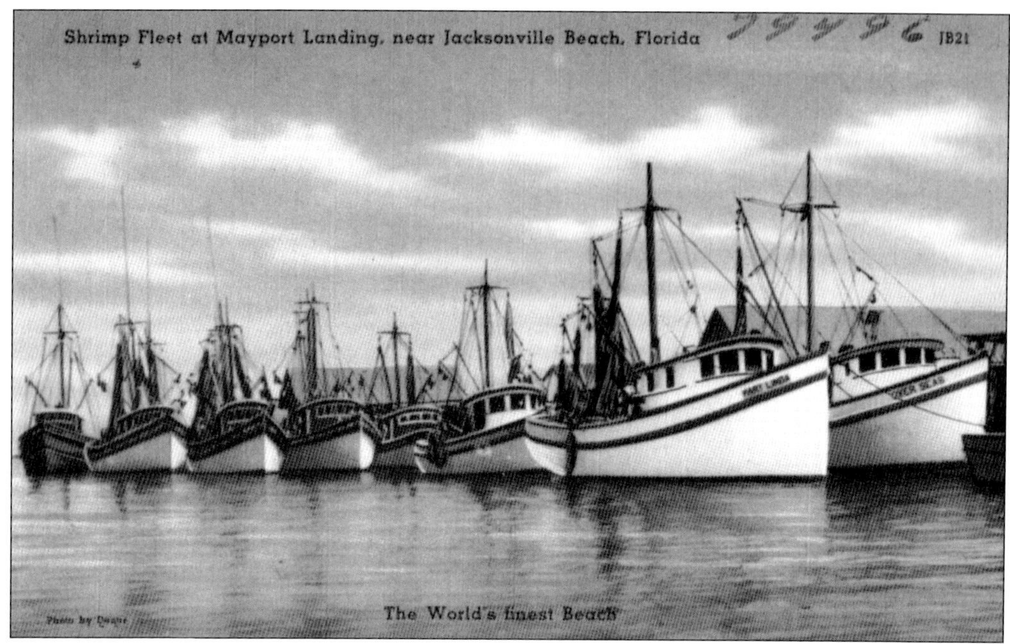

Across Jacksonville and the First Coast, restaurants take pride in serving fresh Mayport shrimp, which is locally caught wild Atlantic shrimp unloaded in the historic fishing village of Mayport. The local waters provide an ideal breeding ground, producing shrimp known for their sweet flavor and freshness. This culinary tradition dates back thousands of years, when the region's Native American inhabitants first harvested shrimp from the abundant coastal estuaries. (Boston Public Library.)

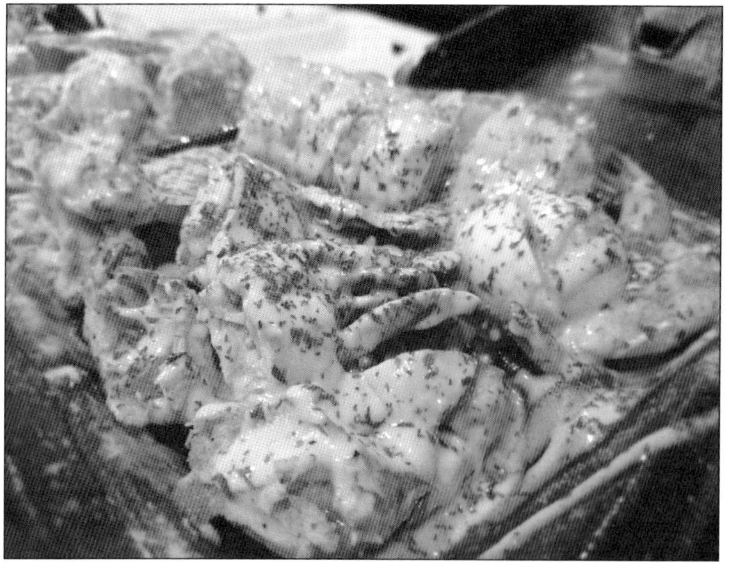

A variant of the well-known seafood boil, garlic crabs are cooked in a melted garlic butter sauce with sausage, corn, eggs, and potatoes. Garlic crabs can be found across the coastal Southeast, but Jacksonville is the world capital of the dish, which is served up at dozens of local crab shacks and restaurants, especially in historic Northside neighborhoods. (Ennis Davis, AICP.)

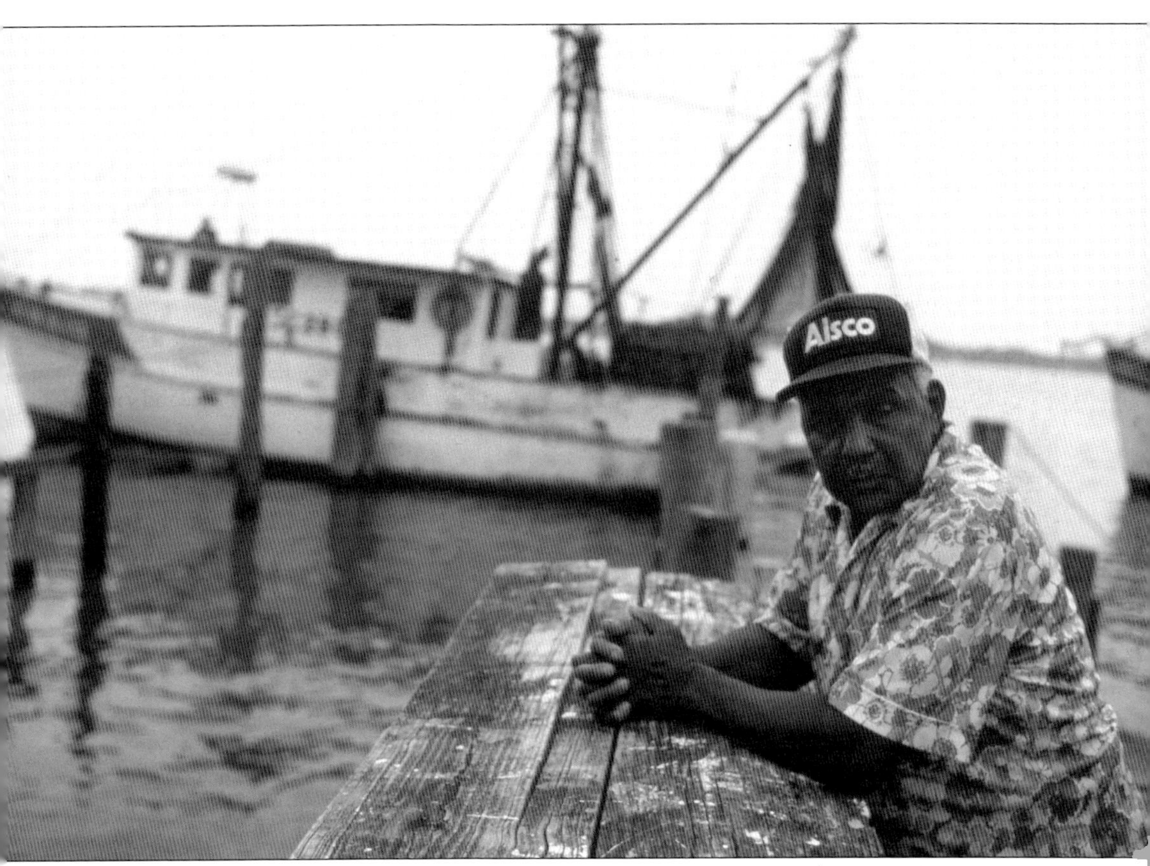

Capt. Eddie Baker is photographed with his shrimp boat, *Miss Alice*, on July 22, 1986, in Mayport. Once called Hazard, Mayport was platted in 1841 by David Palmer and Darius Ferris. Palmer and Ferris operated a mill at Mayport with an enslaved labor force. Early settlers came from the island of Minorca, Portugal, and France, working as bar pilots and fishermen. Mayport's semi-isolation was broken with the establishment of Naval Station Mayport during World War II. By the mid-20th century, Ocean Street had become lined with seafood restaurants, fish houses, and markets. Mayport remains a local favorite because of its laid-back atmosphere, waterfront setting, seafood restaurants, and commercial shrimping industry. (State Archives of Florida)

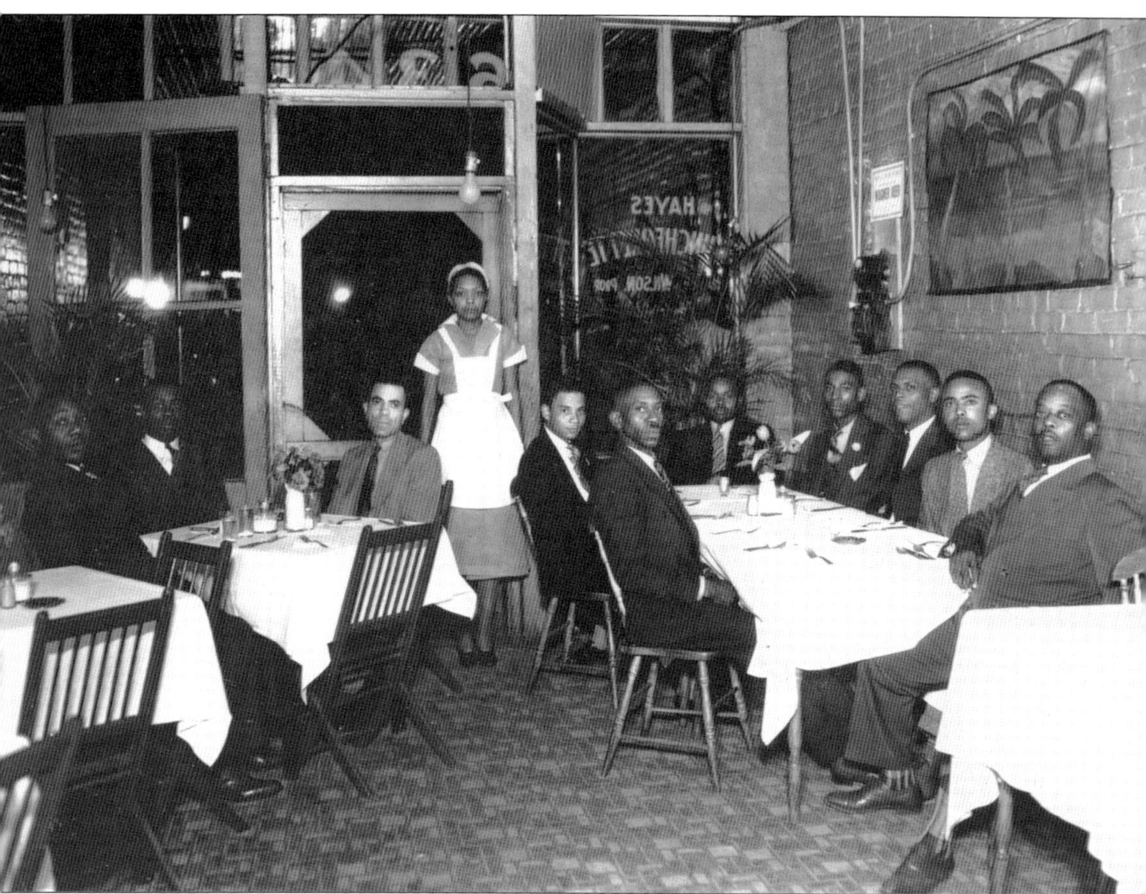

The Hayes Luncheonette in LaVilla, owned by Georgia Wilson and Gibbous Hayes, is seen in this c. 1938 photograph. It was next to the Lenape Bar. Soul food's roots trace to West African cuisine, where staples like okra and rice originated before being brought to the Americas through the transatlantic slave trade. Blending African traditions with available Southern ingredients, it became a hallmark of African American culture. After Reconstruction, freedmen settling in Jacksonville brought these flavors, establishing eateries serving dishes that remain central to local culinary life. This culinary history lives on in local restaurants like Blu Diner, Soul Food Express, and Uncle Gene's Soul & Seafood. (Ritz Theatre & Museum.)

In 1961, Nathan Nesbit Sr. opened a donut and sandwich shop at Myrtle Avenue and Kings Road. In June 1964, he established a new drive-through location at 5913 Avenue B. In 1965, a dining room was added, and the menu was expanded to include seafood, chicken, and hamburgers. Today, Nesbit Restaurant is one of Jacksonville's longest continuously operating restaurants. (Ennis Davis, AICP.)

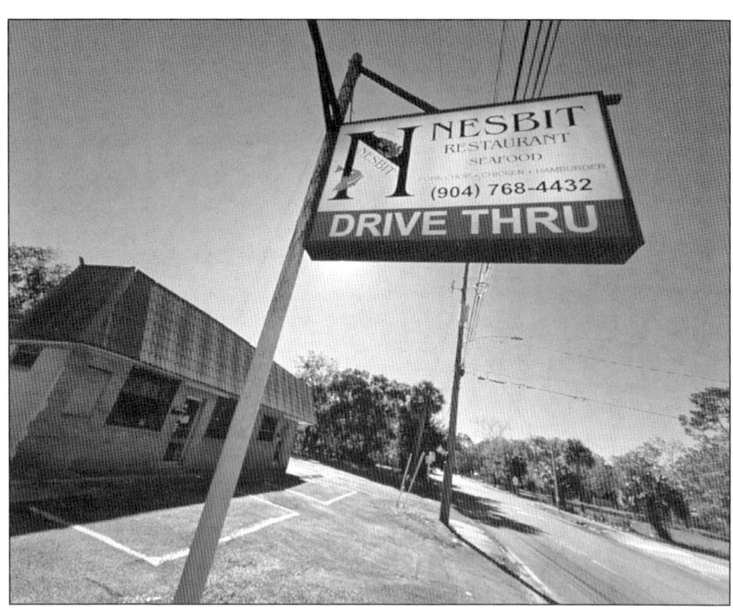

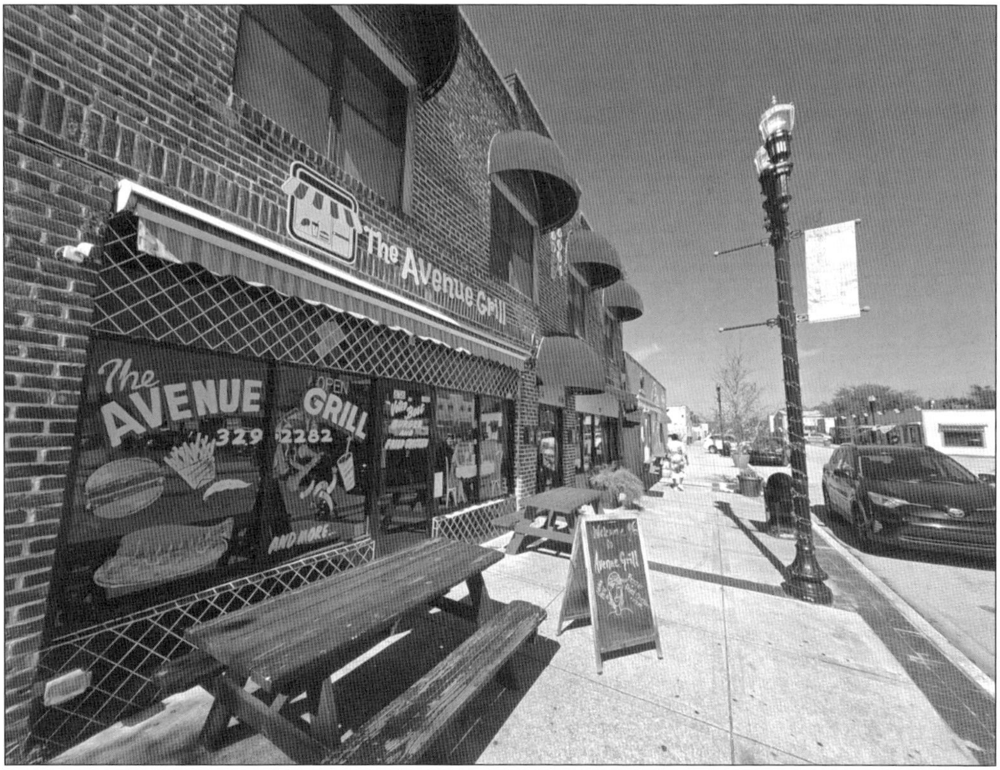

Established in 2013, the Avenue Grill is a beloved Eastside staple located at 818 A. Philip Randolph Boulevard. Owned by Kacheryl "Cookie" Gantt, the restaurant is celebrated for its fried seafood, salmon croquettes, fish and grits, chicken wings, and burgers. For over a decade, the Avenue Grill has nourished both body and spirit, hosting an annual community Christmas breakfast and remaining a cornerstone of neighborhood pride and connection. (Ennis Davis, AICP.)

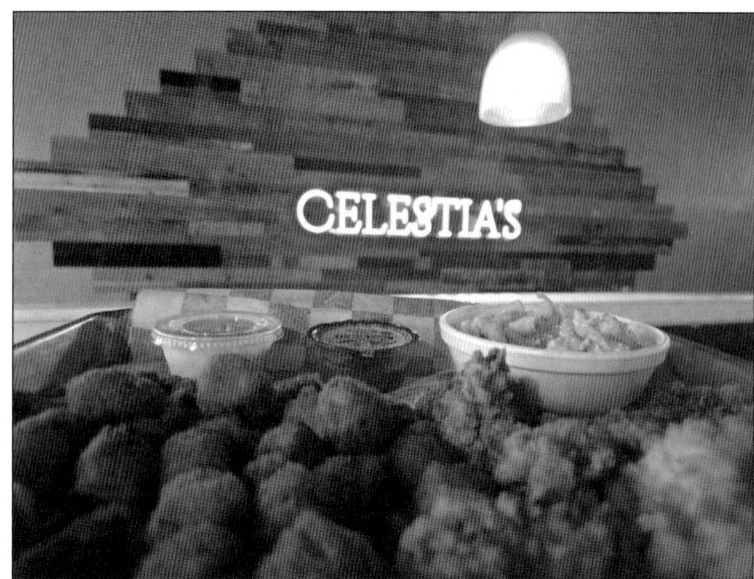

Celestia's Coastal Cuisine is well known for its seafood platters, seafood boils, fried chicken, and fried or smothered pork chops. Located at 6765 Dunn Avenue, the Northside restaurant was established by chef Celestia Mobley and her husband, Varon Mobley, in 2017 and honors the classic soul food of her childhood. (Ennis Davis, AICP.)

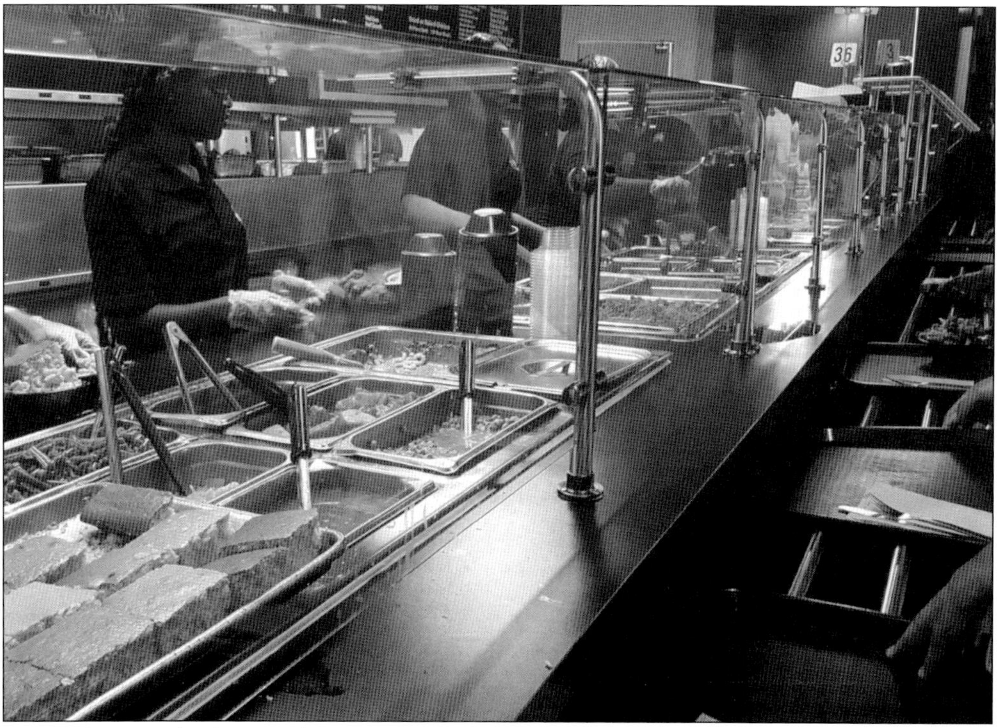

Founded in 1998 by the Potter's House Christian Fellowship of Jacksonville, the Potter's House Soul Food Bistro is one of the city's most popular soul food destinations. Originally called the Potter's House Café, it was expanded and rebranded to anchor the renovated Kingdom Plaza (formerly Normandy Mall). Known for its oxtails and Southern favorites, the restaurant's success led to a second location in Regency. (Ennis Davis, AICP.)

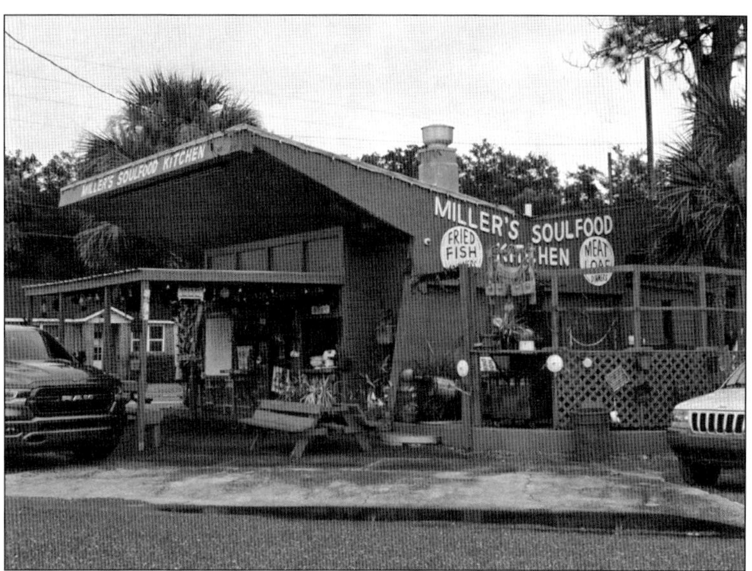

Miller's Soulfood Kitchen is located in an old Skinners' Dairy Milk House at 7303 Pearl Street in North Shore. Originally called Miller's Produce, the business started at the Jacksonville Farmers Market on Beaver Street, selling collard greens and other vegetables. While the menu is expansive, $5 soul food meals are Miller's claim. (Ennis Davis, AICP.)

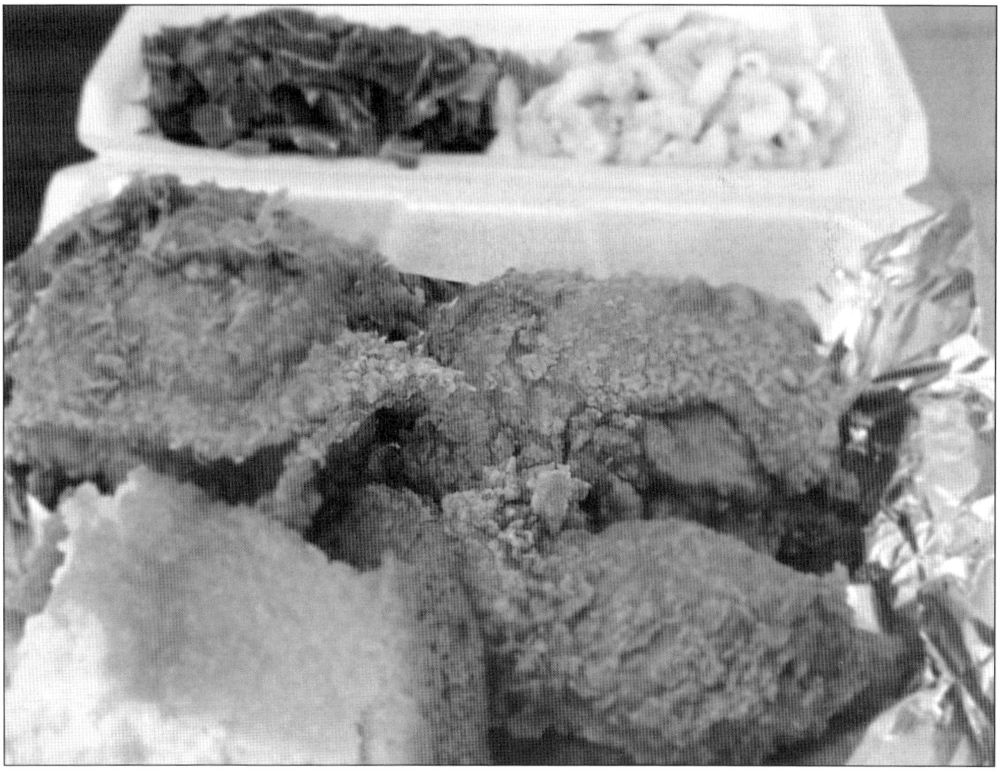

After 27 years in the food and service industry, Richard Jones fulfilled his lifelong dream by founding Shut Em Down Authentic Southern Restaurant in 2014. Joined by his wife, Cathy, and brother, Thomas, he created a place to share his love for food. Built on cherished family recipes passed down through generations, Shut Em Down offers the community a true taste of tradition, warmth, and family-inspired hospitality. (Ennis Davis, AICP.)

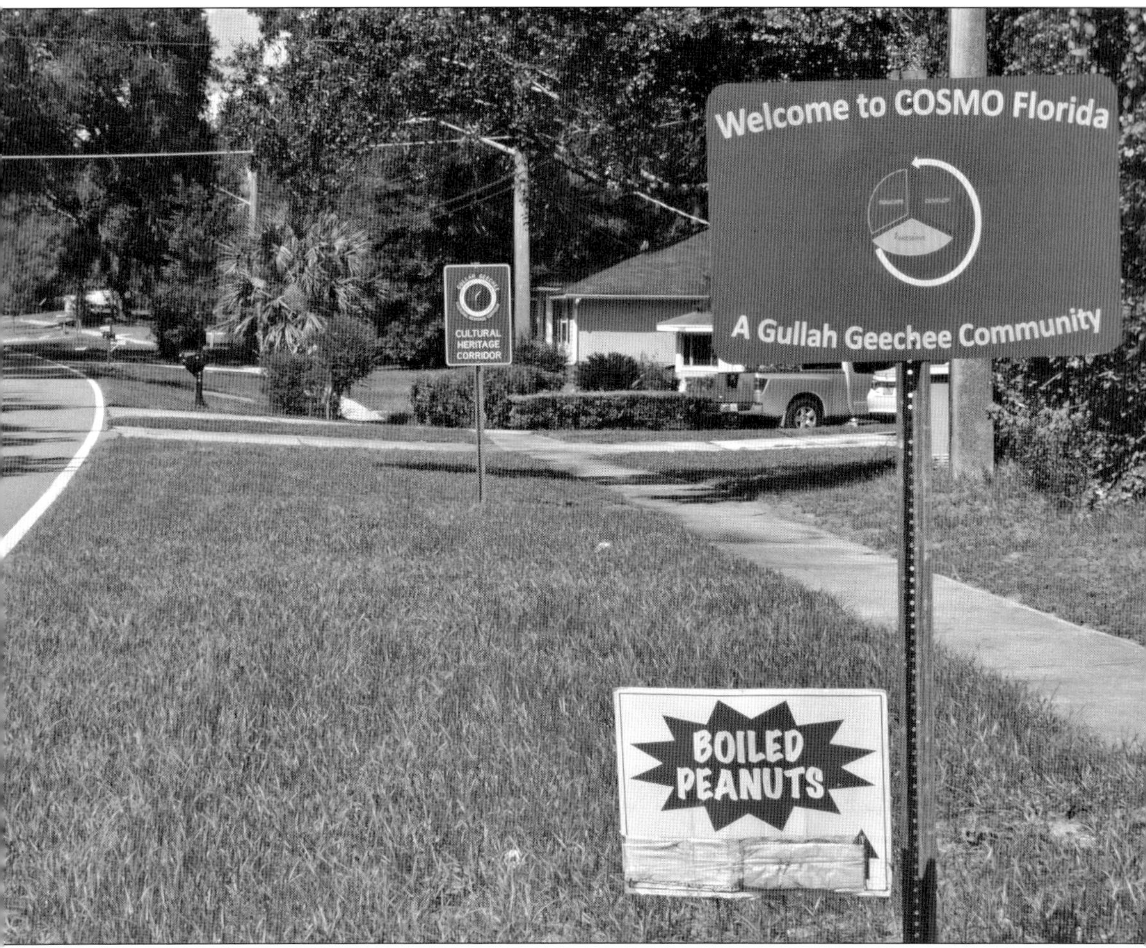

Boiled peanuts, once known as "goober peas," have deep roots in Southern folk culture and Gullah Geechee history. Brought to North America by enslaved Africans in the 18th century, peanuts were initially cultivated in small garden plots for family use. When crops were abundant, communities gathered for lively peanut boils, celebrating with conversation, music, and food. By the early 20th century, peanuts had become a Southern staple. Today, across Jacksonville, this tradition lives on with boiled green peanuts available at roadside stands, farmers' markets, flea markets, and local stores, continuing to connect past and present through a simple, shared delicacy. (Ennis Davis, AICP.)

Five

The Spirit

Faith was and is the heartbeat of Jacksonville's Gullah Geechee community. Spiritual practice for Gullah Geechee people has long bridged the worlds of the seen and unseen. Gullah Geechee spirituality embodies African, Indigenous, and European traditions that arrived on these shores through the various cultures that blended here. Religion and spirituality offered support here on Earth and transcendence beyond. These practices shaped the moral and cultural foundation for Jacksonville's Gullah Geechee descendants.

In the 19th century, praise houses and brush arbors gave rise to the first independent Black Christian churches in the state of Florida. Early Black congregations include Mother Midway AME Church, organized in 1865, and Bethel Baptist Institutional Church, whose congregation secured ownership of their sanctuary after emancipation. These early houses of worship became centers of community power. Churches founded schools, insurance companies, and civil rights organizations that carried faith into public life. Churches like Mount Zion AME, St. Paul AME, and Mount Ararat Missionary Baptist welcomed voices of leadership and protest from local pastors to national figures like Dr. Martin Luther King Jr.

Worship itself reflected the spirit of freedom. Through call and response, congregations built shared dialogue. Through spirituals, people expressed sorrow and hope. Through the ring shout, people embodied African rhythms and movement. Gullah Geechee worship overall reflects joy, determination, and resistance.

Beyond formal religion, Gullah Geechee people also preserved older spiritual systems. Root work, including herbalism, divination, and healing, continued in homes and shops like LaVilla's Eureka Novelty Store, affirming the interconnected nature of body, spirit, and earth.

Death and remembrance carry significant spiritual meaning in Gullah Geechee communities. In cemeteries across Jacksonville, graves face east to greet the rising sun, and loved ones leave offerings to comfort the departed. The same faith that sustained community members in life helped guide the journey beyond.

Together, these practices form a blend of worship and belief that grounds the Gullah Geechee experience. This chapter demonstrates how this sacred inheritance continues to guide Jacksonville's religious and spiritual landscape today.

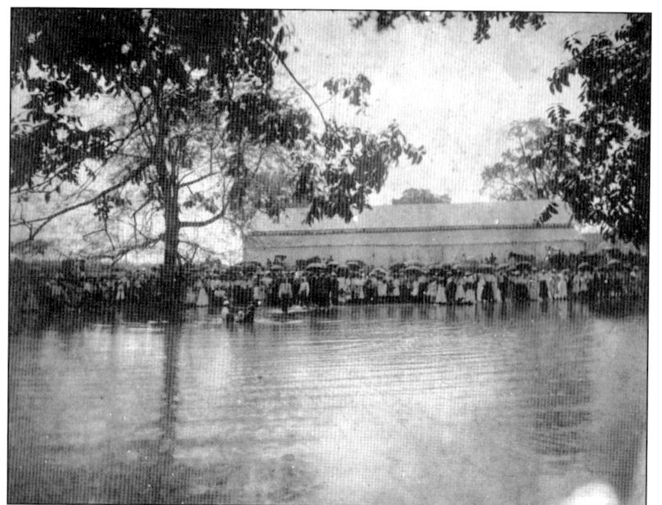

Baptisms typically involved full immersion at the beach or in tidal creeks. Baptisms could be an all-day event and occurred after high tide so that all sins would be washed away with the outgoing tide. This tradition continues today with outdoor baptisms or with baptismal pools inside churches. The Gullah word for baptism is *bactizum* or to *bactize*. (Eartha M.M. White Collection, Thomas G. Carpenter Library Special Collections and University Archives, University of North Florida.)

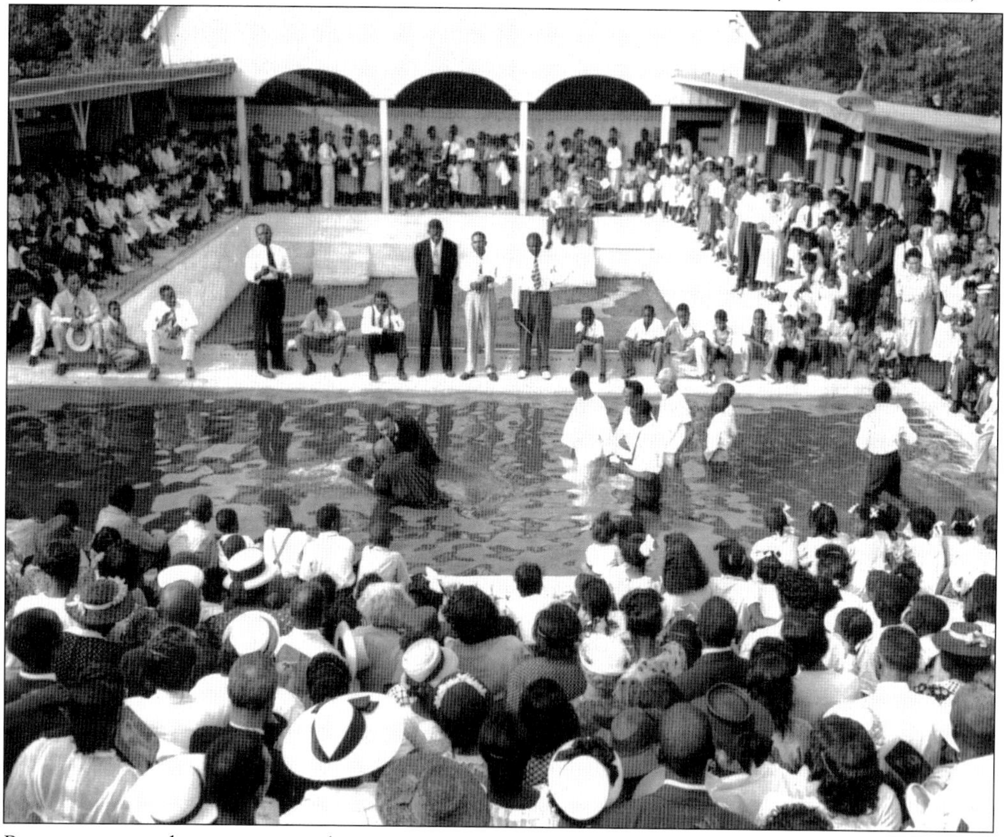

Participants and spectators gather for a baptism at Moncrief Springs, once a popular spot in Jacksonville's Moncrief neighborhood. The area is named after a spring along Moncrief Creek, tied to a local legend of Eugene Moncrief, a French pawnbroker who fled the French Revolution with Marie Antoinette's jewels. Folklore tells of love, betrayal, and hidden treasure. Moncrief's legacy lives on in the mystery of the spring and the neighborhood that bears his name. (Eartha M.M. White Collection, Thomas G. Carpenter Library Special Collections and University Archives, University of North Florida.)

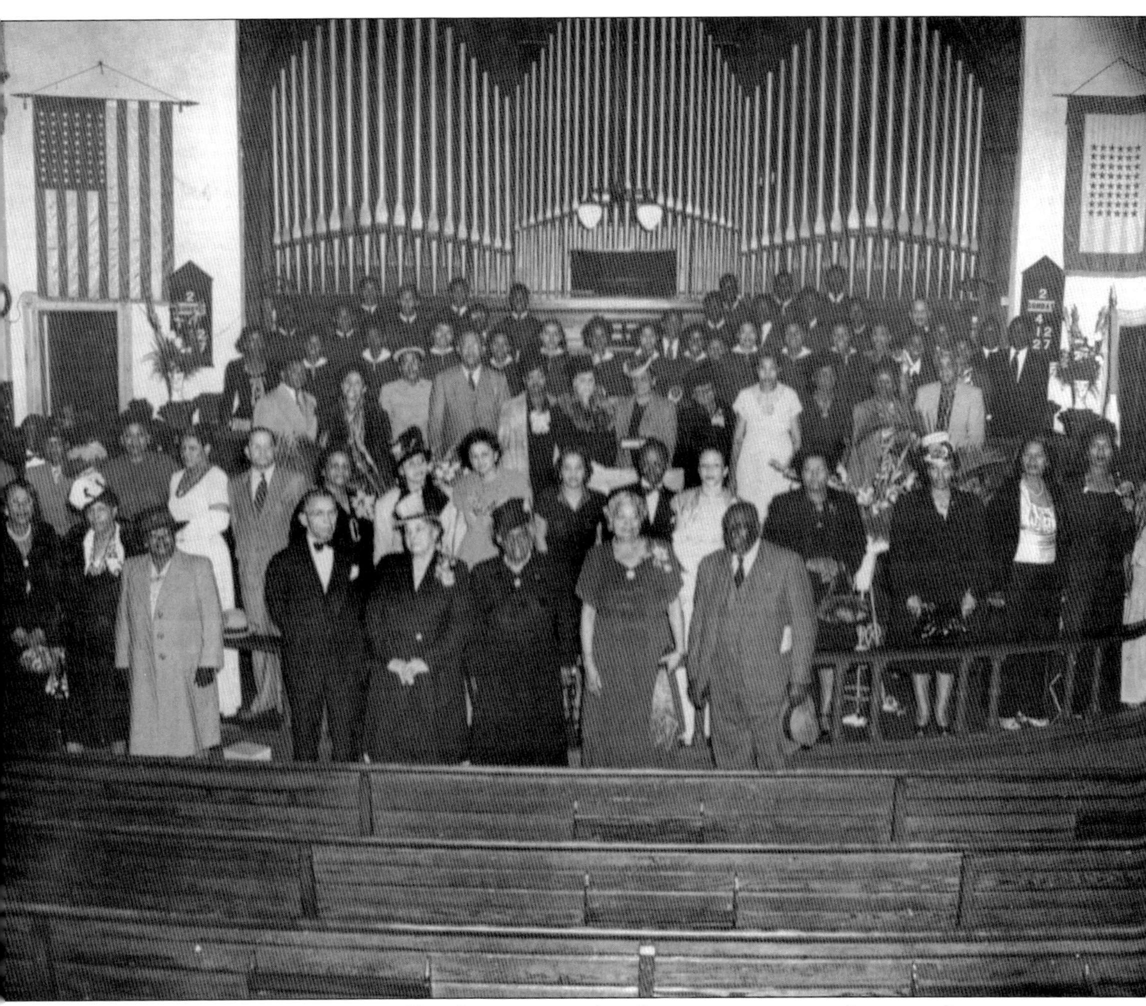

A component of worship is the call-and-response style. This is an interaction between the minister and the congregation, with people responding and adding commentary to the minister's words. Spirituals, group songs intended to invoke the presence of spirit and feeling, are central to Gullah Geechee religious practice. In *The Sanctified Church*, Zora Neale Hurston noted, "Contrary to popular belief their creation is not confined to the slavery period. Like the folk-tales, the spirituals are being made and forgotten every day." In this c. 1940s photograph, Dr. Mary McLeod Bethune and the Bethune-Cookman College Choir attend LaVilla's Ebenezer United Methodist Church. (Bethune-Cookman University.)

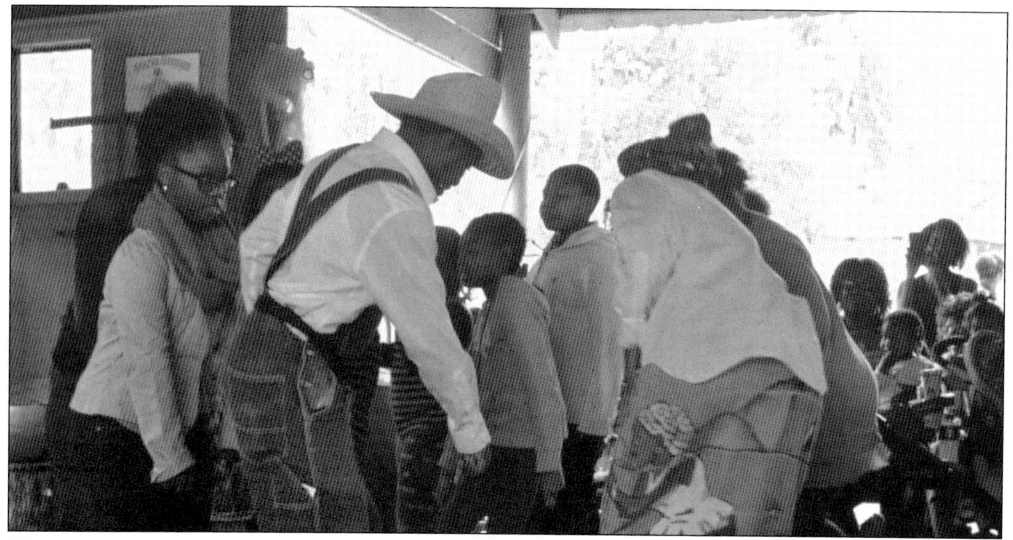

The ring shout is a unique part of Gullah Geechee religious worship that combines music, song, and movement. People move in a counter-clockwise ring and sing, shuffle, stomp, and clap to different rhythms. James Weldon Johnson recalled in his autobiography, *Along This Way*, that Aunt Venie, the champion ring shouter of St. Paul's Church in Jacksonville, "never missed a ring shout" and noted the music was "an African chant and an African dance . . . round and round the ring would go." In this photograph, Griffin Lotson of Gullah Geechee Ring Shouters demonstrates the ring shout. (Heather Hodges.)

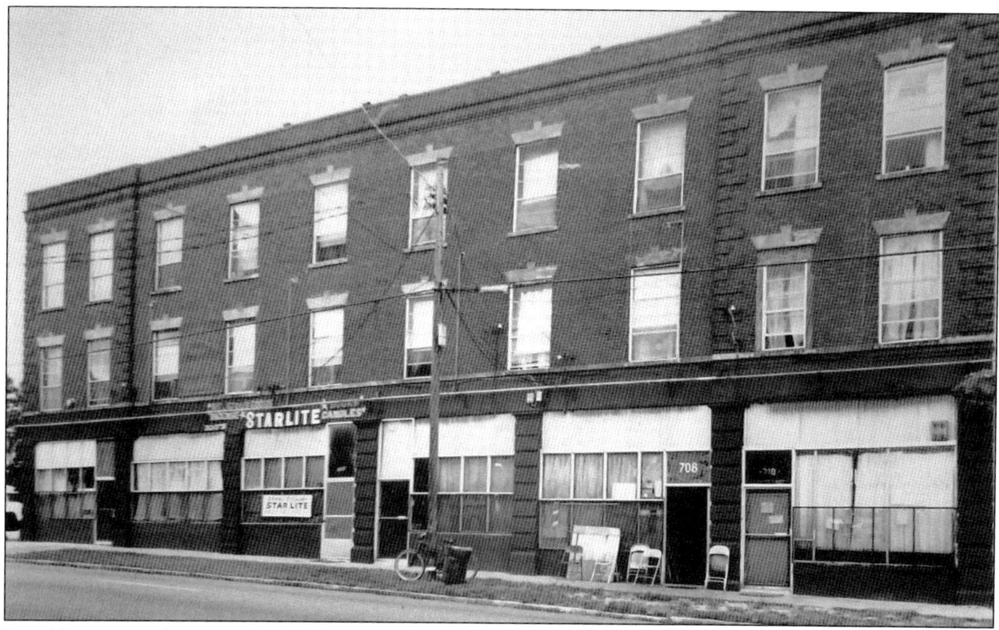

In addition to Christianity, Gullah Geechee people maintain connections to herbalism, spiritualism, and magic. These practices, connected to West African and Indigenous traditions, are called the root. Root doctors are the practitioners. Root doctors use a combination of herbs, other ingredients, and words or songs to assist seekers with various ailments or petitions. Businesses like the Starlite on Broad Street in LaVilla commercialized the root experience for Gullah Geechee descendants in Jacksonville. (University of Florida.)

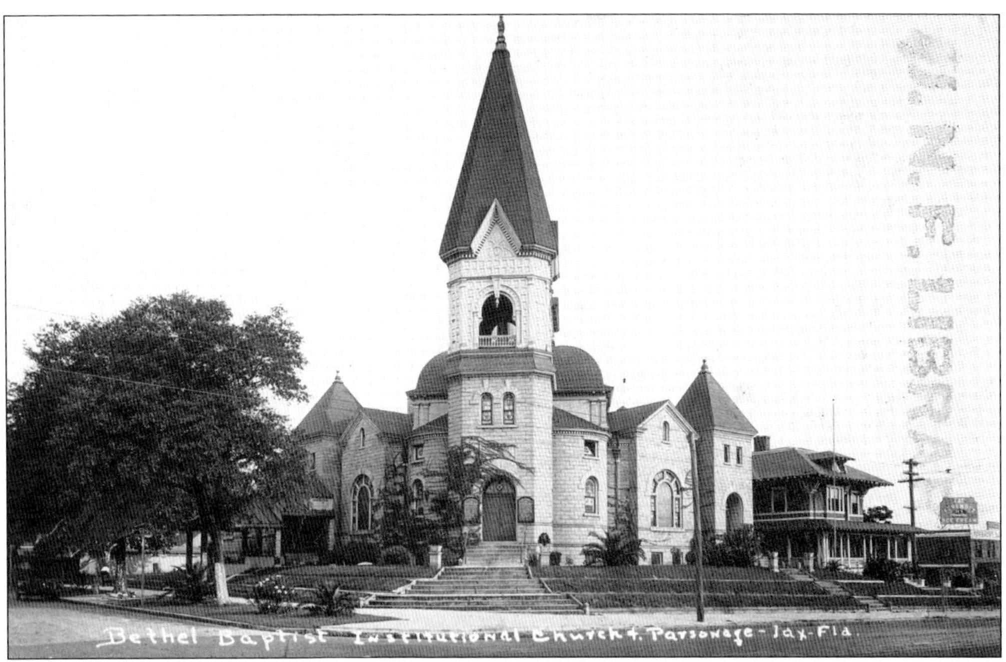

Founded in 1838, Bethel Baptist Institutional Church is Jacksonville's oldest Baptist congregation. Originally comprising enslavers and the enslaved, the church was legally awarded to its Black members after the Civil War. Rebuilt in 1904 after the Great Fire, its grand Greek and Romanesque Revival sanctuary became a cornerstone of Black Jacksonville. With 12,000 members, Bethel fostered institutions like the Afro-American Life Insurance Company and once counted Zora Neale Hurston among its congregation. (Eartha M.M. White Collection, Thomas G. Carpenter Library Special Collections and University Archives, University of North Florida.)

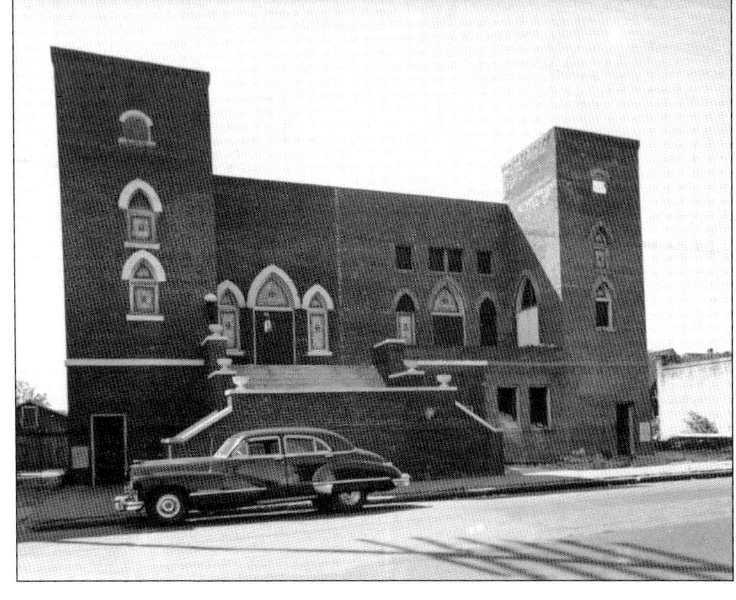

LaVilla's Second Missionary Baptist Church was established in 1848. The church's founders once worshipped with their enslavers at Bethel Baptist before organizing a place of their own. This brick sanctuary, designed by James Edwards Hutchins, was completed under the leadership of Rev. King David Britt. It was designated as a local historic landmark in 2014. (Ritz Theatre & Museum.)

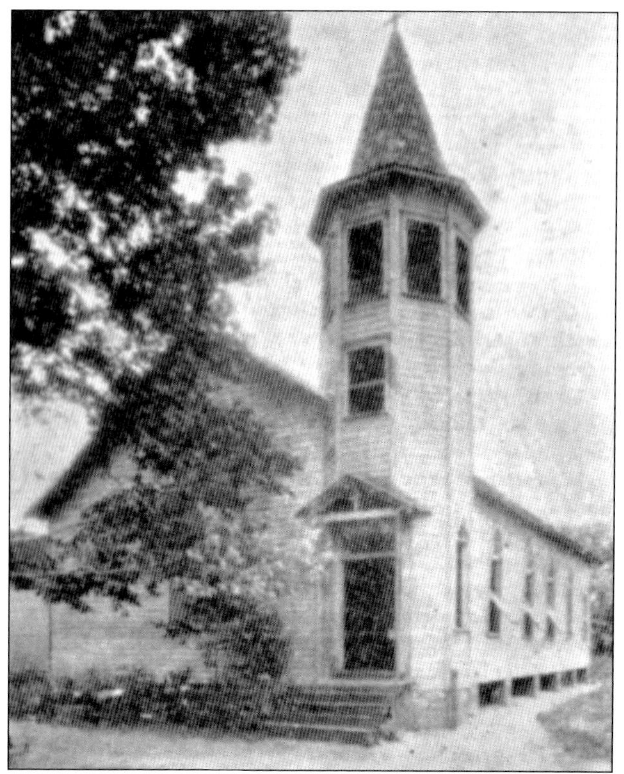

Located in the Eastside, Mother Midway African Methodist Episcopal Church was organized on June 10, 1865, a few weeks after the Confederate army surrendered to the Union in Florida. Mother Midway is the first Black independent church established in Florida. It is known as the "mother" of both the Florida Conference of the AME Church, which was organized in 1867, and the East Florida Conference, which was organized in 1877. (State Archives of Florida.)

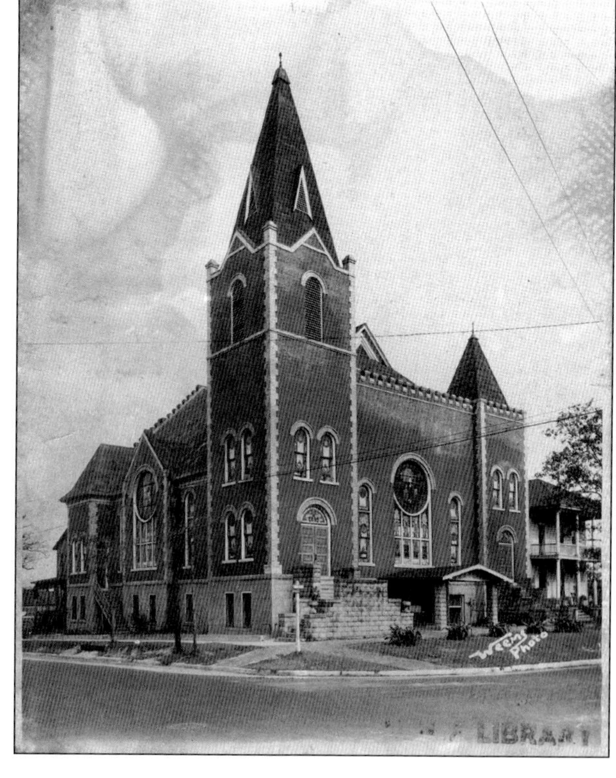

The Mount Zion African Methodist Episcopal Church was founded on July 28, 1866, by formerly enslaved people who organized a society for the purpose of religious worship. Acquiring land at the intersection of Beaver and Newnan Streets before emancipation, the church had built a 1,500-seat sanctuary prior to the Great Fire of 1901. The current Romanesque Revival structure was built between 1901 and 1905 to replace what the fire destroyed. (Eartha M.M. White Collection, Thomas G. Carpenter Library Special Collections and University Archives, University of North Florida.)

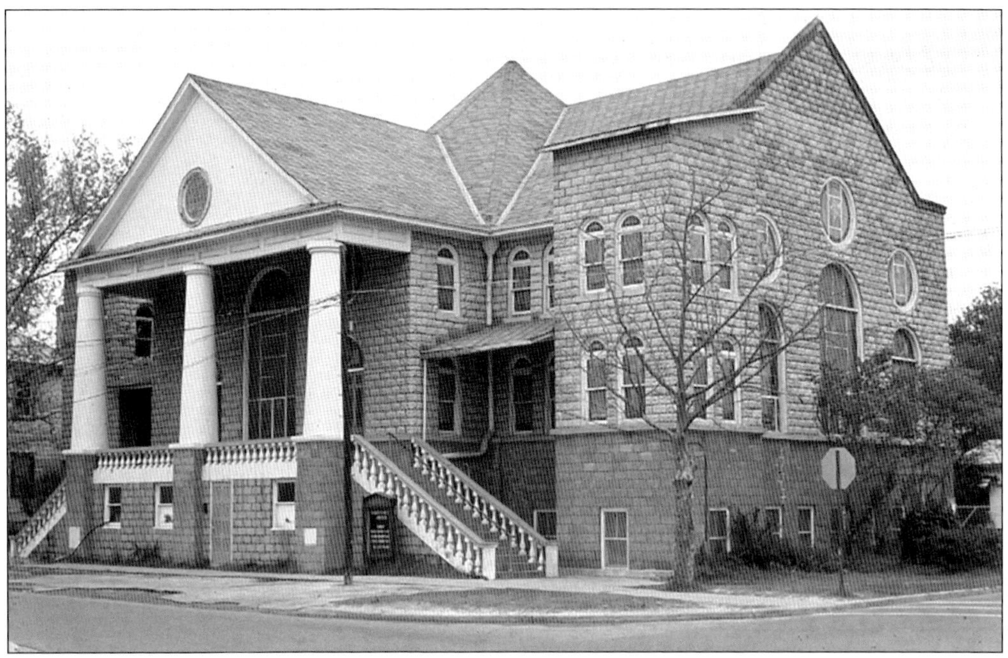

Organized in 1868, Mount Olive African Methodist Episcopal Church began as a brush arbor before this 1922 sanctuary, designed by former enslaved architect Richard L. Brown, rose at Pippen and Franklin Streets. In the early 1900s, young Asa Philip Randolph here observed Rev. Joseph Edward Lee, Jacksonville's first Black attorney and an eloquent orator, whose quiet power inspired Randolph's later leadership in the labor and civil rights movements. (University of Florida.)

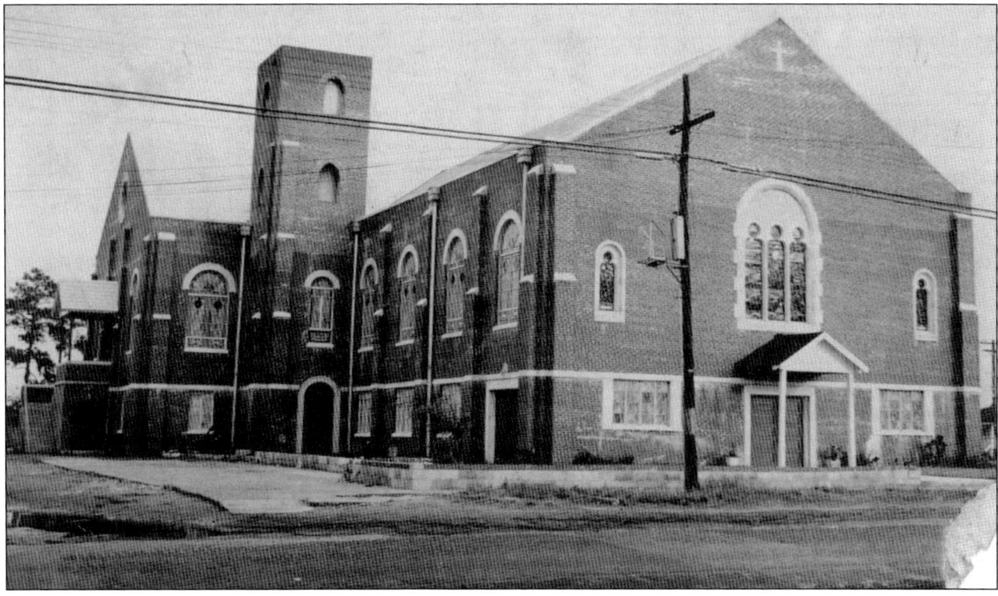

Organized in 1869 at the home of Samuel and Violet Williams, St. Paul African Methodist Episcopal Church began as a humble brush arbor of grass and palmetto leaves in LaVilla. Built in 1956, the church's sanctuary at 2225 North Myrtle Avenue was an important civil rights movement organizational site during the 1960s. This historic sanctuary now houses Harvest Ministries Worship & Community Center. (State Archives of Florida.)

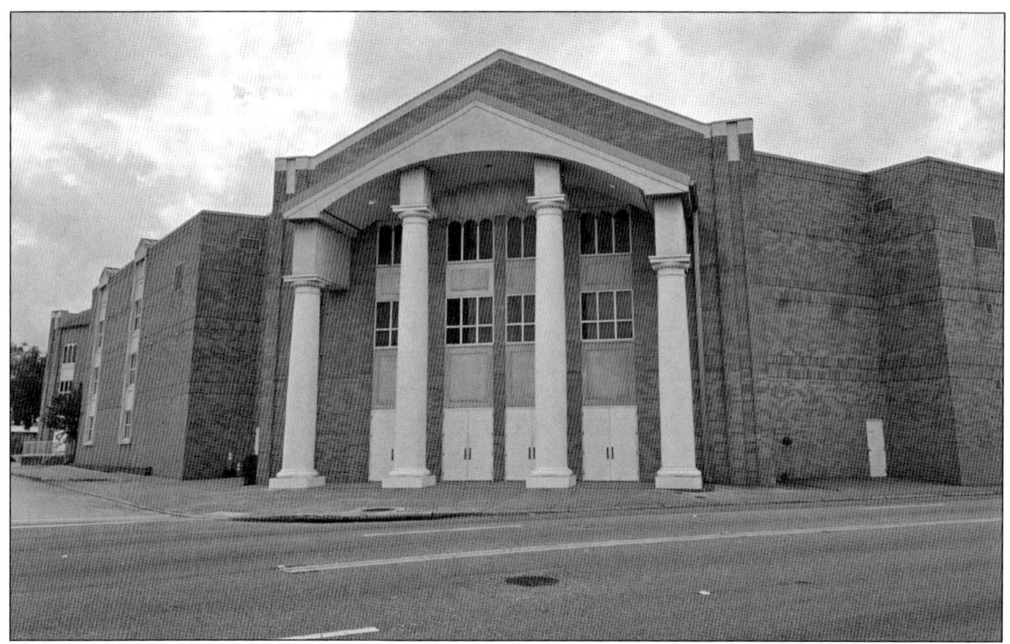

LaVilla's Shiloh Metropolitan Baptist Church was founded as a mission of Bethel Missionary Baptist Church in 1875. Rev. James Johnson, father of James Weldon and John Rosamond Johnson, led the congregation from the 1880s to 1901. In 1953, under Rev. A.B. Coleman Sr., Shiloh moved to its current site, where a 5,000-seat, state-of-the-art sanctuary was completed in 2002. (Ennis Davis, AICP.)

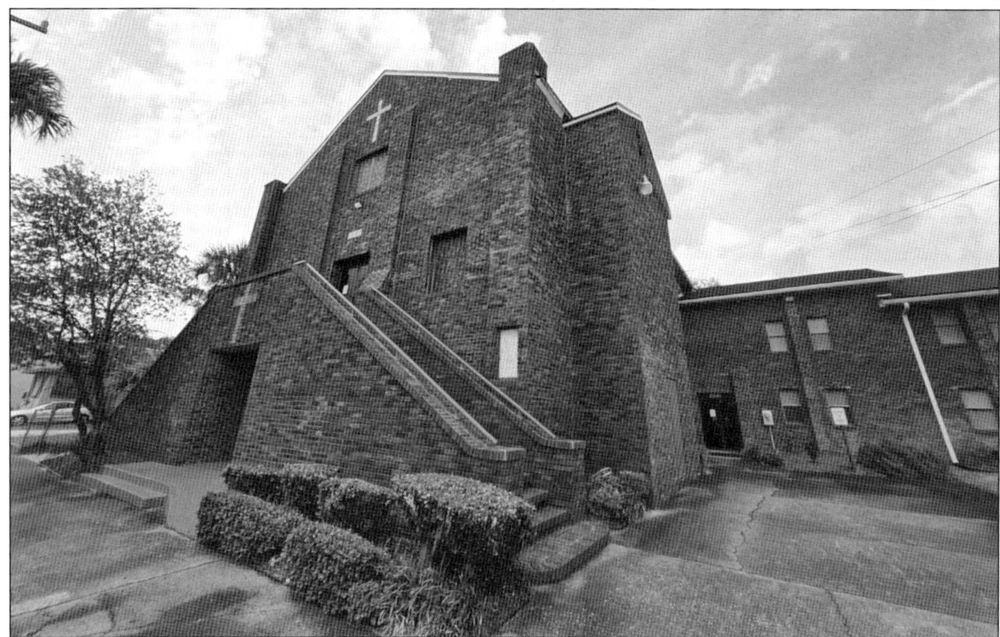

Founded in 1880 as Friendship Baptist Church, the First Baptist Church of Oakland first met in a former dance hall. Renamed in 1916, its current sanctuary was completed in 1944, designed by architect John Henry Rosemond. Born in 1879 in South Carolina, Rosemond settled in Jacksonville around 1915 and was one of a few African American builders before World War II to call himself an architect. (Ennis Davis, AICP.)

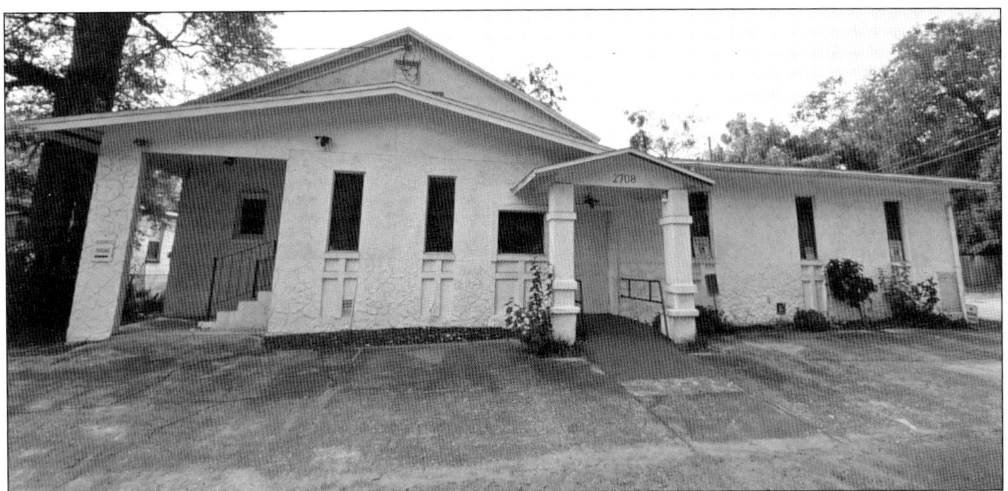

In 1891, Rev. James Williams Randolph moved his family to Jacksonville amid post-emancipation migration. The following year, he began hosting Saturday night fish and chicken fries to fund a new AME church, now Greater New Hope AME Chapel at 2708 North Davis Street. His son, Asa Philip Randolph, later became an international labor and civil rights leader, founding the Brotherhood of Sleeping Car Porters in the 1920s. (Ennis Davis, AICP.)

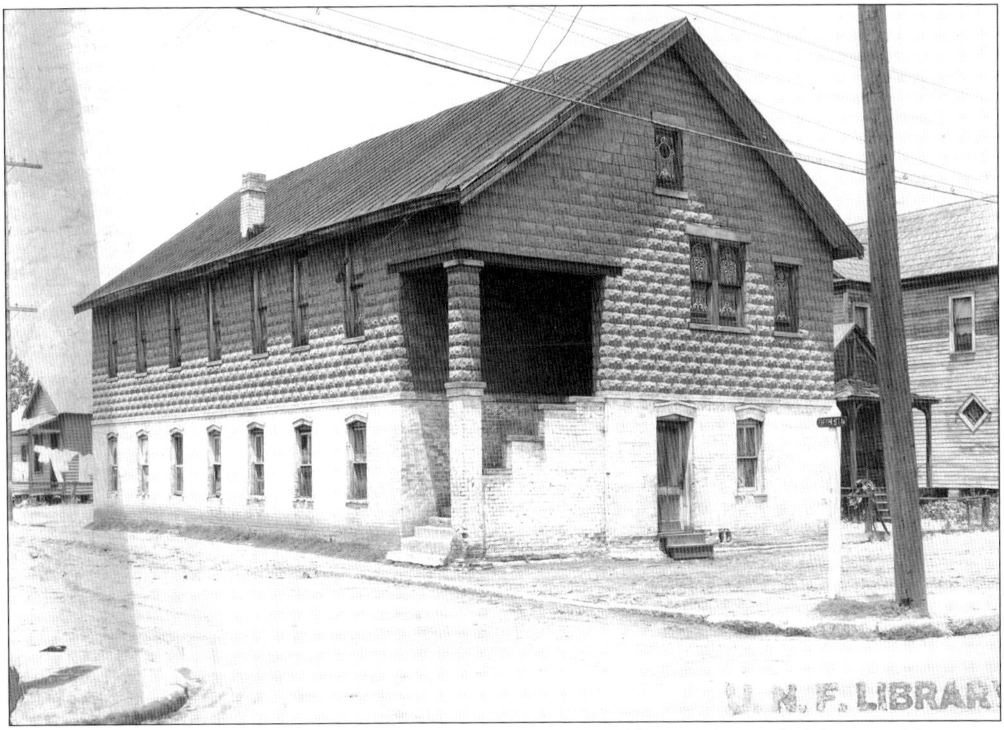

St. Stephen AME Church was founded in 1892, when a small group began holding weekly prayer meetings in a home at Davis and Harrison (now Fourth) Streets. In 1905, the congregation built its first sanctuary, shown in the photograph, at Davis and West Fifth Streets in Hansontown. That structure was later demolished and replaced by the current church building, which was dedicated on August 13, 1961. (Eartha M.M. White Collection, Thomas G. Carpenter Library Special Collections and University Archives, University of North Florida.)

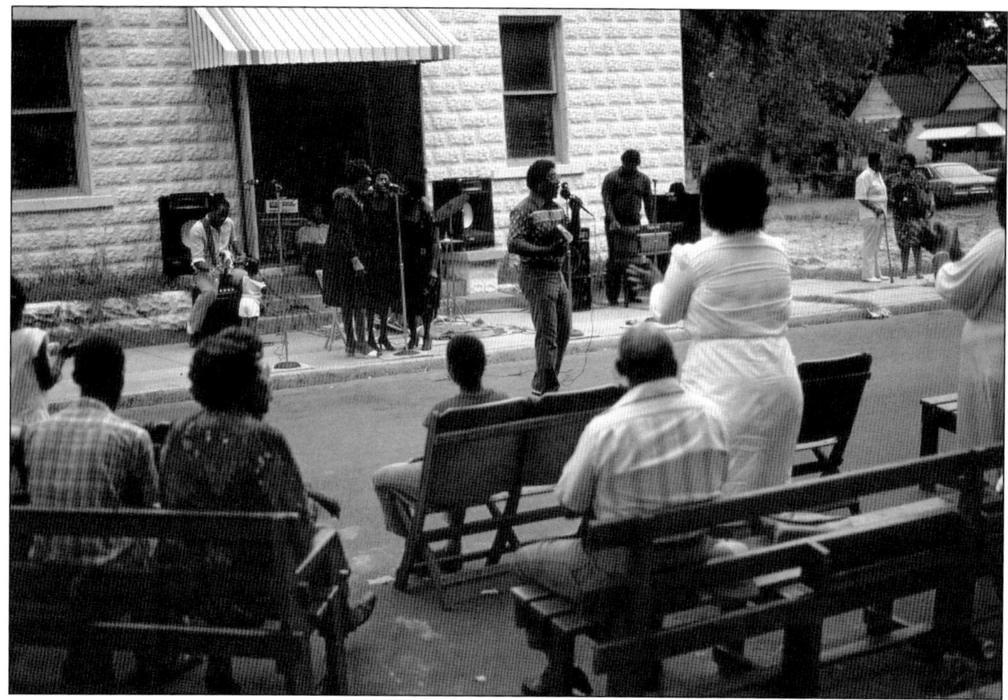

Built in 1911, the property at 723 West Fourth Street is one of the few surviving religious structures linked to the former Hansontown community. For 70 years, it housed the West Fourth Street Church of God, now the Beverly Hills Church of God. Since 1981, it has been home to El-Bethel Divine Holiness Church. Pictured here, Alonzo Hall performs at the church's gospel block party on August 17, 1985. (State Archives of Florida.)

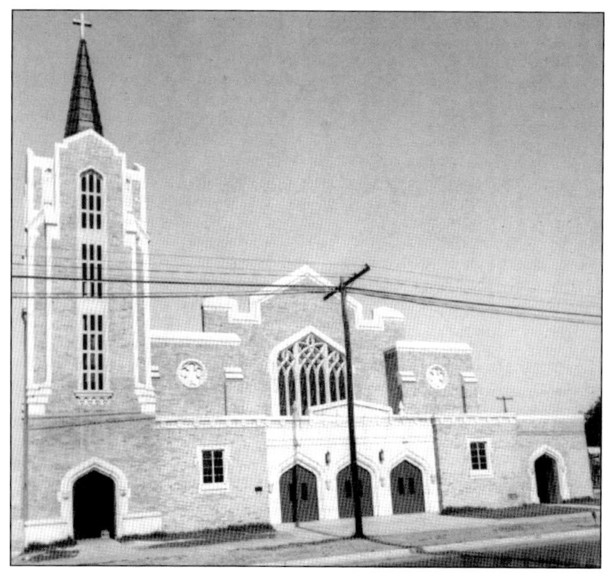

Organized in 1919, Mount Ararat Missionary Baptist Church, at 2502 Myrtle Avenue in Durkeeville, was rebuilt in 1958 under Rev. Dallas J. Graham. On March 19, 1961, Dr. Martin Luther King Jr. delivered his sermon "This Is a Great Time to Be Alive" at the church, urging nonviolent resistance. Sponsored by local civil rights groups, the event took place as Jacksonville's Black community increasingly challenged segregation and demanded equality amid growing racial tension. (Eartha M.M. White Collection, Thomas G. Carpenter Library Special Collections and University Archives, University of North Florida.)

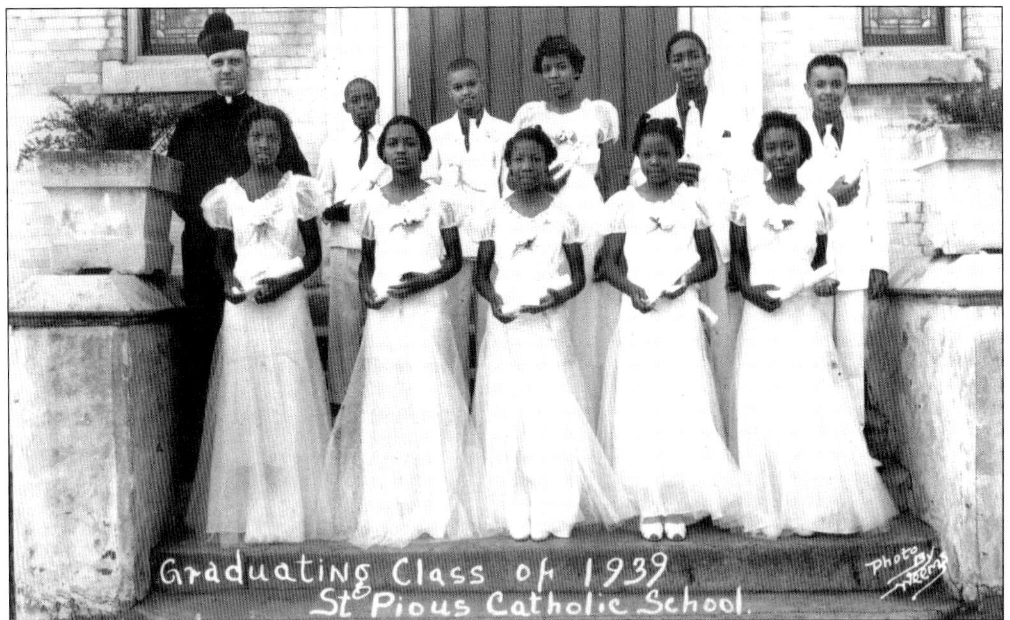

Due to Northeast Florida's Spanish colonial roots, the Catholic Church has played a historic role in the region. Many Gullah Geechee ancestors living during that era were connected to the Catholic faith. This spiritual legacy continues through African American congregations like St. Pius V, established in 1919 for Black parishioners. The parish operated a school for Black children and remains an active parish today. The church and school were located at the southeast corner of West State and Lee Streets in 1939. (Ritz Theatre & Museum.)

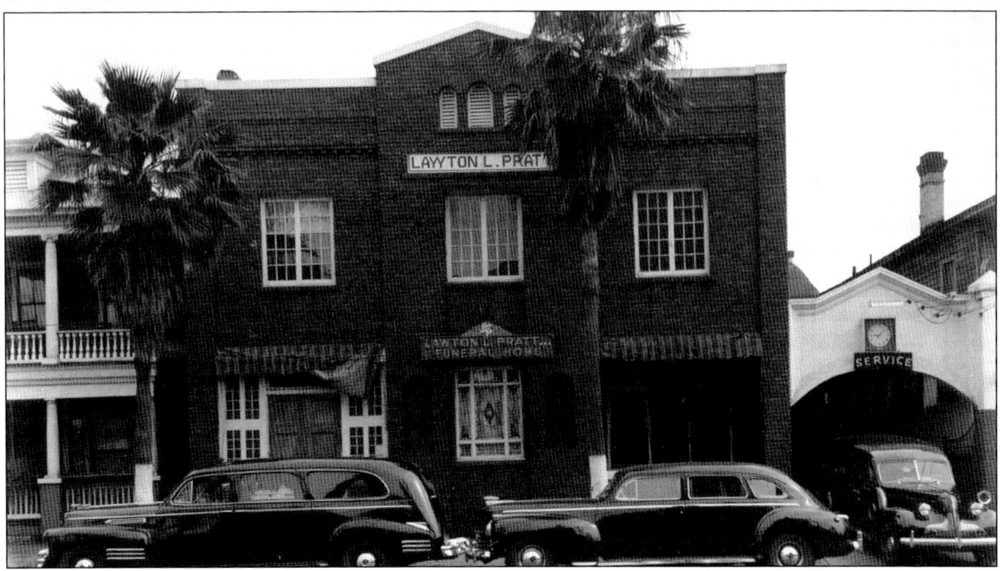

The Pratt Funeral home, like others in Black Jacksonville, served Gullah Geechee descendants during and after segregation. African American funeral directors were pillars of the community as business owners and leaders. They provided culturally sensitive services, coordinated with Black churches, and were often part of other community civic efforts. Black women found career opportunities as funeral directors. Black funeral homes and directors are often multigenerational, with each new generation continuing the family legacy. (Ritz Theatre & Museum.)

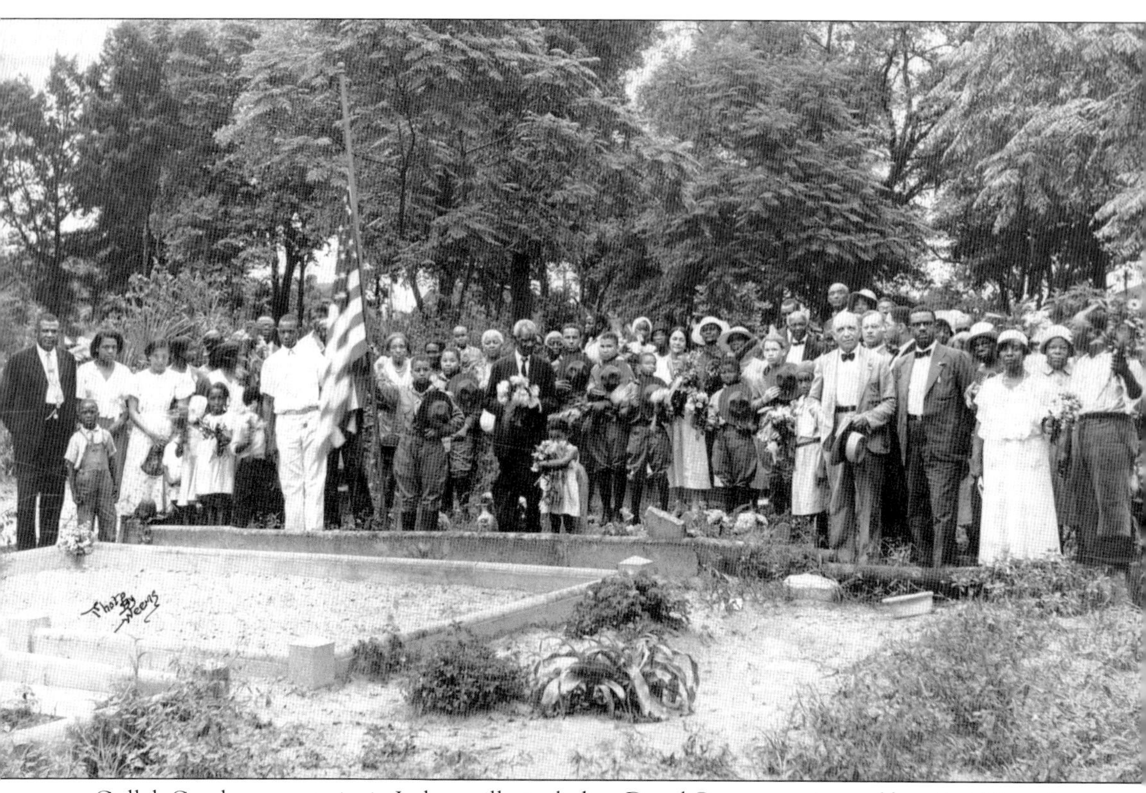

Gullah Geechee cemeteries in Jacksonville, including Duval Cemetery, pictured here in 1933, reflect African and spiritual traditions. Burials typically face east, and grave goods, such as chairs, plates, or personal belongings, were placed on the *grabe* (Gullah for grave). Testimony indicates this was to prevent their spirit from returning home. Families crafted headstones by hand using cement or purchased stones from masons like the Leapheart family. Vault-style burials reflect a burial practice that is connected to West African traditions. Cemeteries connected to Gullah Geechee ancestors in the city include but are not limited to: Old and New Mount Herman, Memorial, Sunset, Pinehurst, Hillside, Greenwood, Mount Olive, Clifton, Lone Star, St. Nicholas Bethel Baptist, St. Nicholas, New Berlin, and Palm Spring. (Eartha M.M. White Collection, Thomas G. Carpenter Library Special Collections and University Archives, University of North Florida.)

Six

The Work

Gullah Geechee labor built the economic foundation of Jacksonville. The skills and knowledge of the Gullah Geechee ancestors and descendants fueled the city's growth over time. Their work encompassed survival and innovation.

The waterways provided the earliest opportunities. Fishermen, shrimpers, and crabbers sustained families and started traditions that endure today along the St. Johns River and local creeks and in Mayport. Others found steady employment on the docks or in the railyards as gandy dancers and longshoremen. The establishment of the Jacksonville Terminal Company in 1919 and International Longshoremen's Association (ILA) Local No. 1408 in 1936 gave structure and dignity to Black labor within a segregated economy. Rural residents worked the pine forests, collecting resin for the naval stores industry that made Jacksonville the "Turpentine Capital of the World."

In the urban core, Gullah Geechee enterprise flourished. Men like Sylvanus Hart and Douglas Watson Onley broke barriers as bankers and industrialists. William and Henrietta Sumter and A.L. Lewis led pioneering Black insurance companies that safeguarded Black families' futures. Businesses like Skinner's Florist, Mercy Hospital, and Eartha White's Service Laundry demonstrated commerce and community care.

Women's work was equally essential. Gullah Geechee women labored as domestic workers, laundresses, midwives, and nurses. These professions demanded skill, resilience, and compassion. They tended White households by day and their own communities by night. Women sustained the institutions that defined Black Jacksonville.

Ultimately, Gullah Geechee workers built livelihoods that shaped the city's physical and social landscape. Their labor powered Jacksonville's growth, from its waterfront and factories to its hospitals, schools, and small businesses. This chapter demonstrates how Gullah Geechee descendants' pursuit of opportunity laid the groundwork for the economic and professional achievements that continue within the community today.

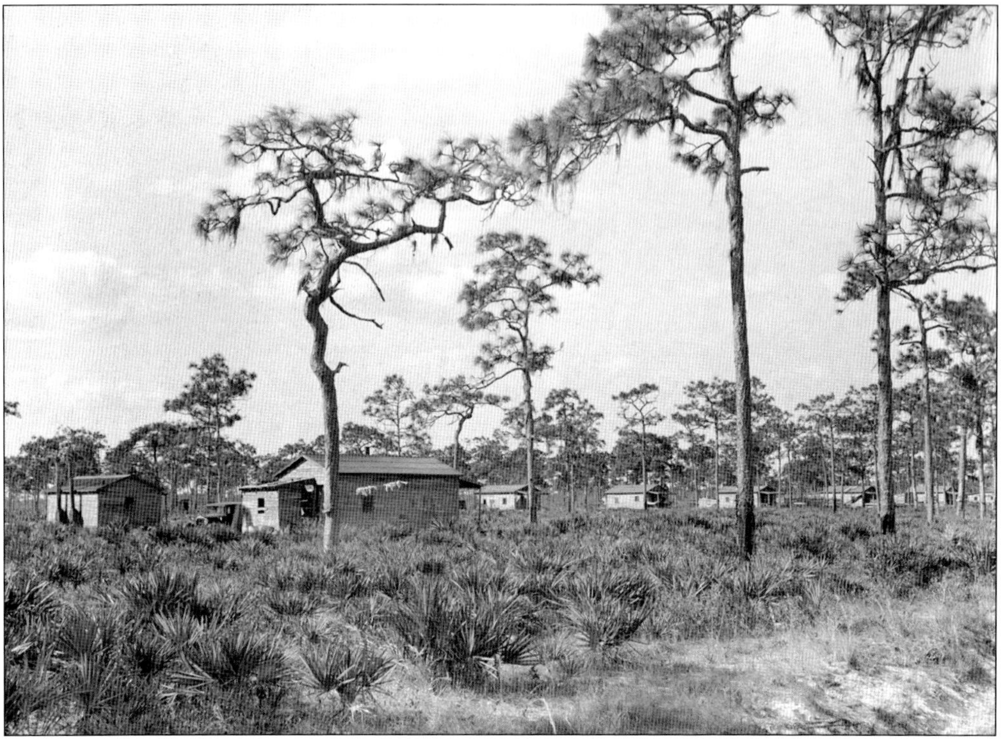

The turpentine and resin industry and its associated camps were a driving economic force for rural North Florida communities during the late 19th century as Jacksonville emerged as the Atlantic capital of the naval stores industry. Collectors were mostly African Americans who scraped gum, or tree sap, in area pine forests into barrels for transportation and ultimate processing in Jacksonville into turpentine. (Library of Congress.)

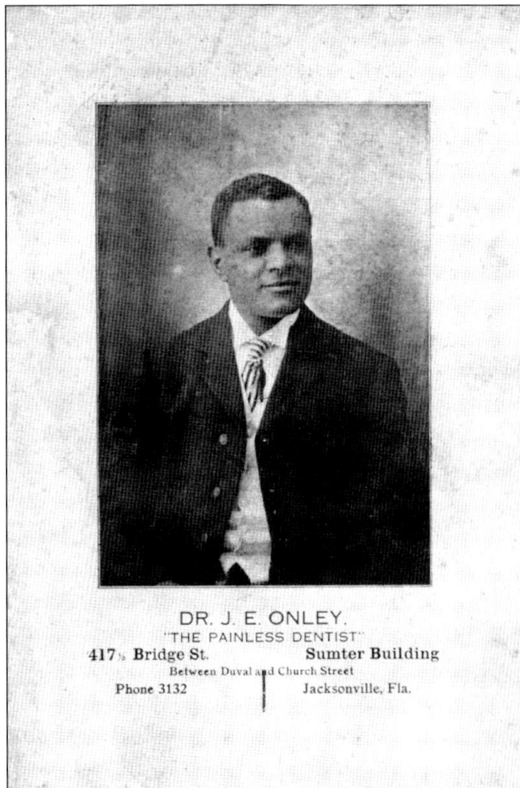

In the late 1880s, Dr. John Edward Onley Jr. and his brother, Dr. Douglas Watson Onley, operated the Onley Brothers contracting business at East Union and Liberty Streets. Next door, Dr. D.W. Onley owned Eureka Industrial Woodworks, the nation's first Black-owned steam sawmill, employing only Black workers. After a fire destroyed the mill in the 1890s, the brothers transitioned from construction to careers in dentistry. (Eartha M.M. White Collection, Thomas G. Carpenter Library Special Collections and University Archives, University of North Florida.)

Jacksonville is a hub for paper production and was once home to several paper mills. The St. Regis Paper Company opened along the Broward River in 1953 as the city's second-largest pulp and kraft mill. Today, it stands as the city's last remaining paper mill, producing 590,000 tons annually. Now operating as a 100 percent recycled facility, it has eliminated the odorous kraft process that once impacted the city's air quality for decades. (State Archives of Florida.)

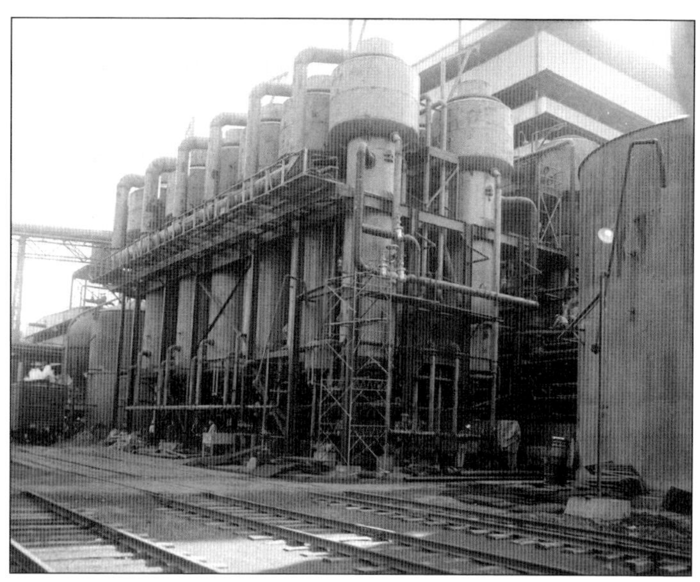

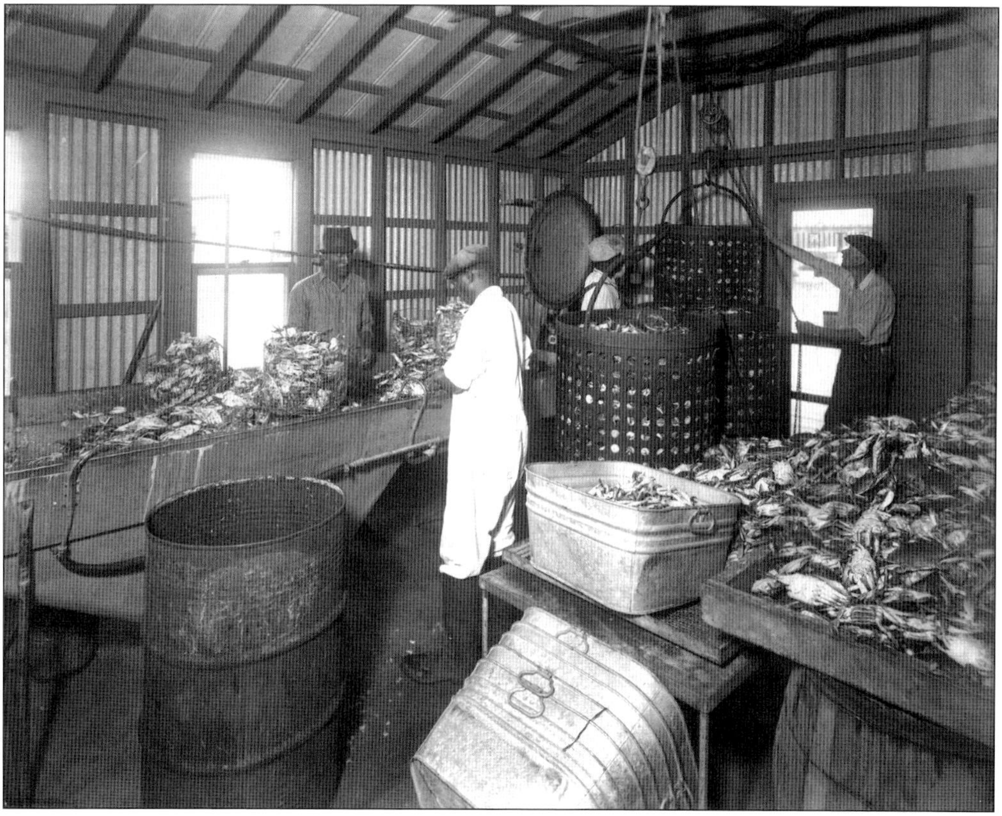

For centuries, blue crabs have sustained Jacksonville families as both a vital food source and an economic staple. The city remains home to Florida's first crab meat processing plant, continuing a long maritime tradition. In 2022, more than 1.2 million pounds of hard- and soft-shell blue crabs were harvested from the St. Johns River. Today, countless crab traps dot Jacksonville's waterways, reflecting a legacy that endures across generations. (State Archives of Florida.)

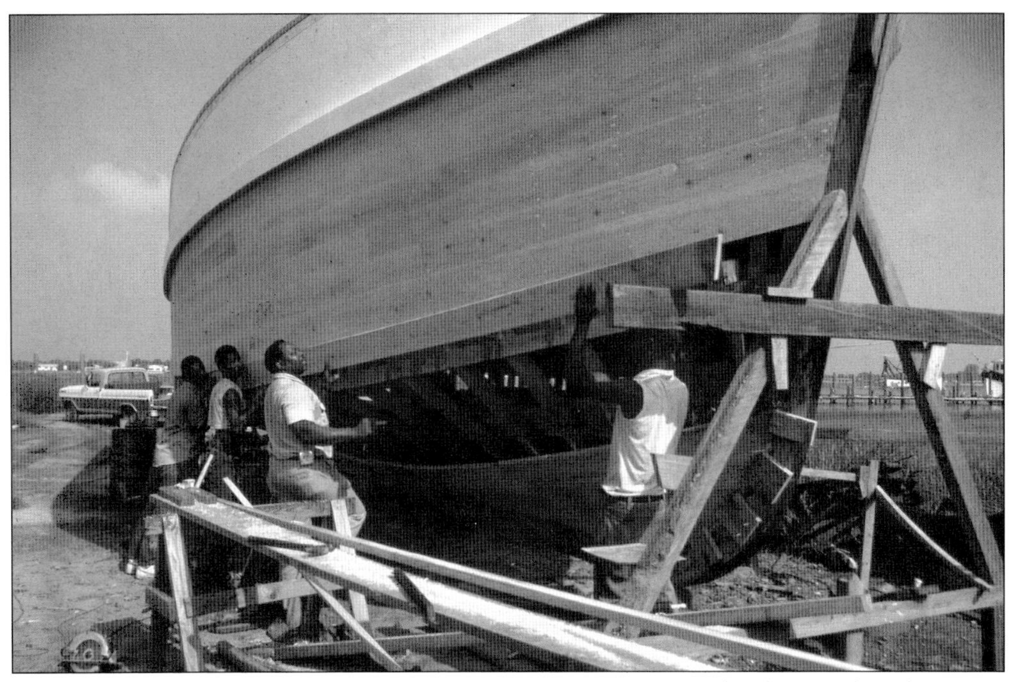

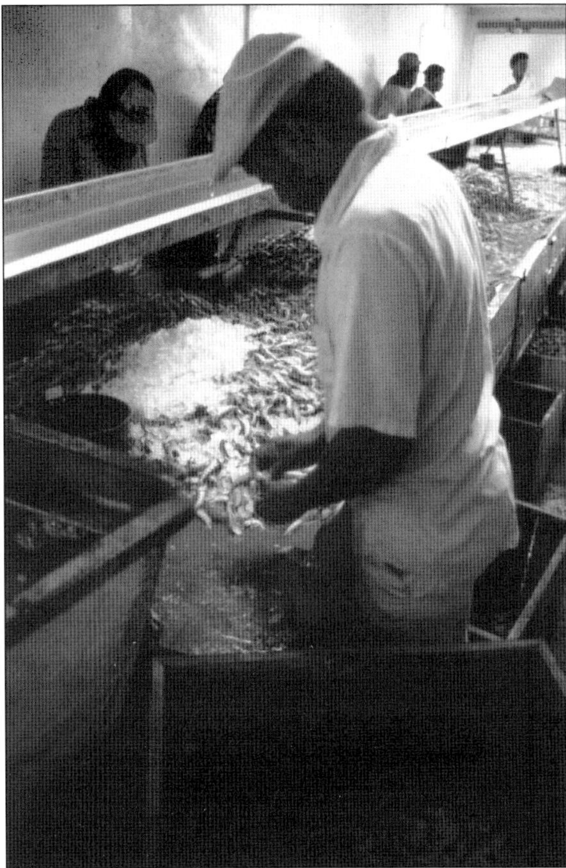

Shrimping has long anchored Jacksonville's economy, sustaining shrimpers, seafood markets, boat repair shops, restaurants, and transport services. Many of these businesses have been run by families for generations. Here, Willie Dunham (second from right) and his crew help with the planking of the 54-foot shrimp boat *Miss Joann* during construction at Mayport in 1985. (State Archives of Florida.)

On August 5, 1986, Roland Seafood worker Arthur Mattox was photographed removing shrimp heads at the Mayport-based Mat Roland Seafood Company. Founded in 1932 by Portuguese immigrant Matias Rolao, who later anglicized his name to Mat Roland, the company traced its roots to his shrimping days between Fernandina Beach and St. Augustine in the 1920s. After nearly 90 years of operation, the historic seafood business closed in 2022. (State Archives of Florida.)

In the 1910s, the Ocean Street Market on Jacksonville's Downtown Northbank thrived as fishermen sold fresh catches along the St. Johns River. This open-air market was vital to the city's food economy, its waterfront location essential for preserving seafood before spoilage. Known for its strong fish scent, the market declined after World War II as aging infrastructure and suburban growth drew residents and commerce away from downtown. (State Archives of Florida.)

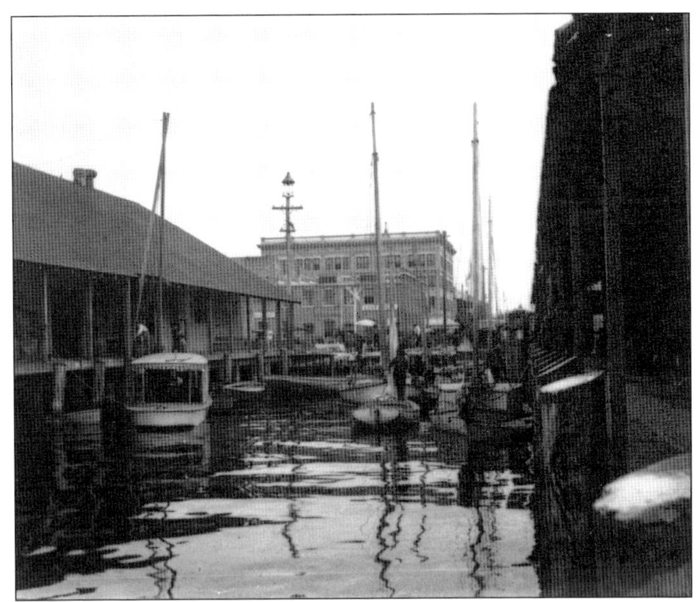

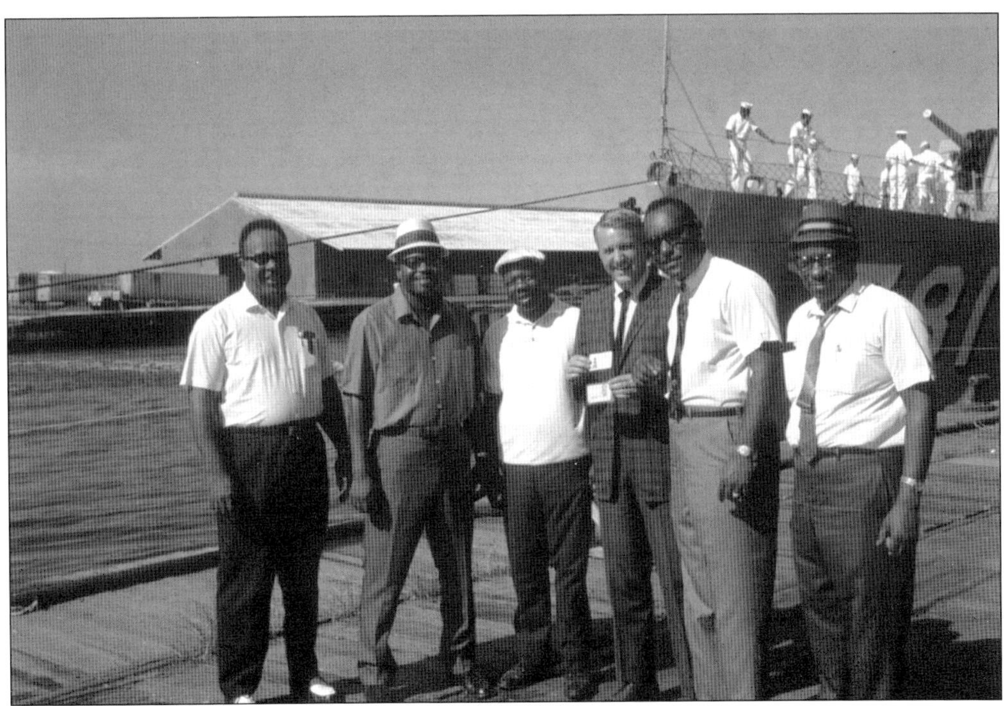

Founded in 1936, ILA Local No. 1408 gave Black dockworkers a collective voice during an era of segregation and harsh labor conditions at the Eastside's Talleyrand docks. Before the union, longshoremen faced low pay, no benefits, and uncertain employment. From left to right, this 1967 photograph captures members Charles Stewart, Paul Fields, Robert Bennett, unidentified, Landon Williams, and Romia Johnson Sr. at a Talleyrand Marine Terminal open house. (JAXPORT.)

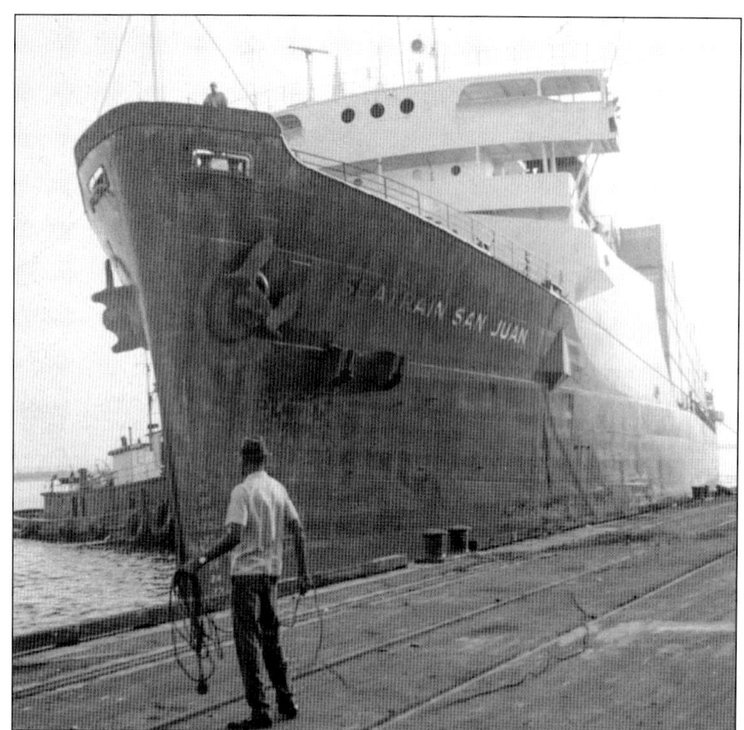

Located in Jacksonville's historic Eastside, JAXPORT's Talleyrand Marine Terminal opened in 1914 as the Municipal Docks and Terminal Company, shifting much of the city's maritime activity from downtown to Talleyrand. Today, the 173-acre terminal remains a vital hub, handling containerized and breakbulk cargo, imported automobiles, and liquid bulk goods like turpentine and molasses, along with steel, lumber, paper, and a variety of frozen and chilled products. (JAXPORT.)

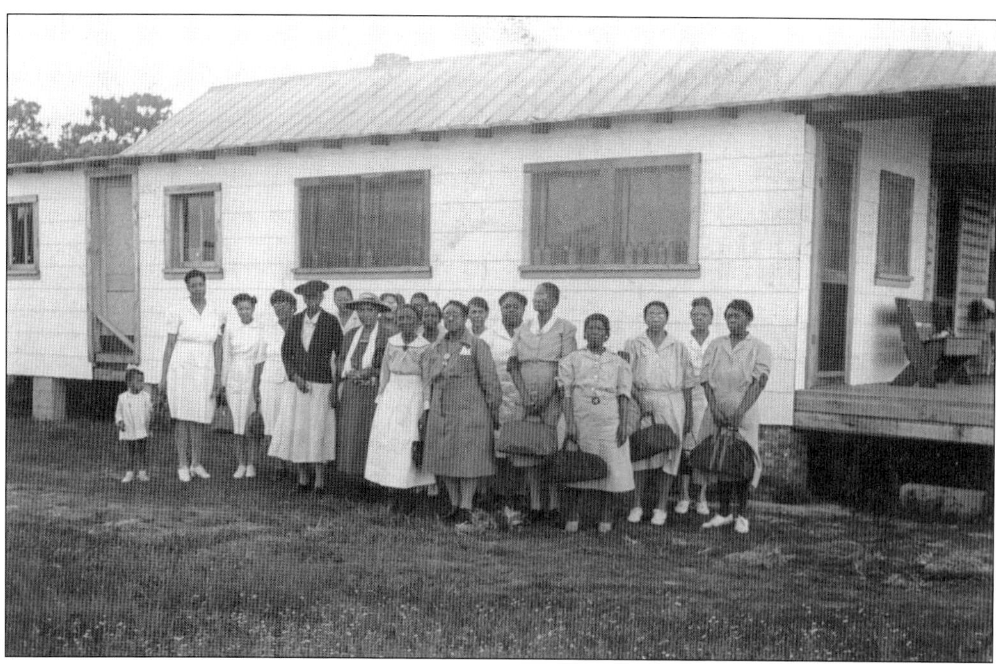

Black midwives in Florida have deep roots in enslaved and post-emancipation Gullah Geechee communities. Mothers depended on these female healers for birth care when formal medical services were denied to them or not accessible. In 1931, the Florida State Board of Health launched a midwife licensing program. Many Black women, such as those pictured here in Jacksonville, participated in this program that standardized midwifery practices. (State Archives of Florida.)

Both the Boylan School and Brewster Hospital trained Black women to be nurses. Brewster Hospital served the Black community in Jacksonville from 1901 to 1966 and ultimately became part of today's University of Florida Health complex. Generations of Black women graduated from Boylan and Brewster, serving the nursing community in Jacksonville and beyond. Brewster Hospital was the primary hospital for Black physicians, nurses, and patients until the Civil Rights Act of 1964 legally ended segregation. (Ritz Theatre & Museum.)

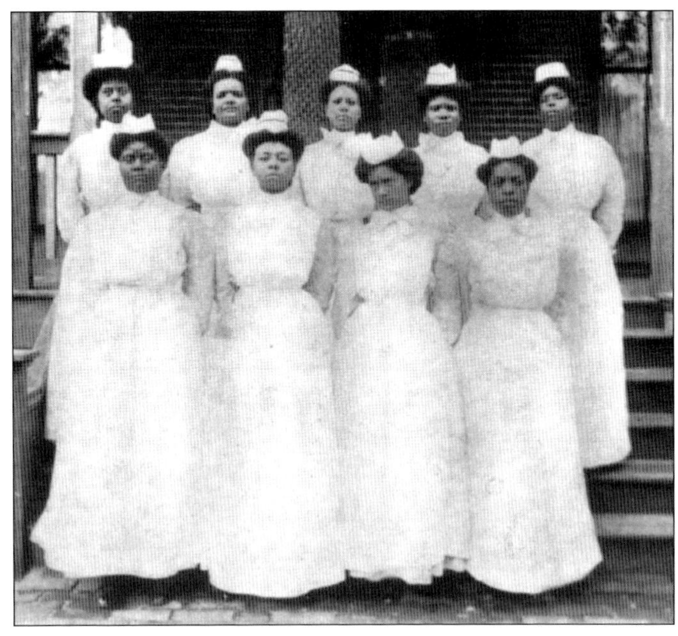

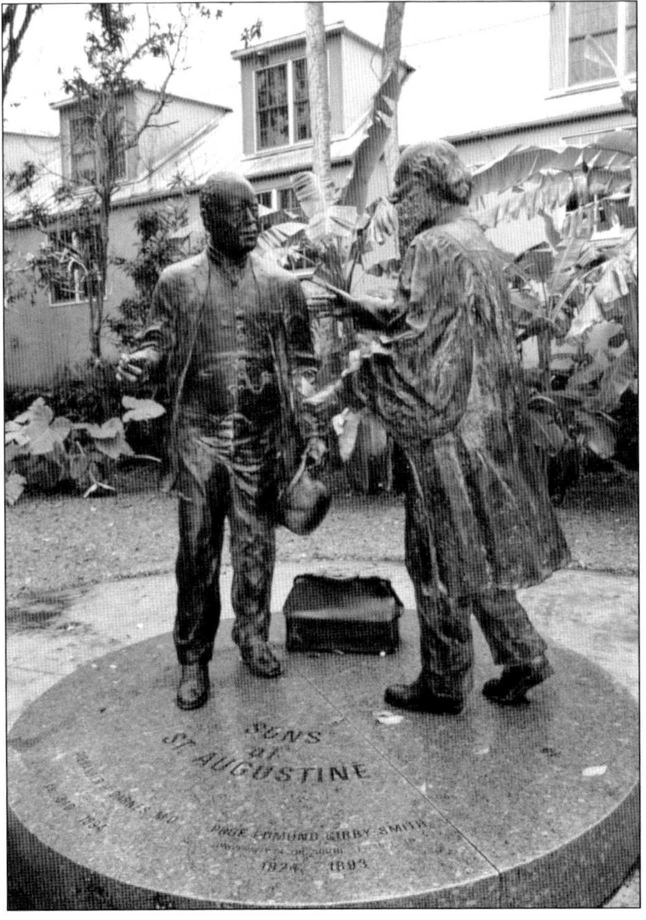

The rise of Black physicians in Jacksonville reflects growing educational opportunities since Reconstruction. Despite limited access to medical schools, Jacksonville produced several pioneering physicians. Among them was Alexander Hanson Darnes (c. 1840–1894), once enslaved by the family of Confederate general Edmund Kirby Smith in St. Augustine. As Jacksonville's first Black physician, Darnes earned acclaim for his courageous service during the city's devastating smallpox and yellow fever epidemics. A sculpture of Dr. Darnes (left) and General Smith was erected by the St. Augustine Historical Society in 2004. (Cosmos Mariner and HMdb.org.)

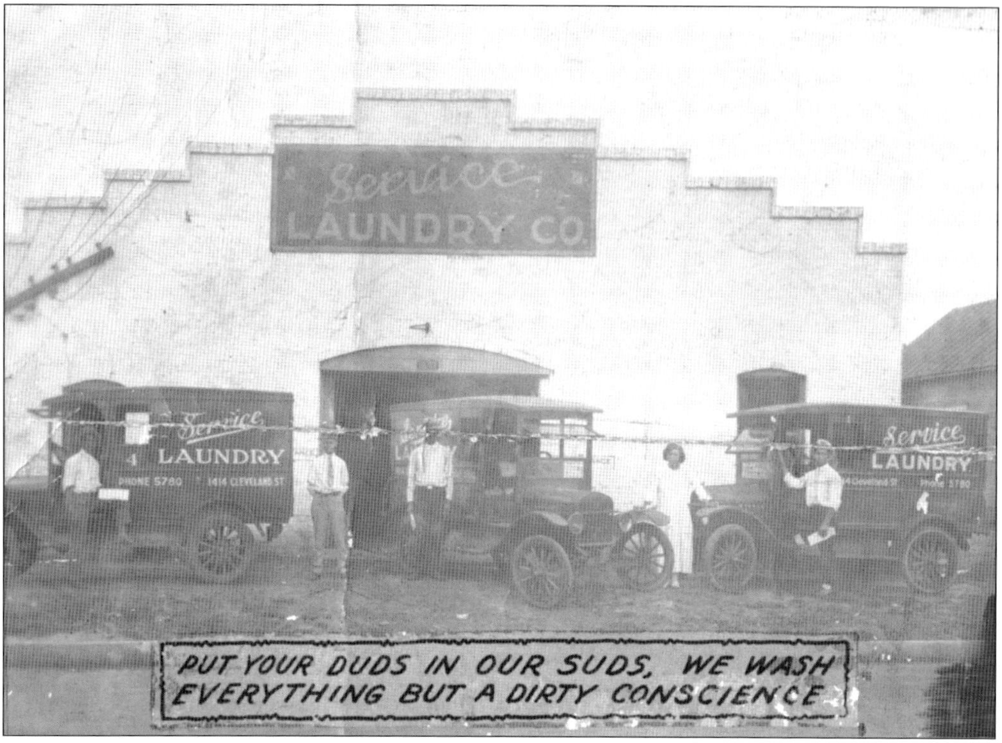

Born in Jacksonville in 1876 to mother Clara, who was formerly enslaved on Amelia Island, Eartha Mary Magdalene White was known as the "Angel of Mercy." She founded LaVilla's Clara White Mission and championed humanitarian causes. Beyond her philanthropy, White was an entrepreneur, owning the Service Laundry Co. at 1414 Cleveland Street in the 1920s. Her business thrived with slogans like "Cleanliness Next to Godliness" and "We Wash Everything but a Dirty Conscience," reflecting her wit and community spirit. (Eartha M.M. White Collection, Thomas G. Carpenter Library Special Collections and University Archives, University of North Florida.)

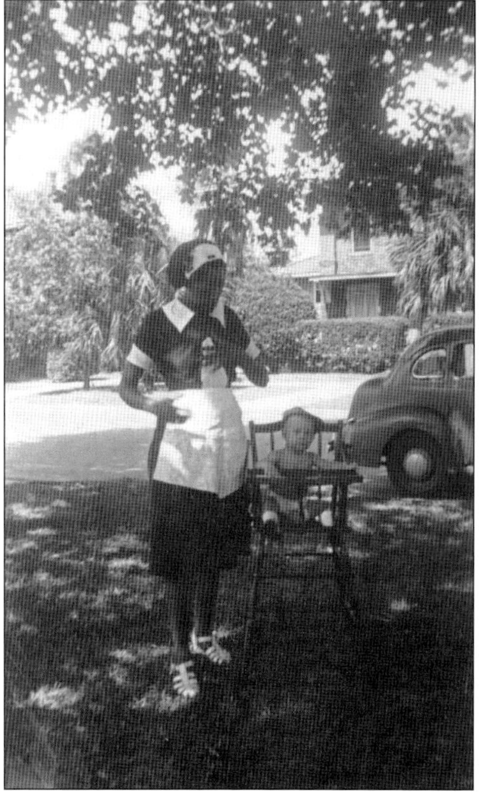

Throughout the 19th and 20th centuries, Black women in Jacksonville, many of them Gullah Geechee descendants, labored as domestics, cooks, laundresses, and nannies in White households while sustaining their own families and neighbors. Domestic work provided steady but limited wages, and treatment varied by household. Black domestic workers built mutual aid networks, helped fund Black community initiatives, and infused domestic labor with dignity and skill. (State Archives of Florida.)

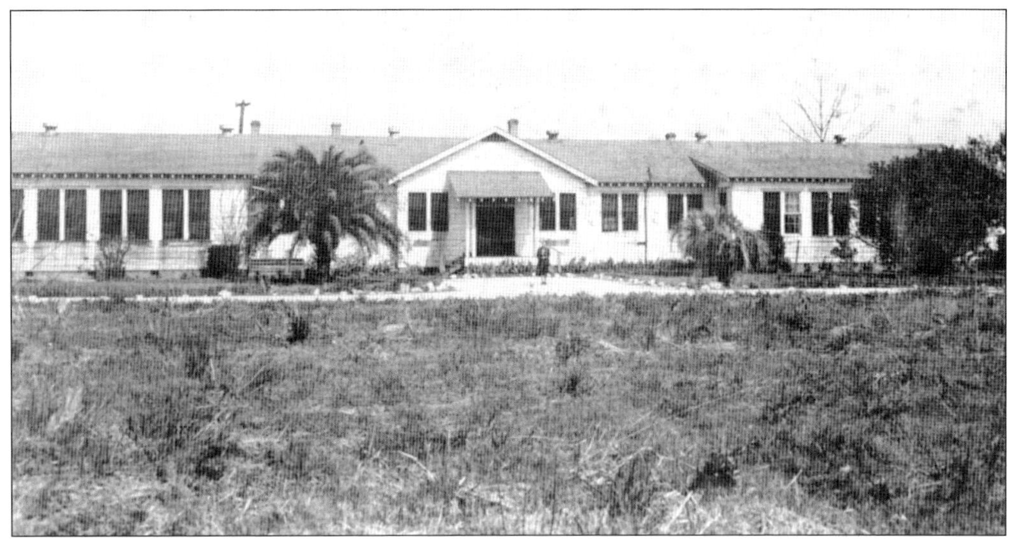

During the early 20th century, Eartha White opened Mercy Hospital at 1449 Milnor Street on the Eastside to care for tuberculosis patients. Along with the Old Folks Home, Mercy Hospital eventually moved across town and became the Eartha M.M. White Nursing Home on Moncrief Road. In 1953, Richard L. Brown Gifted and Talented Academy opened on the hospital's former site. (Eartha M.M. White Collection, Thomas G. Carpenter Library Special Collections and University Archives, University of North Florida.)

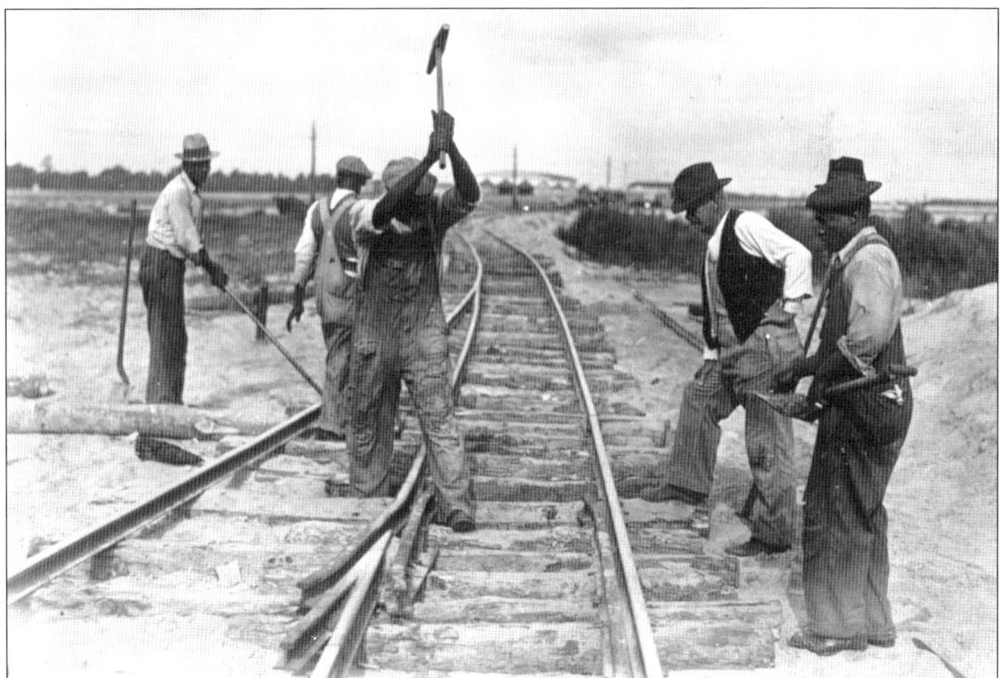

Jacksonville has been Florida's railroad hub since the late 19th century. After the Civil War, many Gullah Geechee men found work maintaining the railways. A 1934 photograph shows a section gang, or gandy dancers, laying track for airport construction. Renowned for coordinating labor through rhythmic work songs, gandy dancers were unique in their use of task-related work chants. (State Archives of Florida.)

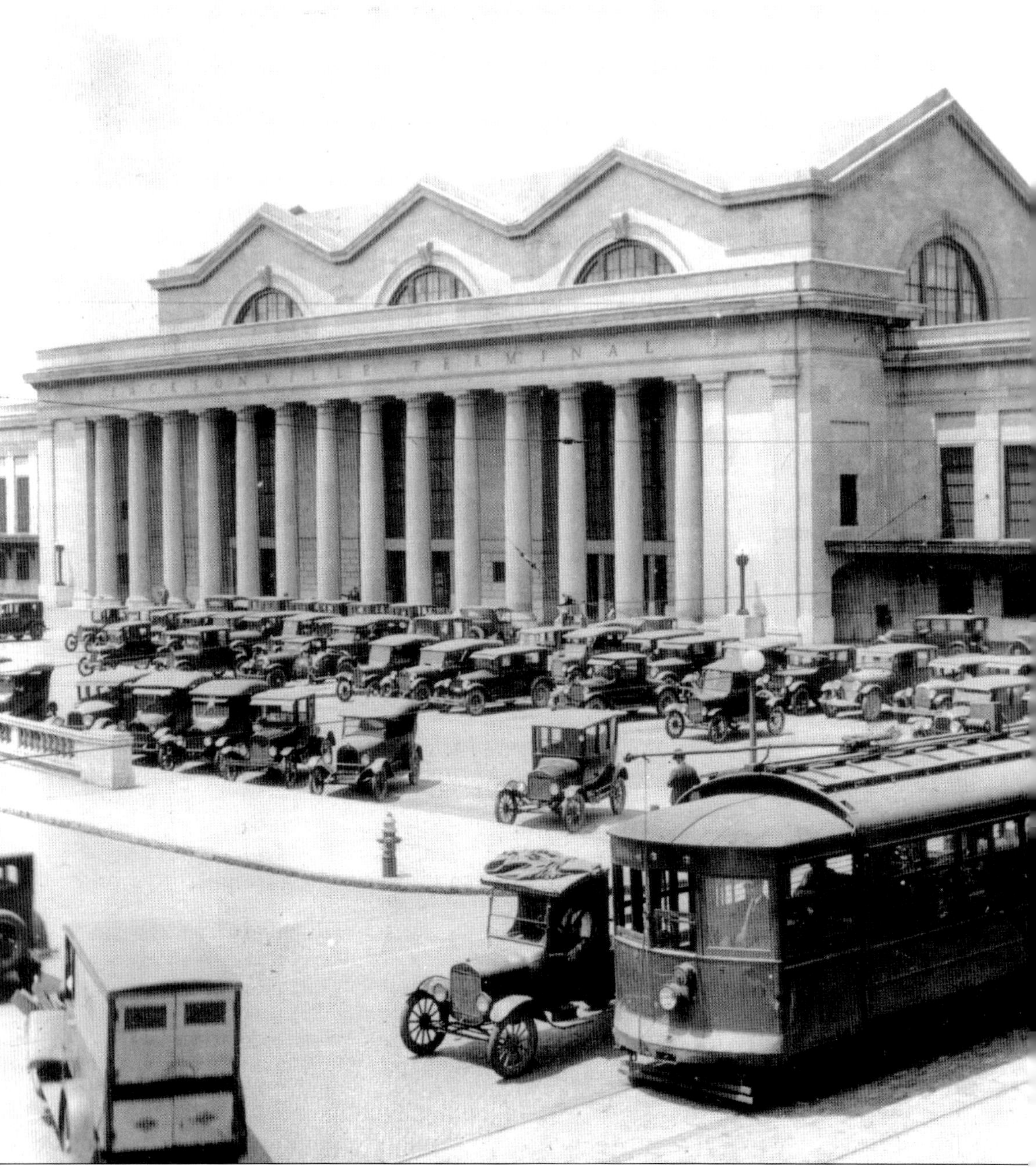

The Jacksonville Terminal Company was the country's largest train station south of Washington, DC, and the main employer for the Gullah Geechee neighborhoods of LaVilla, Brooklyn, Campbell Hill, and New Town. The terminal, which opened in 1919, was first organized by Henry Flagler in the 1890s. With 2,000 workers, it was the city's second-largest employer during its heyday. Traffic peaked in 1944 when 40,000 trains passed through the terminal, carrying nearly 10 million passengers. It was the "Gateway to Florida" for millions of passengers, including the Duke and Duchess of Windsor in 1941 and every US president from 1921 until the terminal's closure in 1974. In 1976, it was placed on the National Register of Historic Places. (State Archives of Florida.)

Raised in Jacksonville's Eastside, Asa Philip Randolph (1889–1979) left for Harlem in 1911 aspiring to become an actor but instead emerged as one of America's most influential civil rights leaders. Once labeled "the most dangerous Black man in the country," he founded the Brotherhood of Sleeping Car Porters, the first Black labor union, and later helped organize the 1963 March on Washington alongside Dr. Martin Luther King Jr. (Library of Congress.)

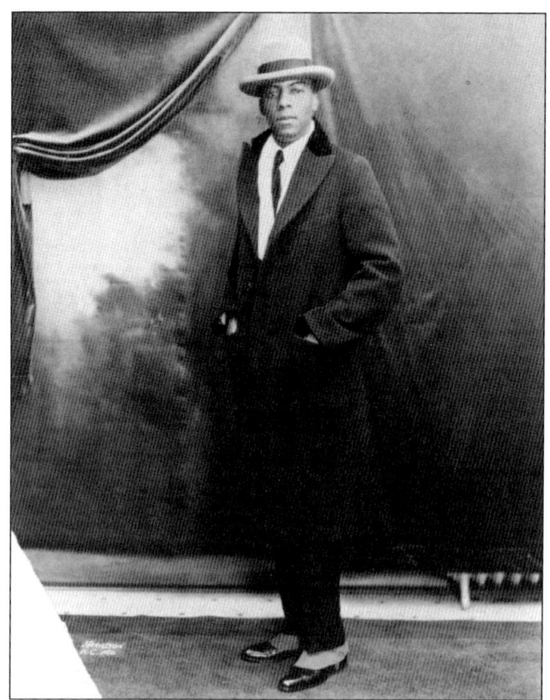

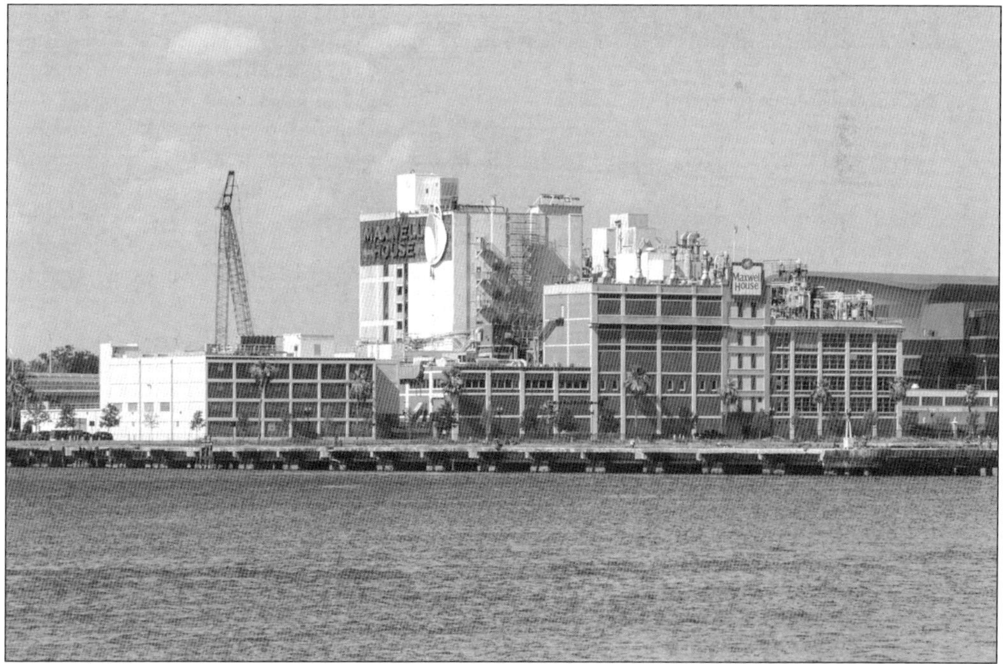

Once home to several major coffee roasters, Jacksonville and its Gullah Geechee community have long been tied to the coffee industry. The Maxwell House plant opened in 1910 as the Cheek-Neal Coffee Company, chosen for its river access to receive beans by barge. Today, it remains one of the world's largest coffee plants and one of Jacksonville's oldest manufacturers, producing up to one million pounds of coffee daily and generating an estimated $600 million annual economic impact. (DXR.)

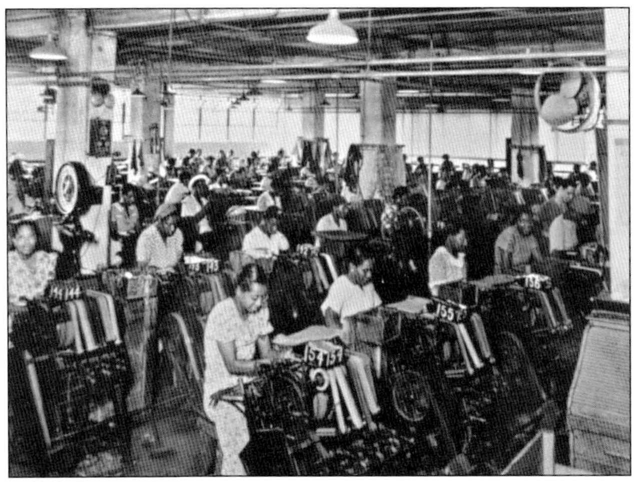

Commercial cigar making in Florida began in the 1830s, flourishing in Jacksonville by the late 19th century. In 1924, John Swisher transformed a former munitions factory in New Springfield into a mechanized cigar plant, the first of its kind. The machines halved cigar prices, making King Edward cigars a global bestseller. By 1941, Swisher's factory was the world's largest and a major employer for nearby Gullah Geechee neighborhoods. (Jacksonville Public Library.)

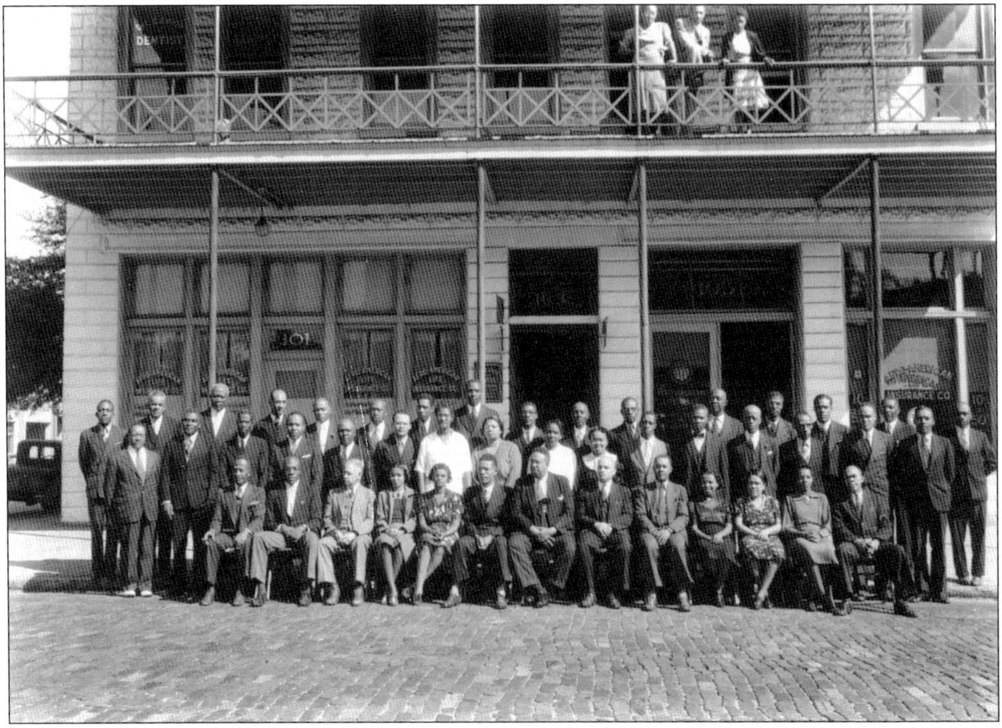

Founded in 1901, the Afro-American Life Insurance Company grew into one of the Southeast's most influential Black-owned businesses. Created to meet the unique needs of the Black community, the Afro extended far beyond insurance, investing in housing, business, and education across the South. In 1941, it financed part of Jacksonville's Main Street Bridge, symbolizing its lasting impact on both the city's growth and the advancement of Black enterprise. (Ritz Theatre & Museum.)

Abraham Lincoln Lewis (1865–1947), shown with first wife Mary Frances Sammis, rose from humble beginnings to become one of Florida's first Black millionaires. After cofounding the Afro-American Life Insurance Company in 1901, he became its president in 1919, leading it to anchor Jacksonville's Black community. A visionary entrepreneur and philanthropist, Lewis founded businesses, cemeteries, and schools, and in 1935, he helped create American Beach, a celebrated resort that welcomed icons like Cab Calloway and Joe Louis. (Eartha M.M. White Collection, Thomas G. Carpenter Library Special Collections and University Archives, University of North Florida.)

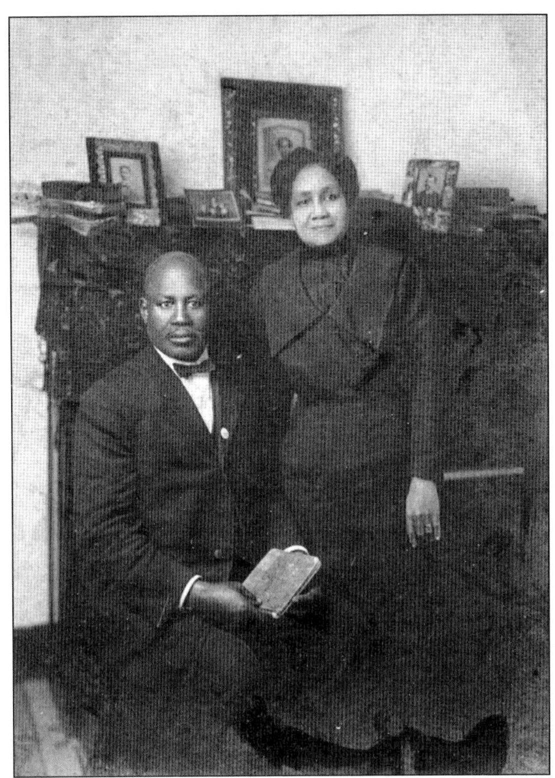

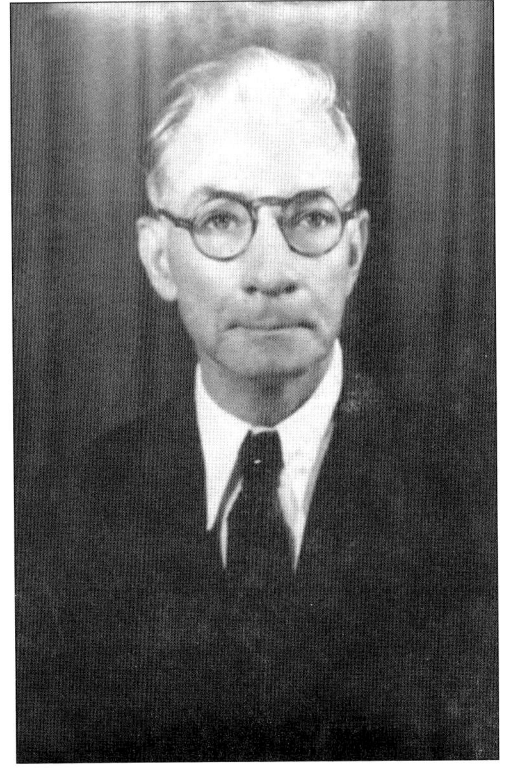

Born in South Carolina in 1860, Sylvanus Henry Hart moved with his family to Jacksonville after emancipation, following his father, Eli Hart, a Civil War veteran. A skilled brick mason and contractor, Hart founded the Capital Trust & Investment Company, Florida's first Black-owned bank, in 1902. His success made him worth over $100,000 by 1912. By 1924, he owned homes in Jacksonville and Harlem. When his bank closed in 1926, all depositors were repaid in full. (Eartha M.M. White Collection, Thomas G. Carpenter Library Special Collections and University Archives, University of North Florida.)

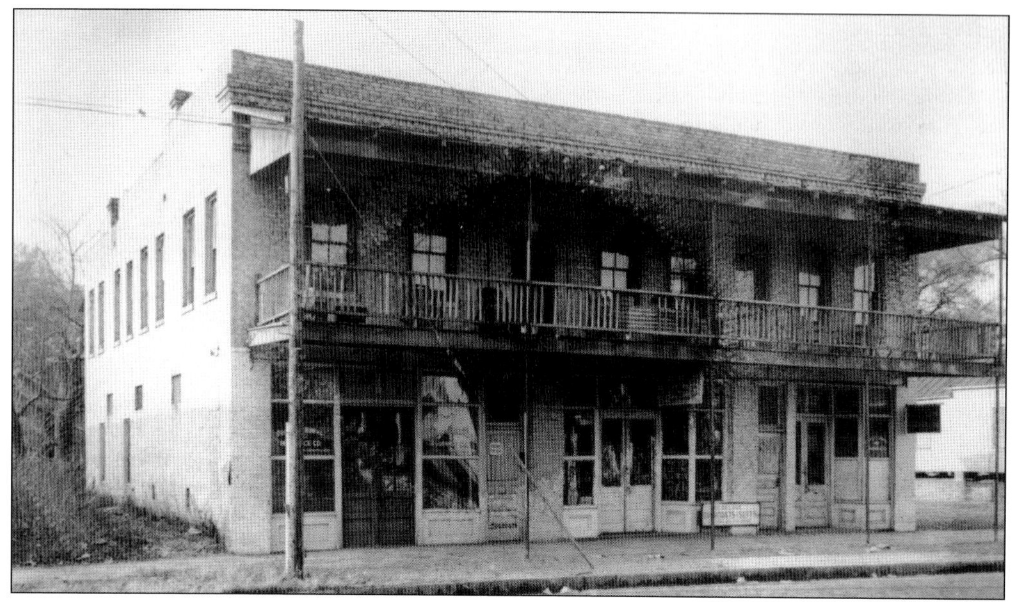

After Jacksonville's Great Fire of 1901, William Sumter moved from Savannah and founded the Union Mutual Insurance Company on Broad Street in LaVilla in 1904. A leader in the Jacksonville Negro Business League, Sumter died in 1918, and his wife, Henrietta Albertina Ewart Sumter, became president. By 1919, she expanded the firm to 125 employees and 40 agencies. In the 1930s, Union Mutual merged with the People's Industrial Insurance Company. (Ritz Theatre & Museum.)

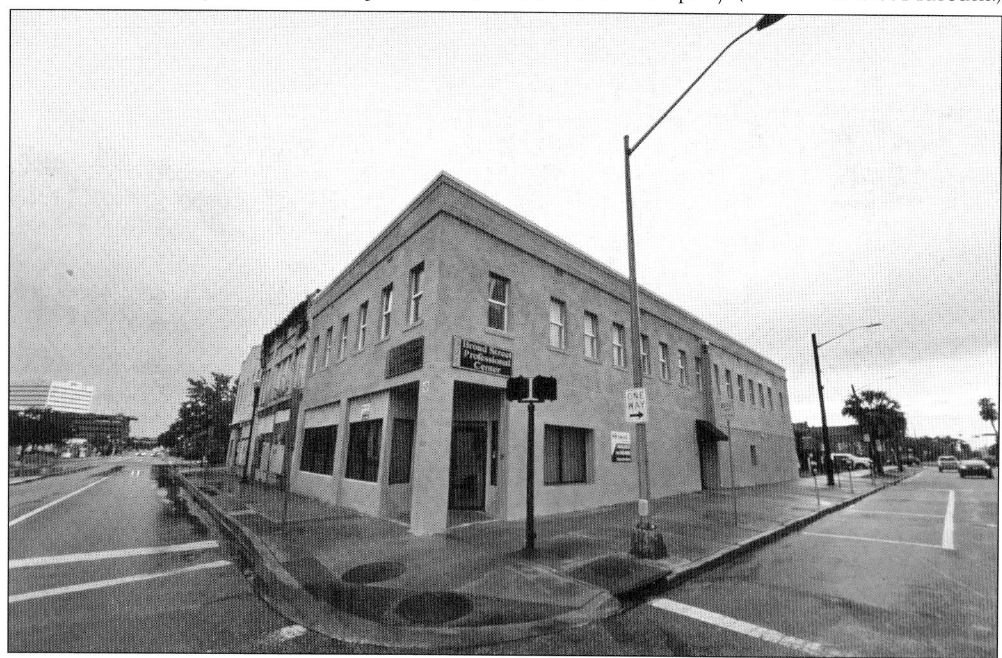

Founded in 1922 by Walter Wilfred Parker and associates, the Citizens Industrial Insurance Company quickly became a leading Black-owned business in Jacksonville. By 1928, it employed 20 home office staff and 175 field workers, operating from this two-story brick building at 610 West Duval Street in LaVilla. In 1931, seeking a better work-life balance, Parker chose to focus on his law career and sold the company to lessen his workload. (Ennis Davis, AICP.)

During Reconstruction, Gullah Geechee men entered Jacksonville's legal profession, providing vital leadership and justice in the face of deep adversity. Their efforts helped pave the way for the 1950s and 1960s civil rights movement. Among them, Simuel Decatur McGill rose to national prominence, arguing more state supreme court cases than any other Black lawyer prior to 1944. His firm, McGill and McGill, became one of the nation's most respected Black law practices. (Eartha M.M. White Collection, Thomas G. Carpenter Library Special Collections and University Archives, University of North Florida.)

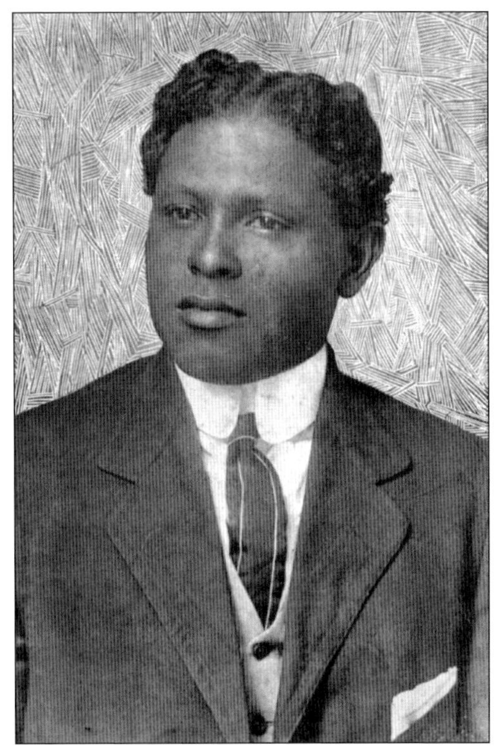

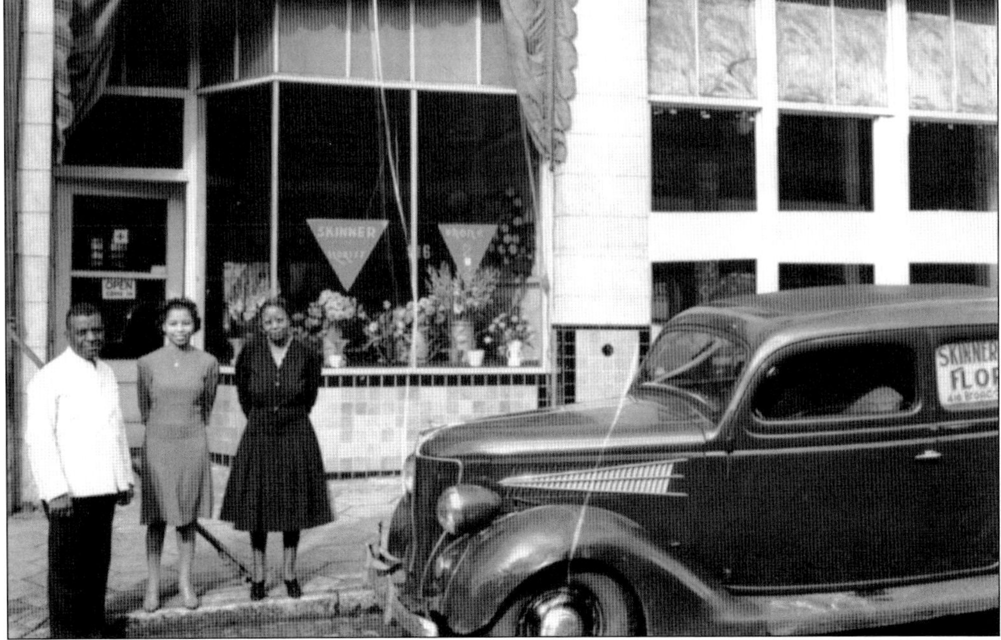

Founded in 1936 by Alex and Wilhelmina Skinner, Skinner's Florist is Jacksonville's oldest operating floral business and representative of the city's segregation-era Black entrepreneur class. This photograph captures Wilhelmina Skinner standing in front of the Skinner's Florist location in the Richmond Hotel at 416 Broad Street in LaVilla between 1938 and 1950. In 1950, Skinner's Florist moved to its current location at 1519 Myrtle Avenue in Durkeeville. (Ritz Theatre & Museum.)

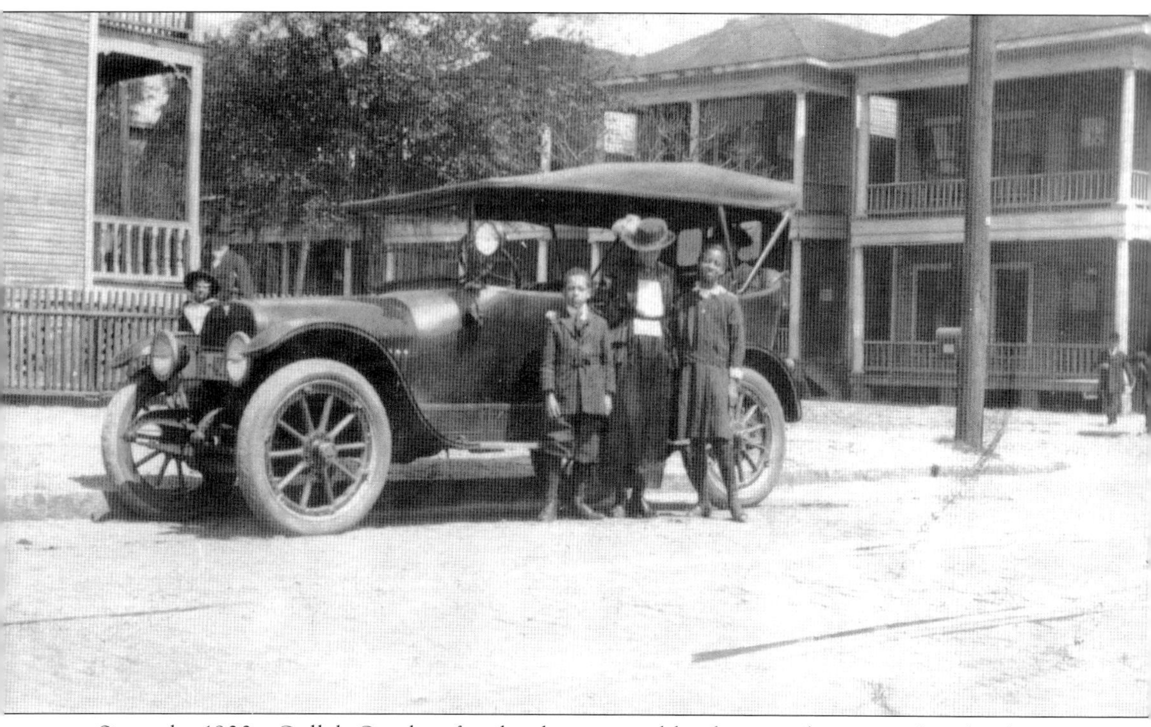

Since the 1800s, Gullah Geechee families have owned land across the region, but development pressures and heirs' property issues have caused significant losses. In the early 1900s, the Florida Home and Investment Corporation, a Gullah Geechee–owned real estate firm based in LaVilla, became a powerful force for land ownership and economic opportunity. The company owned 10,000 acres in Bradford County, selling small farms for vegetable and citrus production, and developed multiple subdivisions in St. Augustine. Prominent Jacksonville leaders, including Black banker Charles H. Anderson, were among its officers. By 1913, investors like G.H. Bowden expanded their influence to Savannah, routinely running ads in the *Savannah Tribune* paper claiming that there was no better investment on earth than the earth itself.

Seven

THE HEART

Jacksonville's Black communities built vibrant, self-sustaining networks rooted in education, faith, entrepreneurship, and collective care. Schools like Stanton, Cookman Institute, and Florida Baptist Academy became more than centers of learning. These schools were training grounds for leadership, cultural pride, and social advancement. Black teachers, many trained in these very institutions, nurtured generations of students through rigorous academics and lessons in self-respect, discipline, and civic responsibility.

Faith, music, and fellowship intertwined through organizations such as the Masons, the Knights of Pythias, and women's organizations, which offered mutual aid, spiritual guidance, and social connection. Institutions led by visionaries like Dr. Eartha M.M. White embodied this ethic of service, blending philanthropy, business acumen, and compassion to uplift the poor, sick, and elderly. Black-owned banks, insurance companies, colleges, and businesses created thriving corridors of commerce and dignity in the Jim Crow South.

Cultural expression flourished through music and dance, from local juke joints to nationally recognized stages. Artists like Augusta Savage and Frankie Manning carried Jacksonville's creative spirit to the world, shaping the Harlem Renaissance and American popular culture. The buzzard lope, the Lindy Hop, and the jazz rhythms that filled the Knights of Pythias dance hall linked the city's cultural pulse to the wider Gullah Geechee continuum stretching along the Atlantic coast.

Community life also unfolded on the playing fields and beaches. The Jacksonville Red Caps baseball team and Manhattan Beach, Florida's first African American beach, reflected joy and perseverance. These recreational spaces provided Gullah Geechee descendants a place to gather with pride and solidarity.

Together, these schools, churches, businesses, and cultural venues reveal how Gullah Geechee descendants in Jacksonville, denied equal access to public institutions, built parallel, heart-led systems that educated minds, nourished spirits, and strengthened communities. This chapter explores how community care influenced Black life in Jacksonville.

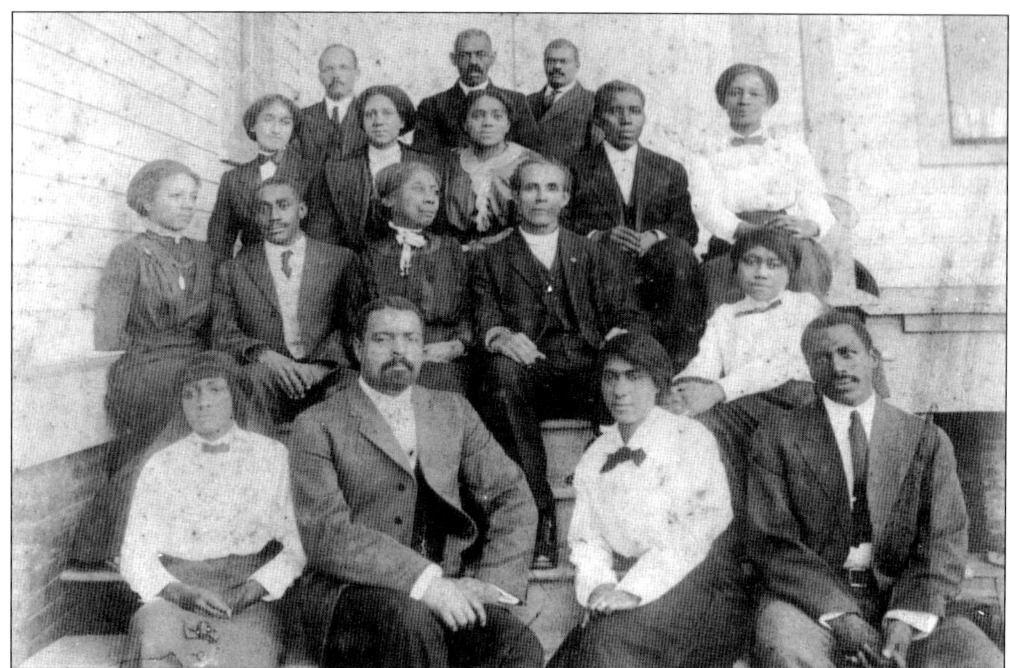

Amid segregation, Black educators were pillars of resilience and progress. Leading schools such as Stanton, Gilbert, and West Lewisville nurtured literacy, faith, and civic engagement while shaping generations through discipline and pride. Their classrooms served as sanctuaries of learning and cultural affirmation, empowering students to rise above systemic inequality. Here, the principal and teachers of Stanton High School are pictured in 1914. (Ritz Theatre & Museum.)

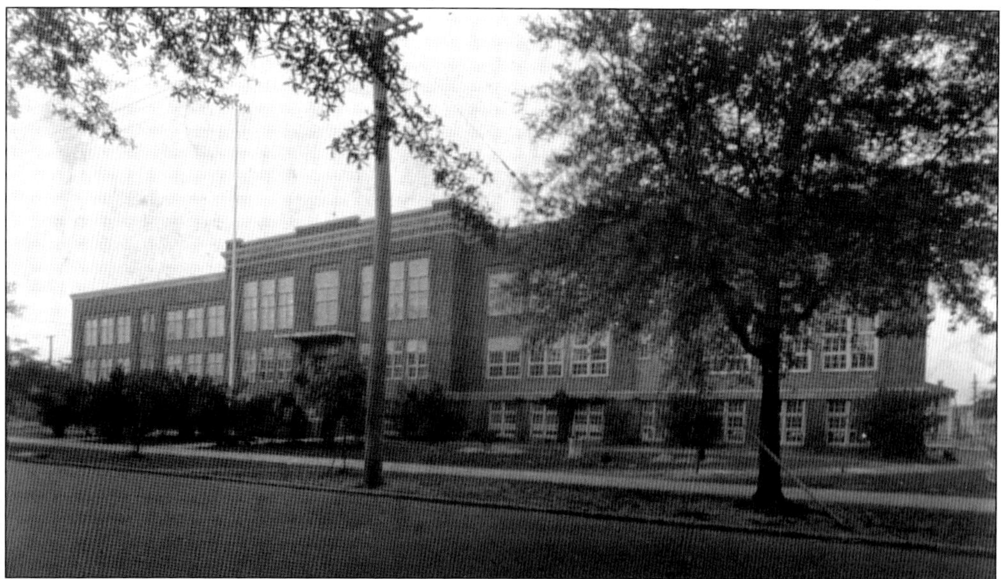

Founded in 1869 with aid from the Freedmen's Bureau, Stanton became Florida's first school for Black children, named after Lincoln's secretary of war, Edwin M. Stanton. James Weldon Johnson, later principal, helped make it Jacksonville's only Black high school and premiered "Lift Ev'ry Voice and Sing" there in 1900. Rebuilt in 1917, Stanton evolved into a vocational high school and remains a landmark of education and civil rights. (University of Florida.)

Founded in 1892 on Jacksonville's Eastside, Florida Memorial University began as Florida Baptist Academy, established by Rev. Matthew Gilbert, Rev. J.T. Brown, and Sarah Ann Blocker. In 1900, composer J. Rosamond Johnson, renowned for the Black national anthem, "Lift Ev'ry Voice and Sing," joined the faculty. The institution later relocated to St. Augustine in 1918 and finally to Miami in 1963, continuing its legacy of Black educational excellence. (Eartha M.M. White Collection, Thomas G. Carpenter Library Special Collections and University Archives, University of North Florida.)

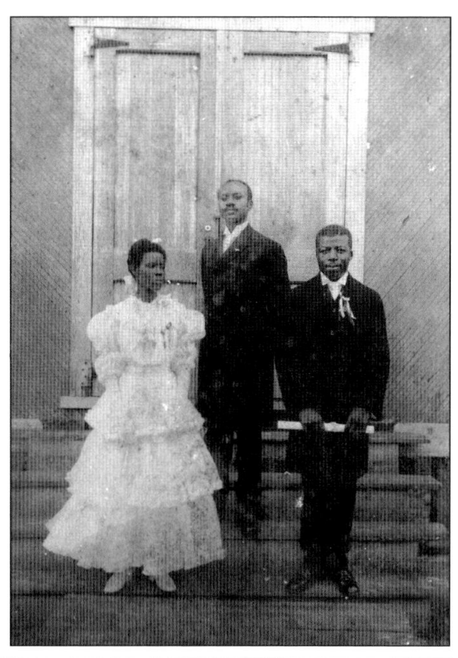

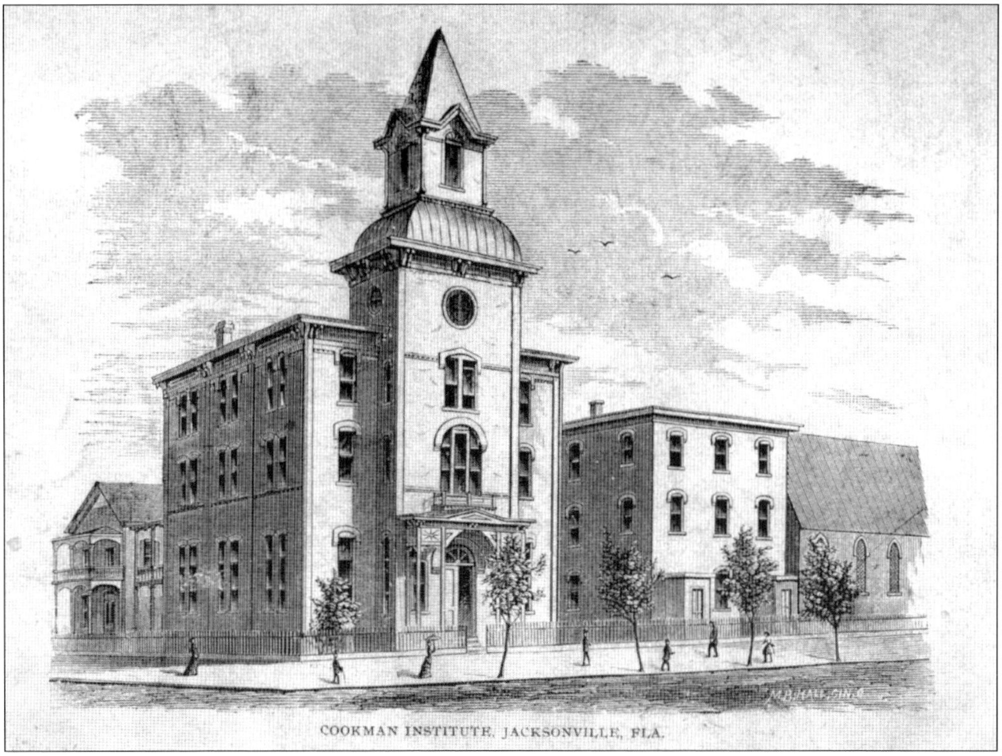

COOKMAN INSTITUTE, JACKSONVILLE, FLA.

Founded in 1872 by Rev. S.B. Darnell, Sugar Hill's Cookman Institute was named for Rev. Alfred Cookman, whose donation funded its first building. Shown in 1910, among its distinguished students was A. Philip Randolph, later a leader in the Harlem Renaissance and the civil rights movement. In 1925, the school merged with Dr. Mary McLeod Bethune's Daytona Normal and Industrial Institute, officially becoming Bethune-Cookman in 1931. (State Archives of Florida.)

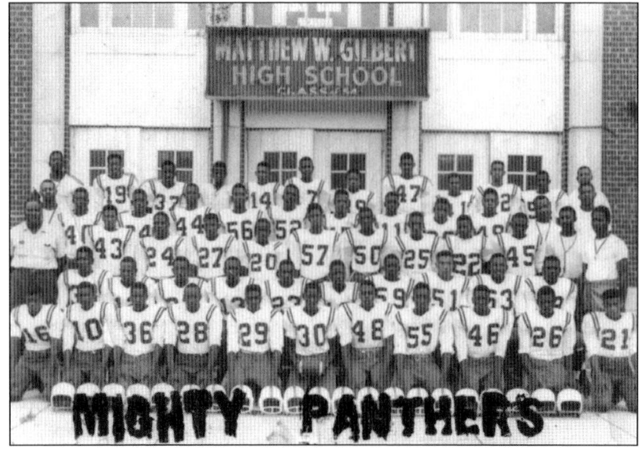

When Florida Baptist Academy left the Eastside in 1918, residents successfully lobbied for a new school. Built in 1927, the Franklin Street Public School No. 146 later became Matthew W. Gilbert High School, honoring the Baptist Academy president. Expanded in 1950 into a junior-senior high, it produced notable alumni like Judge Henry Lee Adams Jr. and Olympian Bob Hayes before reverting to a junior high in 1971. (Ritz Theatre & Museum.)

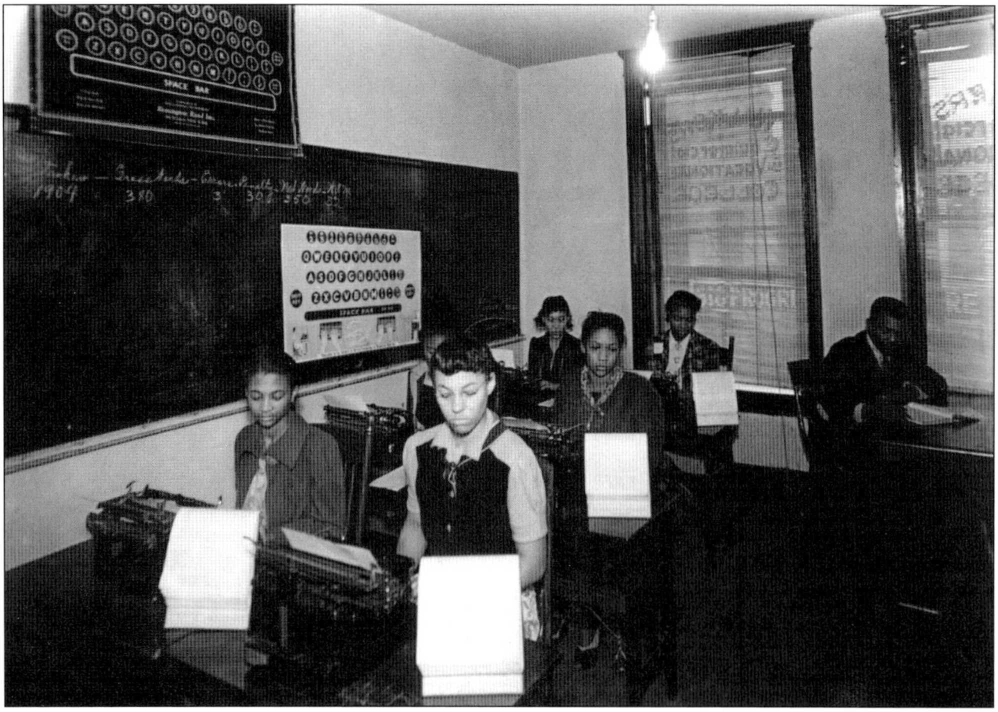

In 1916, Dr. Julia Walker Brown opened the Walkers Commercial and Vocational College on LaVilla's Broad Street. The school served as a bridge for veterans leaving service and offered courses in bookkeeping, accounting, insurance, office machines, secretarial training, dressmaking, tailoring, and upholstering. In 1950, the college relocated to Myrtle Avenue in Durkeeville. The school survived until 1970. (Eartha M.M. White Collection, Thomas G. Carpenter Library Special Collections and University Archives, University of North Florida.)

In 1958, Matthew Gilbert High became the first all-Black school to win a state football championship, an achievement ignored at the time due to segregation. Among its players was Robert Lee "Bullet Bob" Hayes, who later became the only athlete to win both an Olympic gold medal and a Super Bowl ring. Fifty years later, in 2008, the team finally received long-overdue recognition, letter jackets, and championship rings. (Ritz Theatre & Museum.)

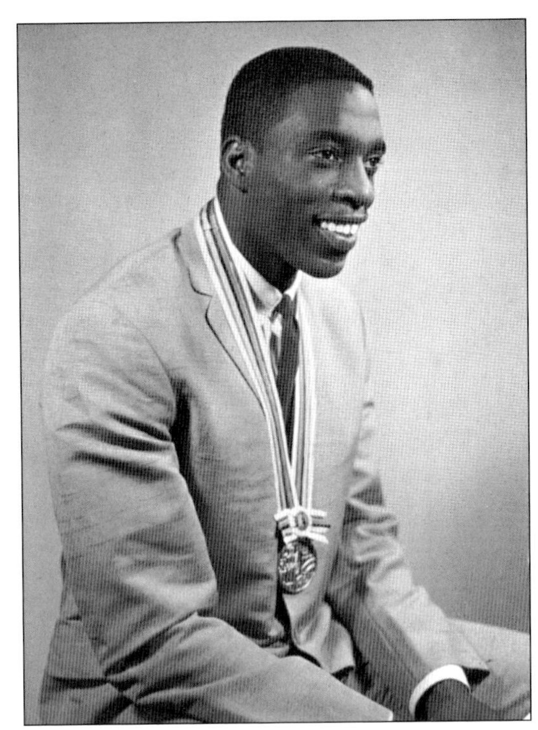

The Jacksonville Red Caps baseball team posed for this Ellie Lee Weems photograph in 1938. The Negro Leagues baseball team began as an independent team organized by the Jacksonville Terminal Station. The players all worked at the station as porters. Porters were nicknamed "redcaps" for the hats they wore, hence the team's name. (Ritz Theatre & Museum.)

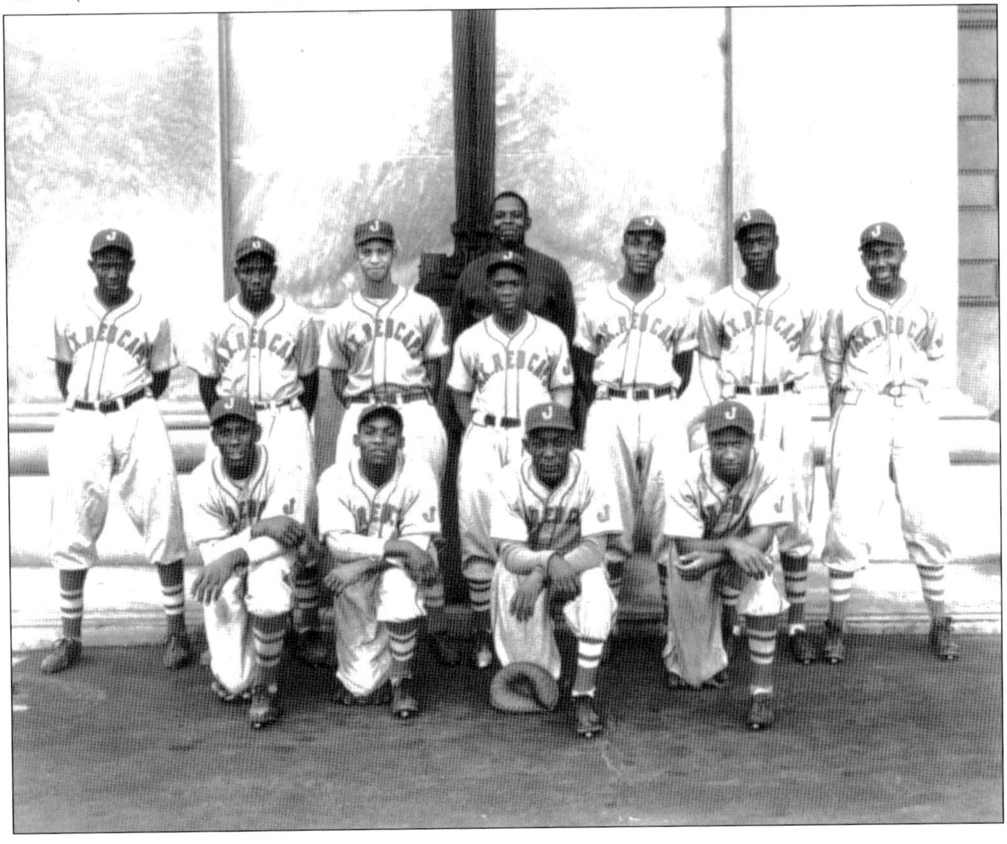

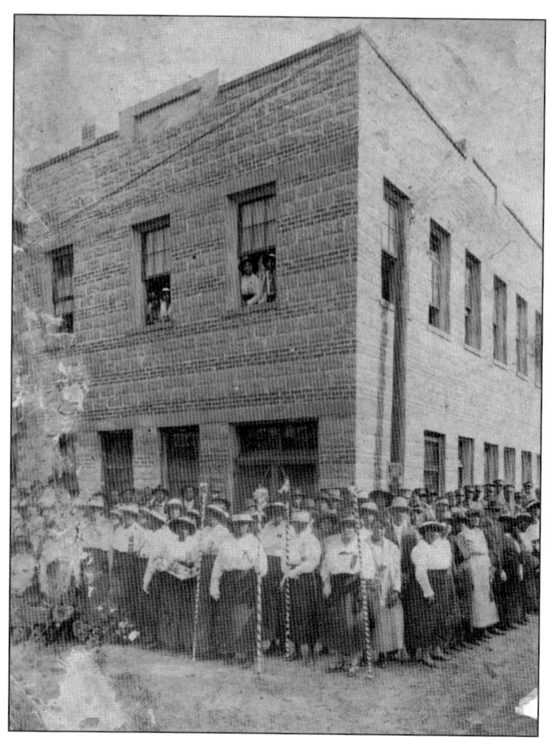

Fraternal organizations provided vital networks of mutual aid, leadership, and community pride. Groups such as the Masons, Elks, and Odd Fellows offered financial assistance, burial support, and educational opportunities. These lodges fostered dignity and solidarity, serving as spaces for social connection, civic engagement, and resistance to racial exclusion. Photographed in 1922, the St. Joseph's Aid Society and women's auxiliary groups like the Masonic Eastern Stars and Elks' Daughters provided similar outlets for women. (Ritz Theatre & Museum.)

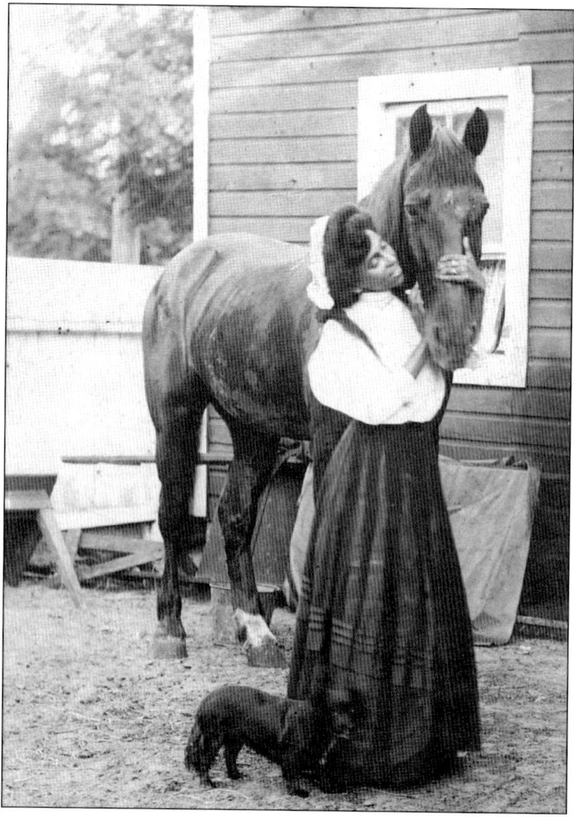

In addition to being a successful businesswoman, Eartha Mary Magdalene White was one of Northeast Florida's most influential philanthropists and humanitarians. Beginning in 1904, White established a hospital, nursing home, childcare centers, boardinghouses, a mission for the poor, and a community center. These institutions transformed Black Jacksonville through compassion, service, and an unwavering commitment to human dignity. Eartha White was appointed to the National Center for Voluntary Action by President Nixon in 1971 and honored as a Great Floridian in 2000. (Clara White Mission.)

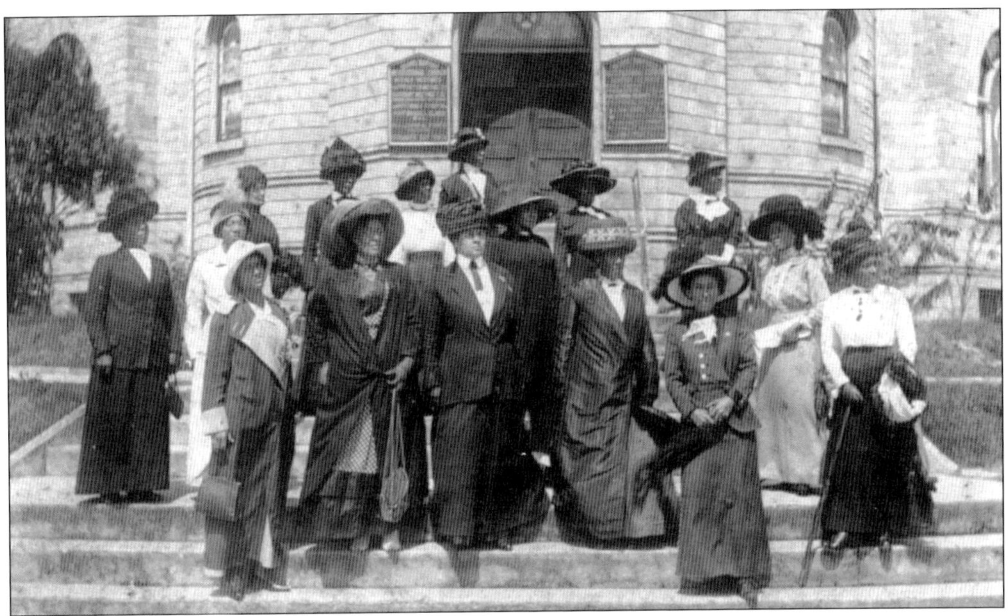

Margaret Murray Washington (first row, third from left) and Dr. Eartha M.M. White (first row, fifth from left) are pictured with members of the Women of City Federation of Colored Women's Clubs at Bethel Baptist Institutional Church in 1925. Margaret Murray Washington was the wife of Booker T. Washington and a prominent antilynching activist and cofounder of the National Association of Colored Women in 1896. (Thomas G. Carpenter Library, University of North Florida.)

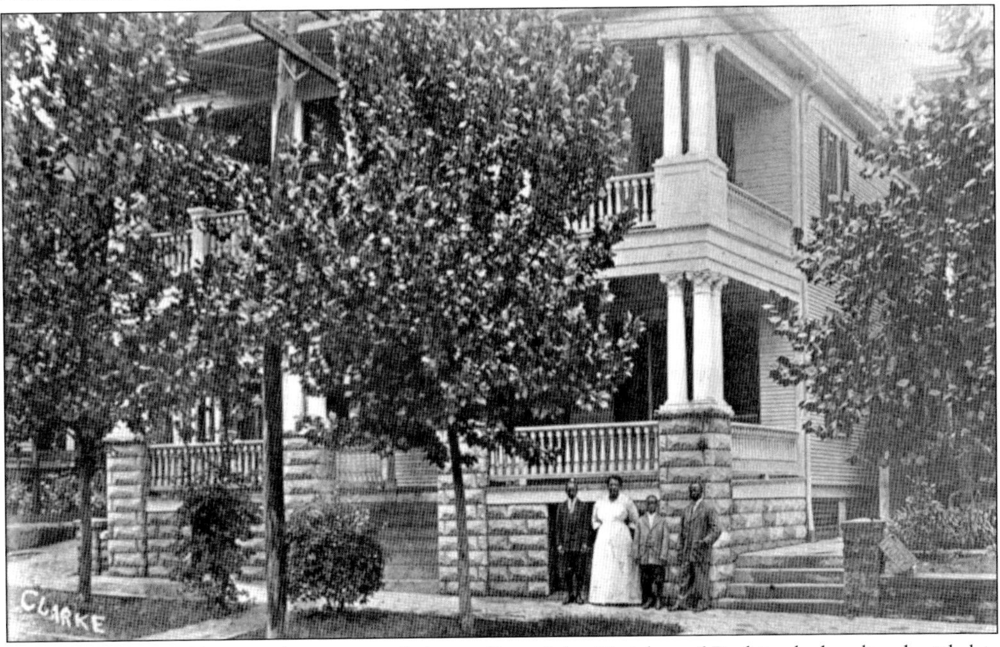

Gen. William Wallace Andrews, grand chancellor of the Knights of Pythias lodge, lived with his family at 511 Clay Street in LaVilla. A pioneering entrepreneur, he founded the *Florida Sentinel Bulletin* in 1919. After moving to Tampa in 1934, his son C. Blythe Andrews revived the paper in 1945. Today, it remains Florida's only Black-owned newspaper that prints twice weekly and operates with fully owned printing equipment. (State Archives of Florida.)

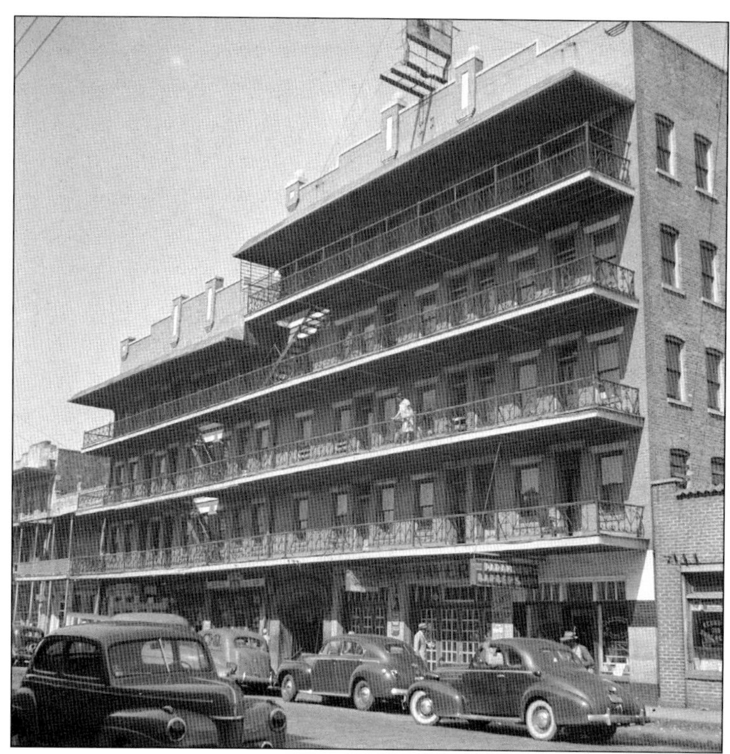

Built in 1924, LaVilla's Knights of Pythias Building was a major entertainment hub on West Ashley Street. The Knights were one of the local fraternal organizations. Its famous fourth-floor dance hall hosted national stars like Louis Armstrong, Ella Fitzgerald, Duke Ellington, Cab Calloway, Earl "Father" Hines, Jimmy Lunceford, Walter Barnes, and Fletcher Henderson, making it a vital part of the Chitlin' Circuit. The building's prominence declined in the 1940s, and it was demolished in 1957. (Library of Congress.)

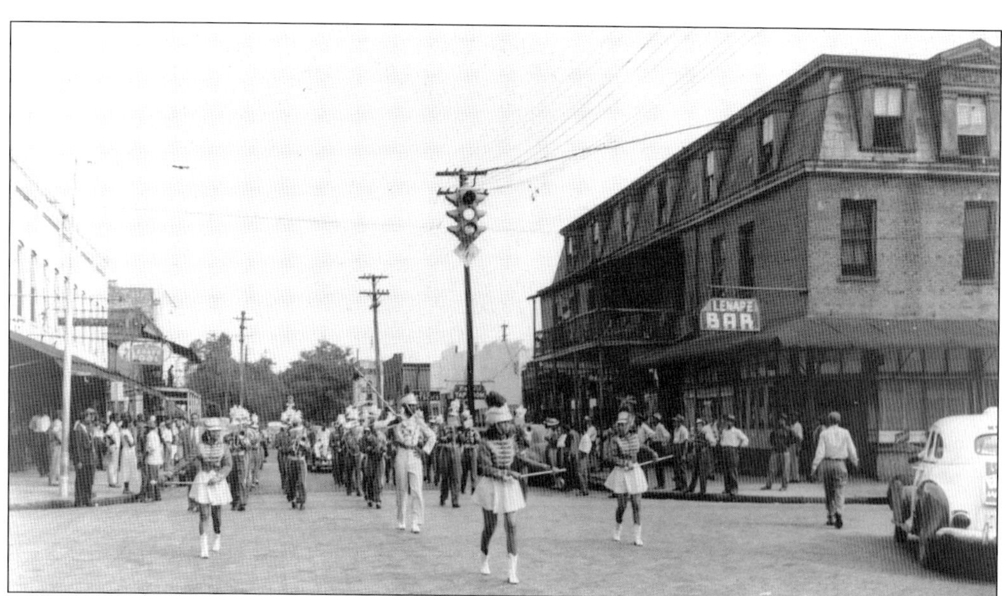

Built in 1895, the Wynn Hotel and Lenape Bar was a stop listed in the *Negro Motorist Green Book*. Louis Armstrong favored the Wynn during his visits to Jacksonville. In the 1940s, two hitching rails outside were "the rails of hope," where young musicians waited for gigs, including a local teen named R.C. Robinson, later famed as Ray Charles. The Lenape's stage also welcomed legends such as Walter Barnes, Dizzy Gillespie, and Billie Holiday. (Ritz Theatre & Museum.)

Alice Kilpatrick, shown here, opened the Richmond Hotel with husband, George, in 1909. The hotel became one of Jacksonville's premier hotels for African Americans during the Jim Crow era. With 48 guest rooms and a 65-seat restaurant, it hosted legends like Duke Ellington, Ella Fitzgerald, and Billie Holiday. Musicians often serenaded crowds from its balcony, most famously Cab Calloway, who sang his signature "Hi-De-Ho" to adoring fans on Jacksonville's streets below. (Ritz Theatre & Museum.)

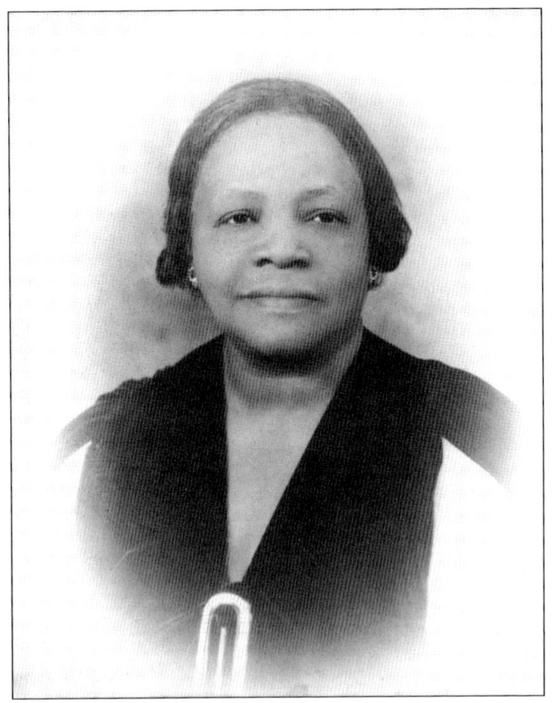

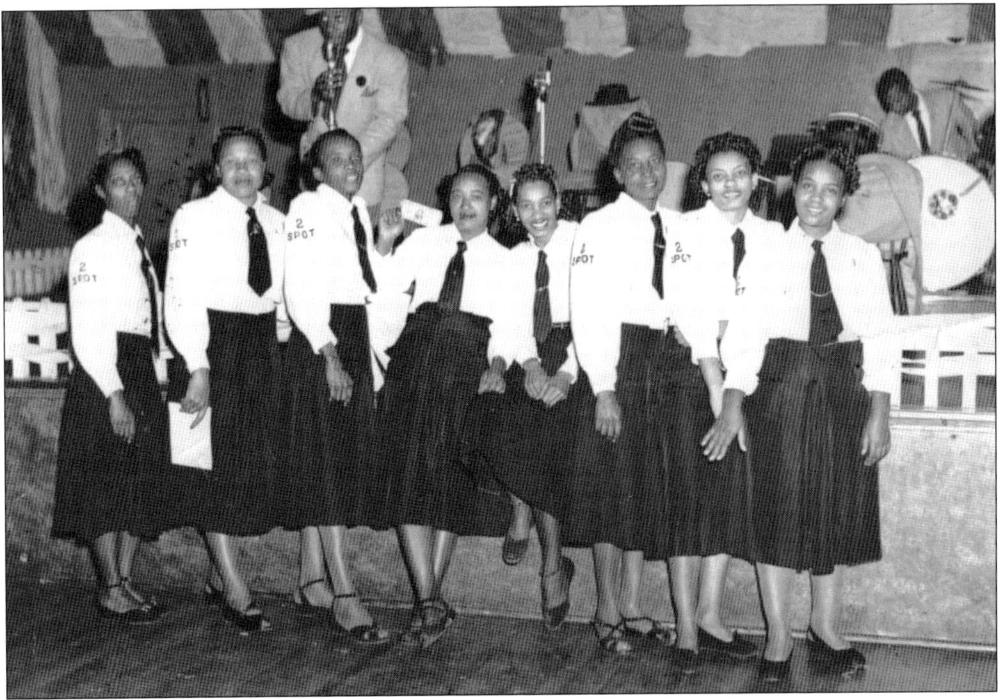

James Brown called the Two Spot "one of the biggest venues to perform as a Black musician during the 1960s segregation." Built by James "Charlie Edd" Craddock, the "kingpin" of West Ashley Street, the club opened on December 25, 1940, near West Forty-Fifth Street and Moncrief Road. With room for 3,000 guests, it hosted legends like B.B. King, Sam Cooke, Ray Charles, Lionel Hampton, Dinah Washington, and Jackie Wilson. (Ritz Theatre & Museum.)

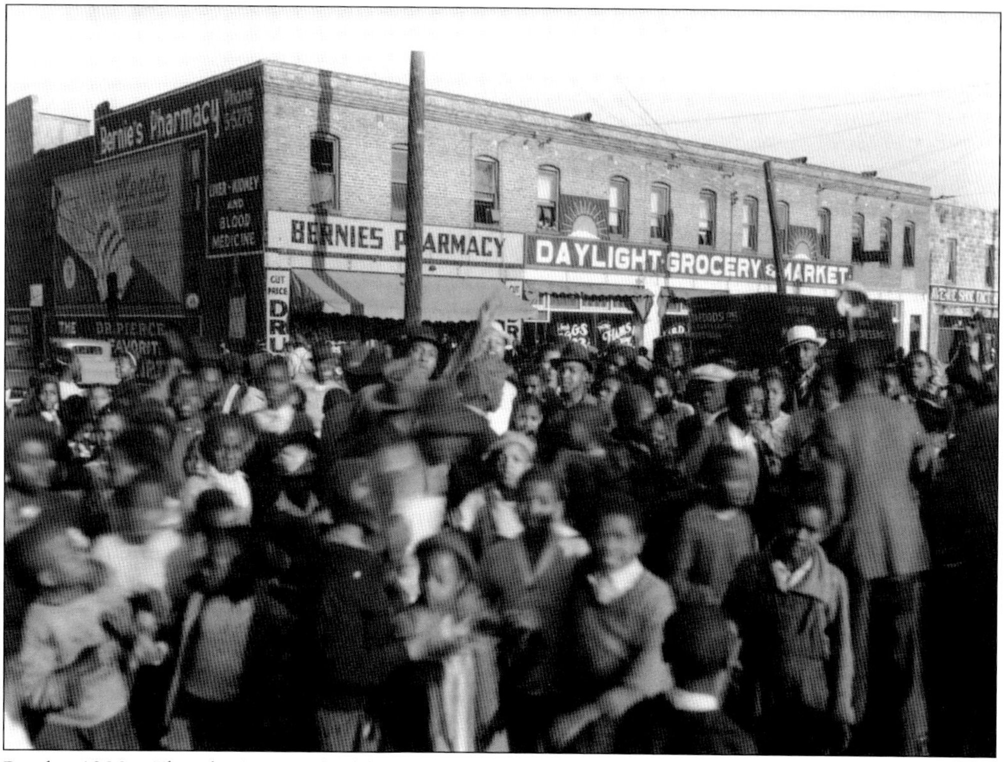

By the 1920s, Florida Avenue had become known as a center of Black commerce for residents living east of Hogans Creek. Affectionately known as "the Avenue," its line of mixed-use buildings was occupied by small businesses, restaurants, and clubs, including the Blue Ridge Inn, Charlie Joseph's grocery store, and Johns Furniture and Bill's Clothing. Famed neighborhood residents who once frequented this strip include A. Philip Randolph, Zora Neale Hurston, A.L. Lewis, and Bullet Bob Hayes. (Ritz Theatre & Museum.)

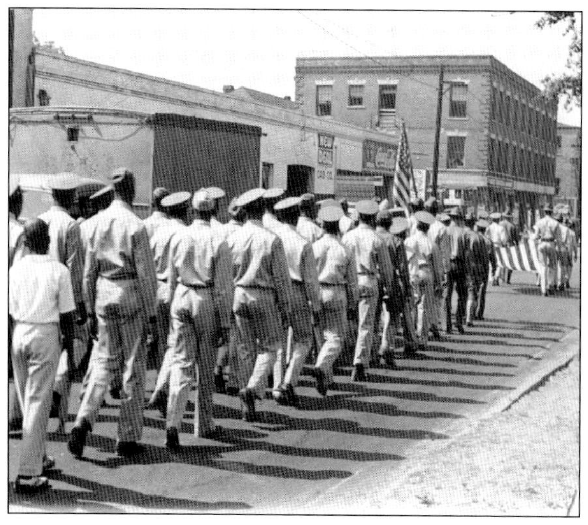

LaVilla's Broad Street was a major route for the Patriotism Parade during World War II. At its height, Broad Street's Black-owned businesses were a major focal point of Black life, culture, and the fight for civil rights in Florida. Black-owned businesses included banks, insurance companies, restaurants, theaters, mutual aid societies, boardinghouses, seafood markets, grocery stores, hotels, furniture stores, and professional offices. (Eartha M.M. White Collection, Thomas G. Carpenter Library Special Collections and University Archives, University of North Florida.)

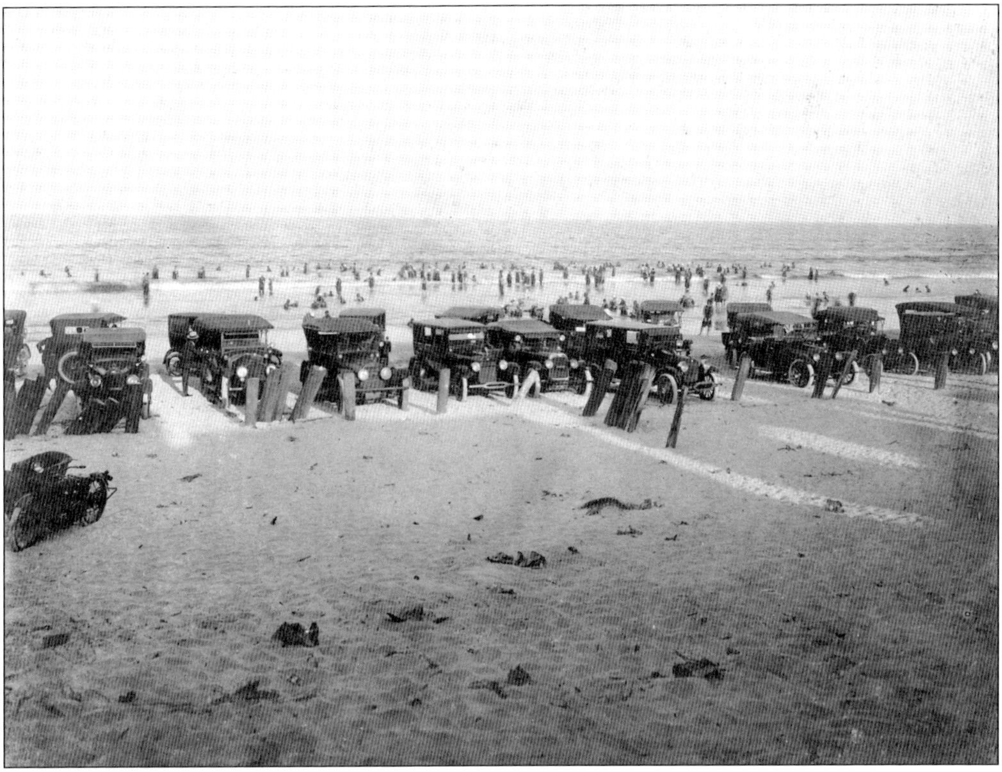

In the 1920s, vehicles parked on Manhattan Beach, which was Florida's first African American beach. Established around 1900 by industrialist Henry Flagler for his Black railroad and resort workers, it became a vibrant destination with food, lodging, and entertainment at two pavilions run by Mack Wilson and William Middleton. The beach closed in 1938. The site is now part of Kathryn Abbey Hanna Park. (Eartha M.M. White Collection, Thomas G. Carpenter Library Special Collections and University Archives, University of North Florida.)

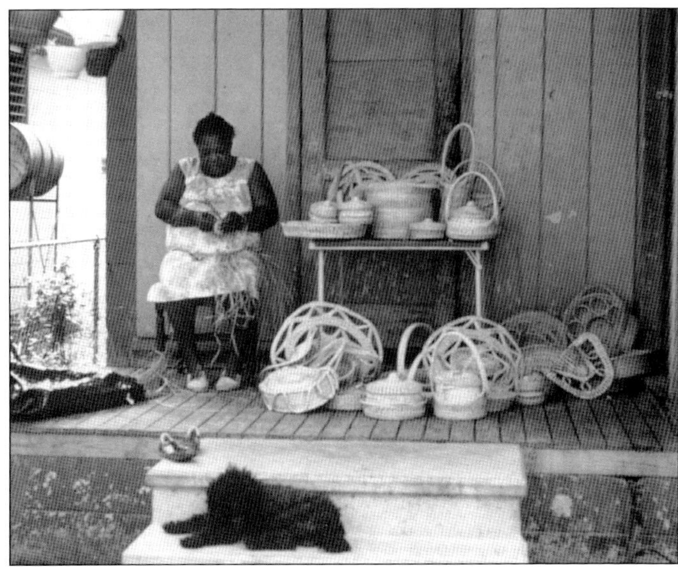

The art of sweetgrass basket weaving, rooted in Gullah Geechee traditions, has flourished for centuries in coastal communities from North Carolina to Florida. Once used for storing food and crops, these baskets are now celebrated as cultural artworks. On July 19, 1979, Lucille Jones (1906–1980) was photographed at her Jacksonville home skillfully crafting a sweetgrass basket, surrounded by her intricate creations, a testament to a heritage preserved through artistry and tradition. (State Archives of Florida.)

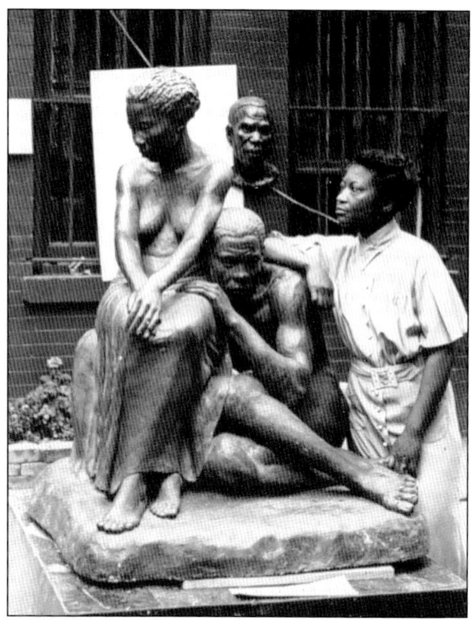

Augusta Savage (1892–1962) stands with her sculpture *Realization* in 1938. As a child growing up in Green Cove Springs, she taught herself to sculpt using the red clay of the local brickyard. In 1921, she left Jacksonville and moved to Harlem, where she became a sculptor associated with the Harlem Renaissance. (Archives of American Art, Smithsonian Institution.)

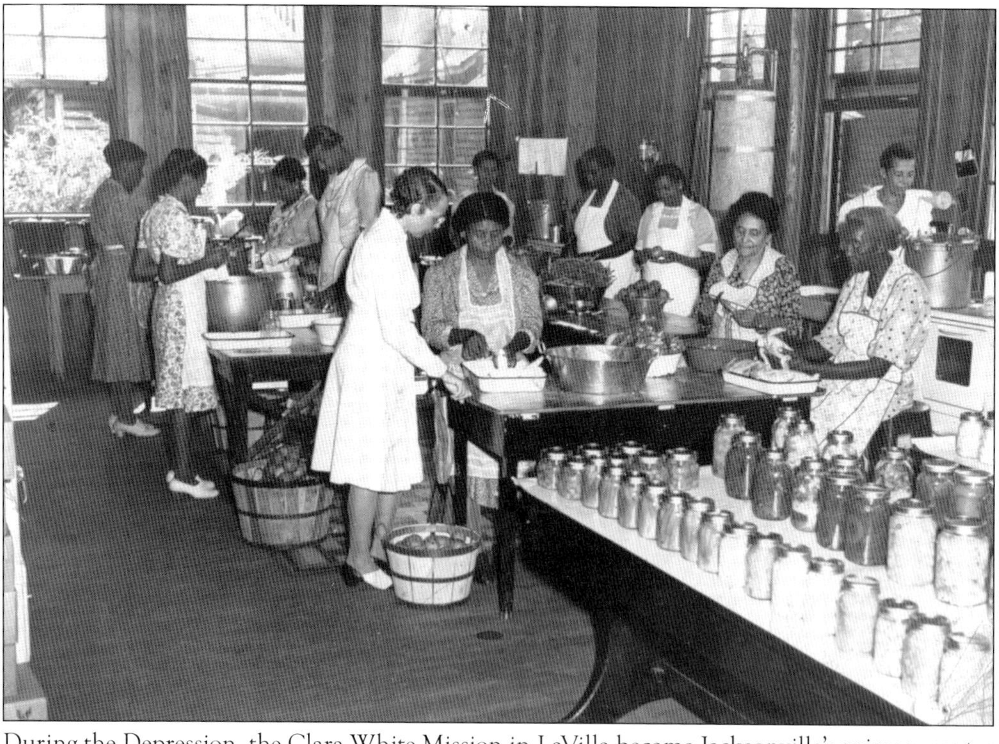

During the Depression, the Clara White Mission in LaVilla became Jacksonville's primary center of relief for the Black community. It hosted WPA offices and the Federal Writers' Project Colored Division and provided housing for mothers and children. A sewing room employed 100 women, while training programs taught domestic service and crafts for the blind, making the mission a vital hub of hope, employment, and empowerment during hard times. (Eartha M.M. White Collection, Thomas G. Carpenter Library Special Collections and University Archives, University of North Florida.)

Eight

The Journey

Gullah Geechee heritage in Jacksonville is not a memory of the past. It is a living legacy that continues to shape the city's journey over time. This heritage is embedded in the landscapes, buildings, food, and community spaces that are seen today. Visiting these places offers a way to connect with centuries of history that remain visible and rooted in the everyday life of Jacksonville.

Many of Jacksonville's cultural landmarks grew from the self-determination of Gullah Geechee people during and after Reconstruction. The Masonic Temple on Broad Street, designed and financed by Black builders and fraternal leaders, stands as a monument to community leadership, progress, and Black excellence. Nearby, the Clara White Mission and Eartha M.M. White Historical Museum preserve the legacy of one of Jacksonville's most visionary philanthropists and entrepreneurs. Churches, schools, and homes in neighborhoods like Durkeeville, Eastside, and LaVilla reveal the craftsmanship of builders such as Joseph Haygood Blodgett and the history of residents who made these places thrive.

Preserved landscapes like Cedar Point, Reddie Point, and Kingsley Plantation link today's visitors to sites of ancestral labor and survival. New spaces, such as Freedom Park at Cosmo, mark an ongoing commitment to recognition and education. Cultural and educational centers like the Ritz Theatre & Museum, Norman Studios, and Edward Waters University connect Gullah Geechee history to the arts, scholarship, and public memory.

These places are not static monuments but part of a living cultural network. From Lift Ev'ry Voice and Sing Park to the Melanin Market on the Avenue, Gullah Geechee heritage is celebrated through food, movement, music, storytelling, and entrepreneurship. Visiting these sites provides an invitation to witness a cultural legacy that continues to define Jacksonville's spirit and story.

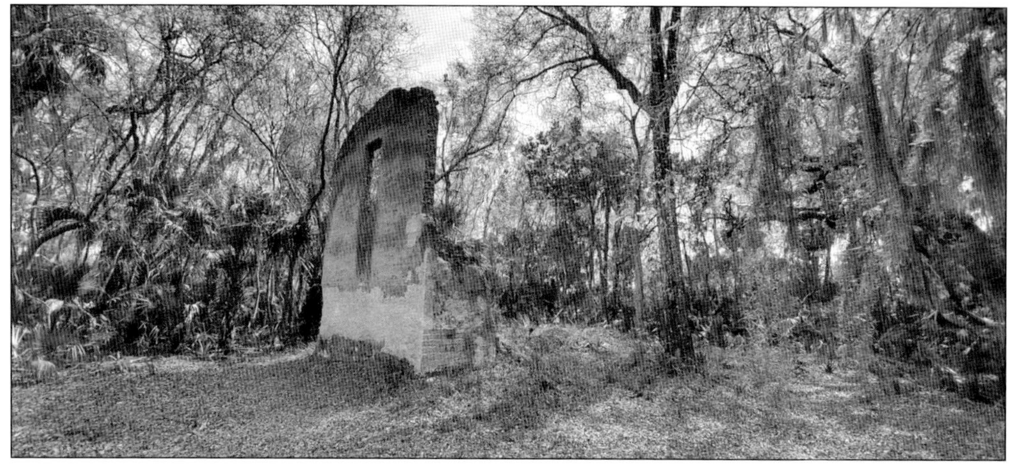

The ruins of the Fitzpatrick Plantation at Cedar Point, built in the late 1700s, are near the southern tip of Black Hammock Island. The land was originally granted to Samuel Mills and later acquired by the Fitzpatrick family. Enslaved African laborers were forced to produce salt by boiling seawater. The plantation was destroyed by Union forces during the Civil War. Today, Cedar Point is a part of the National Park Service's Timucuan Ecological and Historic Preserve. (Ennis Davis, AICP.)

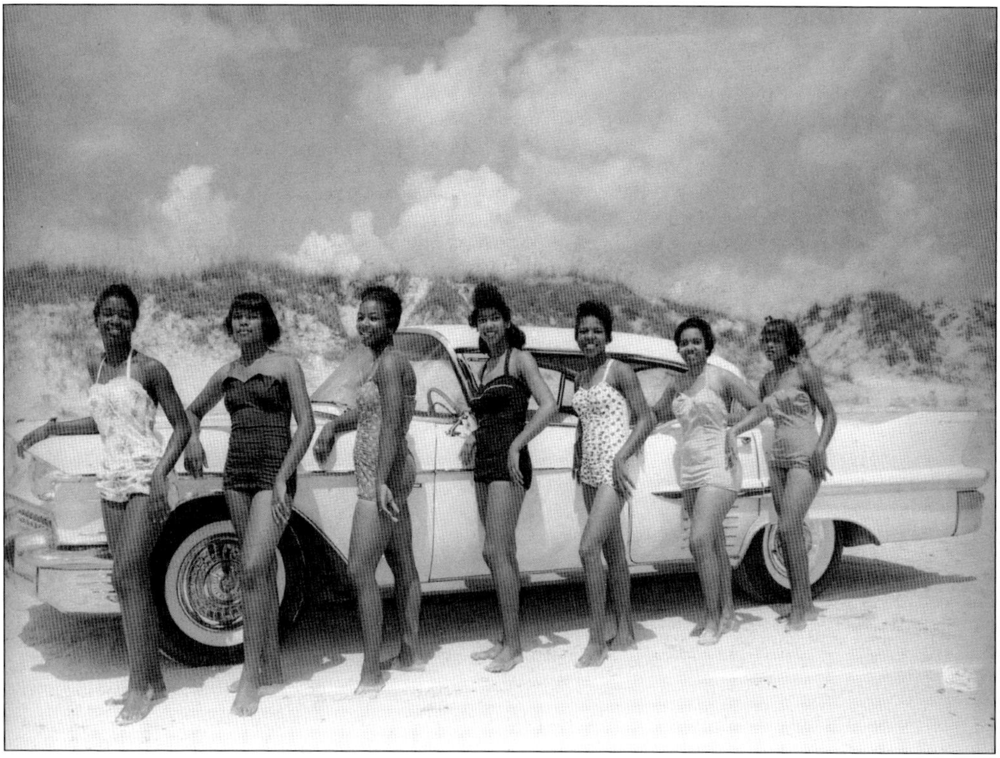

Founded in 1935 on Amelia Island by the Afro-American Life Insurance Company, American Beach became a 216-acre seaside haven where Black families enjoyed "Recreation and Relaxation Without Humiliation." During its mid-century heyday, it drew crowds and celebrities like Zora Neale Hurston, Ray Charles, and Joe Louis. Listed on the National Register of Historic Places in 2002, it is now home to the A.L. Lewis Museum at American Beach, opened in 2014. (Special Collections, Thomas G. Carpenter Library, University of North Florida.)

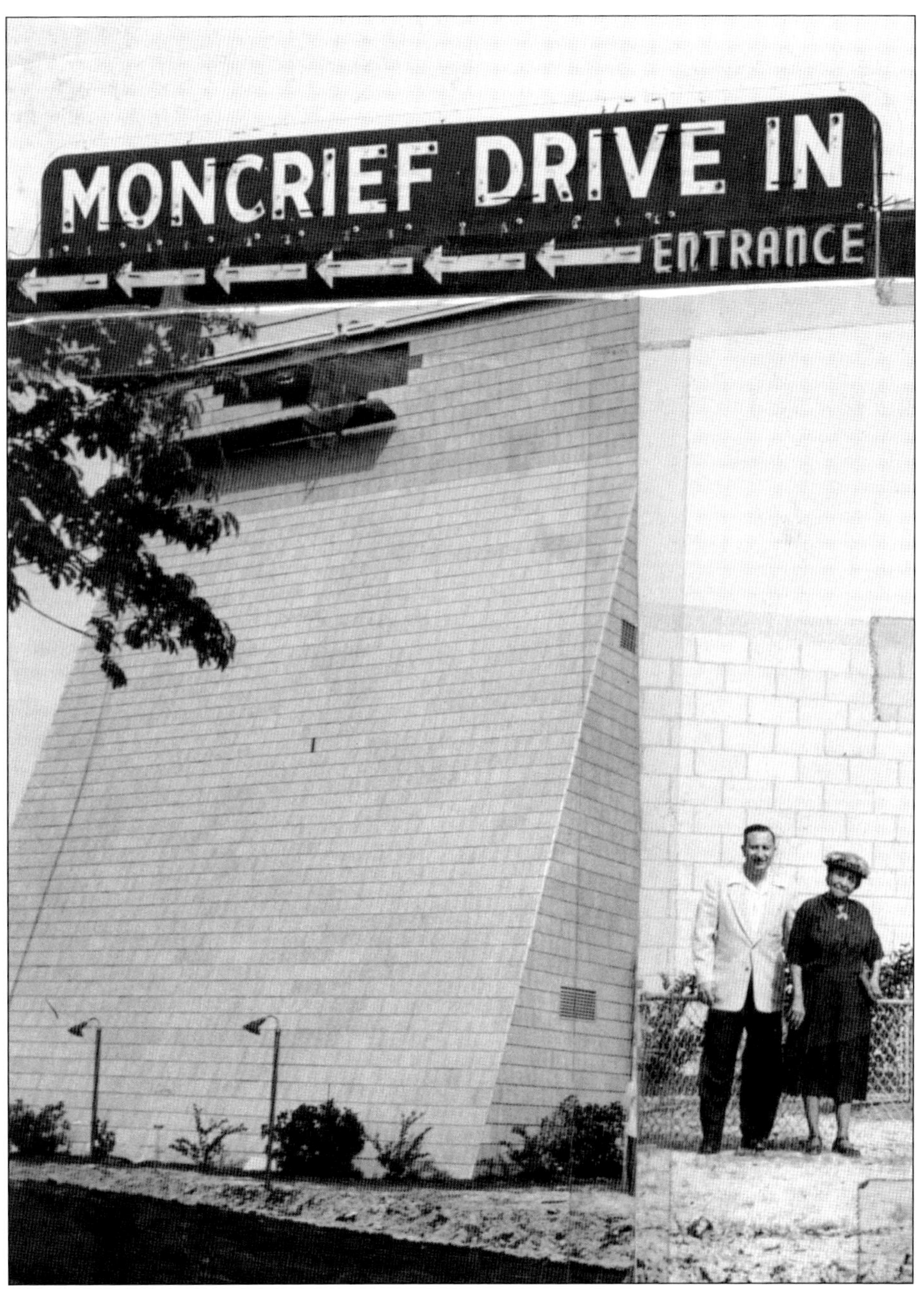

Moncrief Road has long served as a social destination for Jacksonville's Black community. Opening to the public in March 1953, the Moncrief Drive-In was a 350-vehicle drive-in theater for Black patrons. The Moncrief Drive-In closed and was replaced by multifamily housing in 1971. Today, cultural destinations in the immediate vicinity include Eartha's Farm & Market. Established in 2012 at 4850 Moncrief Road on property once owned by Eartha White, the purpose of Eartha's Farm & Market is to increase the production of healthy fruits and vegetables, improve food access in the community, and provide training and educational programming to the local residents. The 10.5-acre urban farm is open to the public every Saturday from 10:00 a.m. to 2:00 p.m. (Thomas G. Carpenter Library, University of North Florida.)

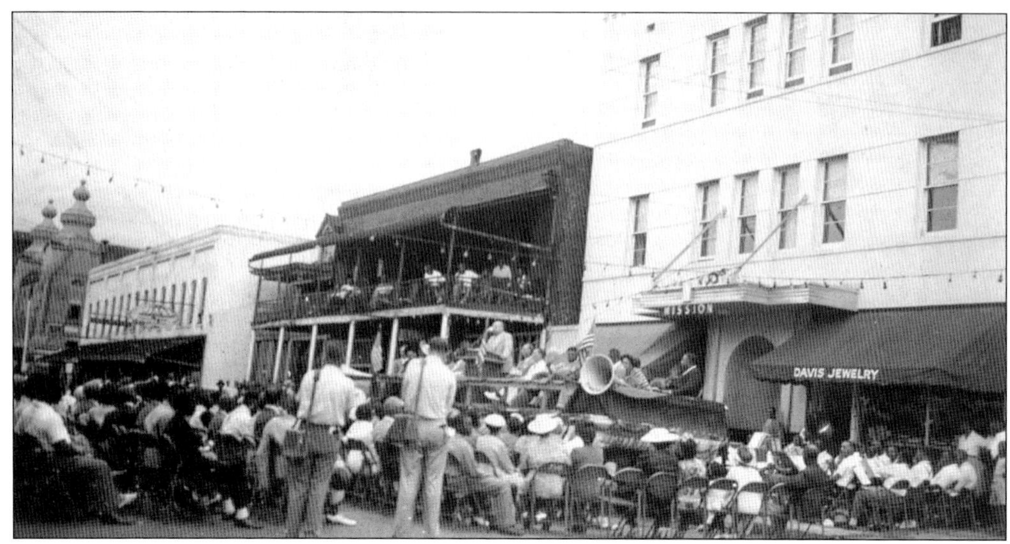

The Clara White Mission was dedicated in 1947 at 613 West Ashley Street in LaVilla. The Eartha M.M. White Historical Museum celebrates the legacy of Dr. Eartha Mary Magdalene White, Florida's first Black female millionaire. This second-floor museum features photographs, artifacts, and stories highlighting her remarkable life and connections to figures like Booker T. Washington, Dr. Martin Luther King Jr., Dr. Mary McLeod Bethune, Ray Charles, and Eleanor Roosevelt. (Thomas G. Carpenter Library, University of North Florida.)

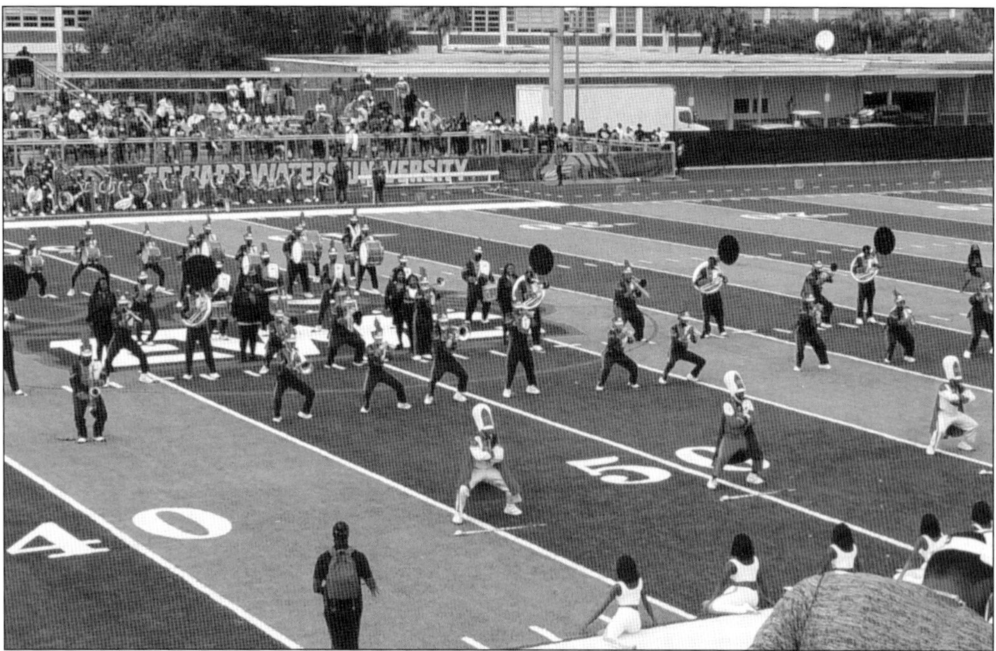

Founded in 1866, Edward Waters University (EWU) is the state of Florida's first independent institution of higher learning and Florida's first institution established to educate African Americans. Featuring buildings designed by late-19th- and early-20th-century African American architects, the campus was added to the National Register of Historic Places in 2022. In this image, the EWU Triple Threat Marching Band performs during a football game at Nathaniel Glover Community Field and Stadium. (Ennis Davis, AICP.)

A partnership between the City of Jacksonville and nonprofit Groundwork Jacksonville, the Emerald Trail is an ambitious plan to connect 14 urban core neighborhoods, parks, schools, and the St. Johns River with 30 miles of connected multi-use paths. Completed segments connect the historic Gullah Geechee neighborhoods of West Lewisville, Brooklyn, Campbell Hill, LaVilla, Durkeeville, Robinson's Addition, New Town, and Eastside. (City of Jacksonville.)

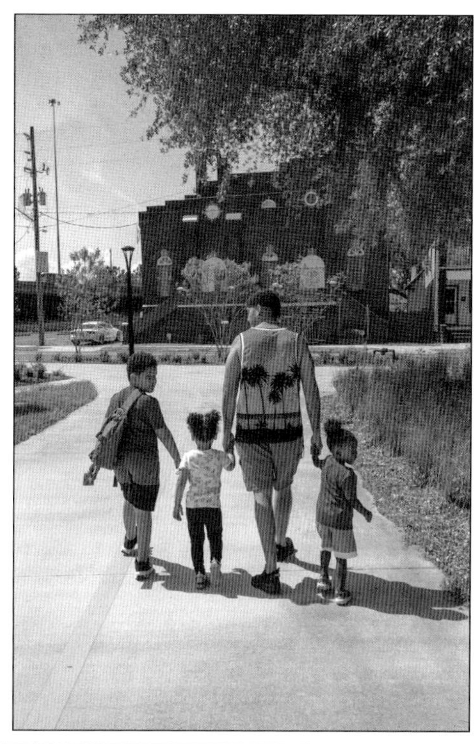

The Fort Caroline National Memorial, at 12713 Fort Caroline Road, commemorates the 1564 French settlement led by René Goulaine de Laudonnière, which included free African Moors. In 1565, the Spanish captured the fort, ending the French presence. Though its true site remains lost, a replica now stands within the 50,000-acre Timucuan Ecological and Historic Preserve, which includes the Timucuan Preserve Visitor Center, pictured here. (State Archives of Florida.)

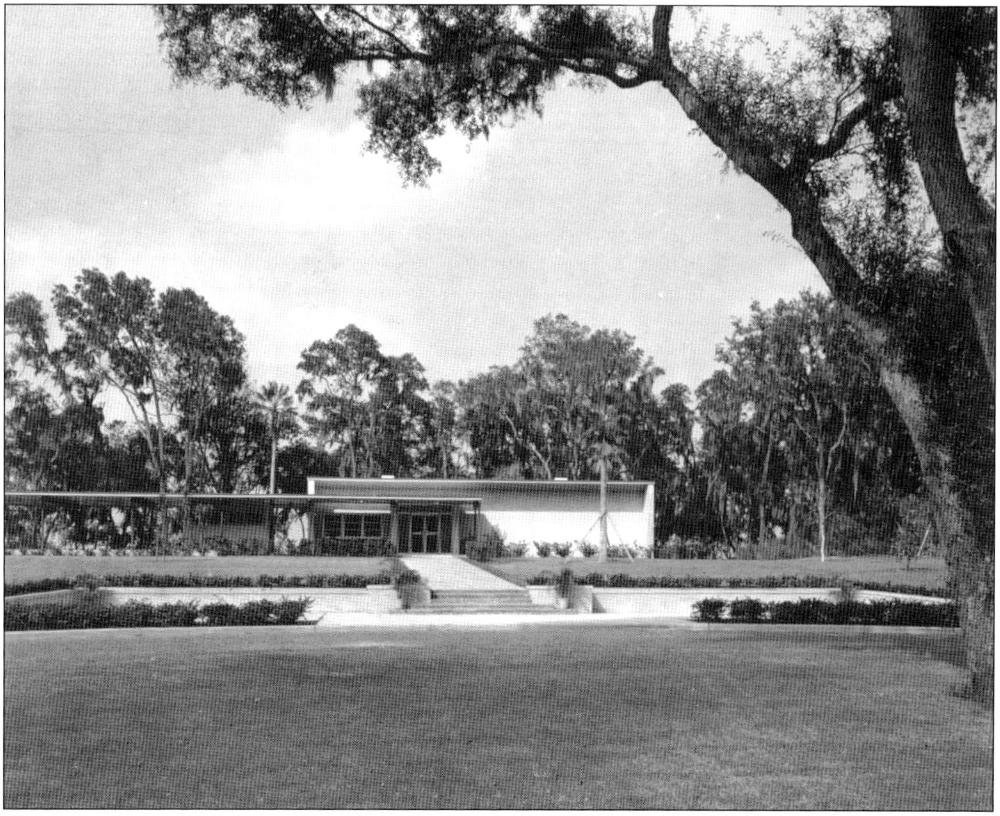

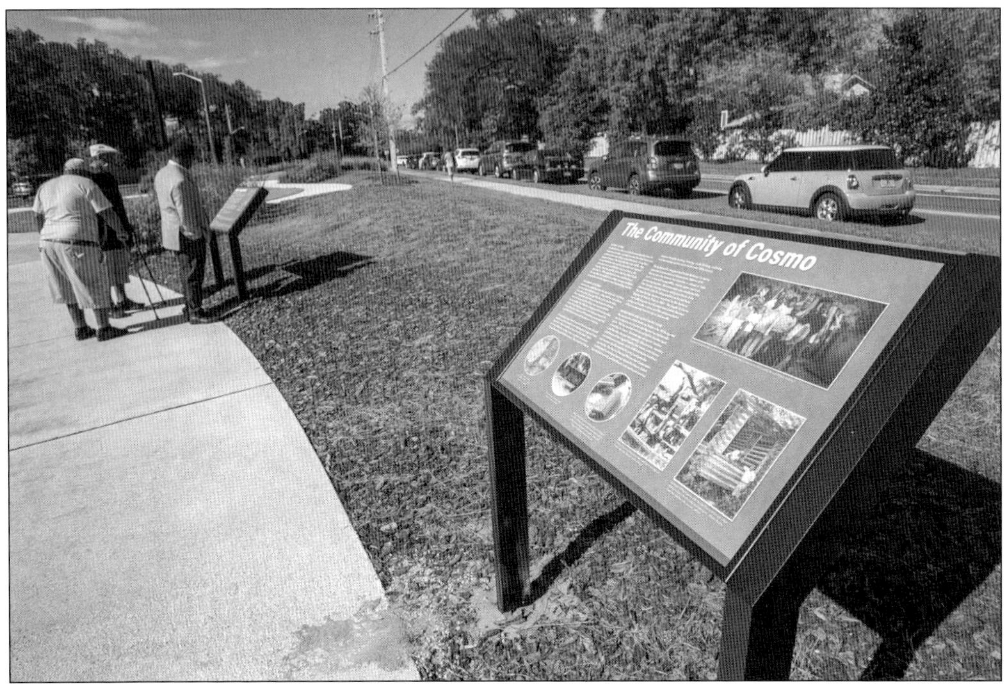

The settlement of Cosmo was established in 1877 by Gullah Geechee families and remained in isolation until the construction of the Mathews Bridge and the development of Arlington as a popular suburb during the 1950s. In 2022, the City of Jacksonville established Freedom Park in Cosmo, featuring the first public markers in Jacksonville honoring Gullah Geechee people. The park stands as a testament to the work of the Cosmo Historical Preservation Corporation. (City of Jacksonville.)

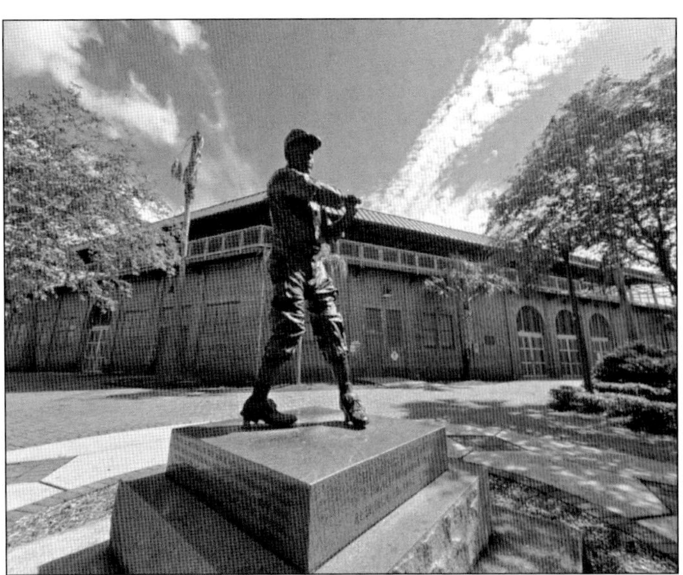

Built in 1912 at 1701 Myrtle Avenue, Durkee Field was home to the Negro League's Jacksonville Red Caps, Florida's first major-league team. Baseball greats like Babe Ruth, Lou Gehrig, and Henry Aaron once played here. Now known as Hank L. Aaron Field at James P. Small Memorial Stadium, the ballpark's baseball museum and children's playground capture the rich history of the sport in Jacksonville and the surrounding Durkeeville neighborhood. (Ennis Davis, AICP.)

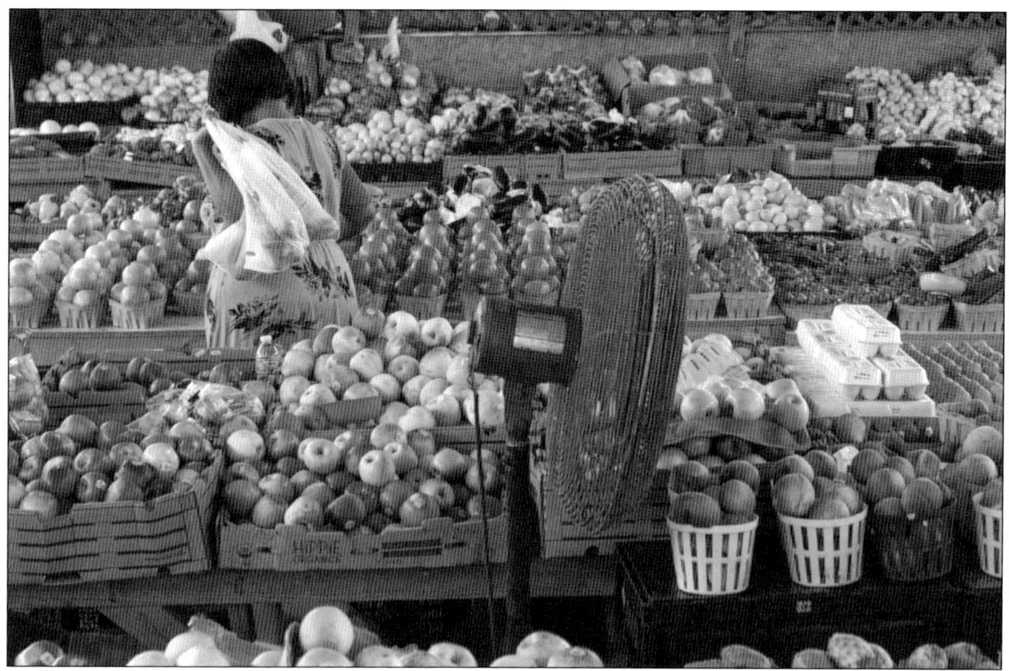

Just west of downtown Jacksonville, the Rail Yard District encompasses the historic Gullah Geechee neighborhoods of New Town, Robinson's Addition, and Mixtontown. At its center stands the Jacksonville Farmers Market, Florida's oldest continuously operating market since 1938. This open-air market draws over 25,000 visitors each week and offers an authentic shopping experience where farmers, wholesalers, and local vendors sell everything from fresh produce and seafood to flowers, spices, and even live chickens and goats. (City of Jacksonville.)

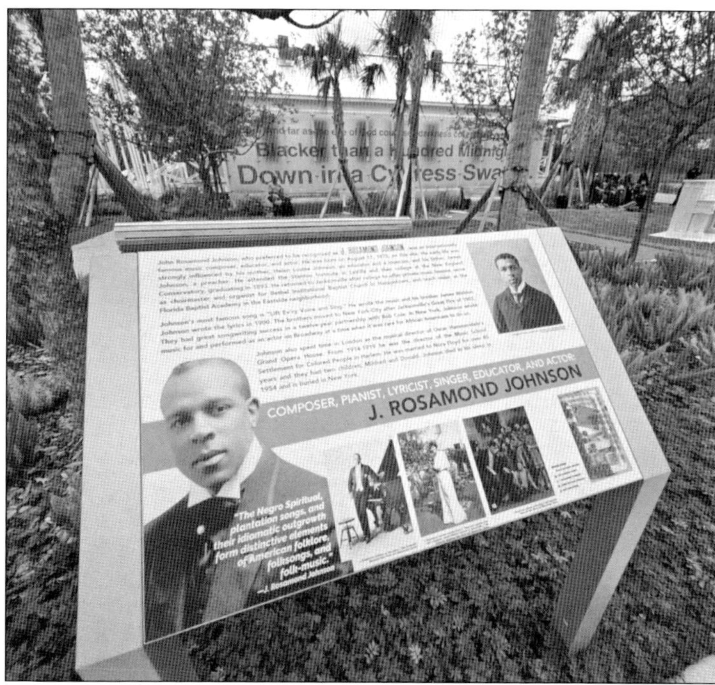

Lift Ev'ry Voice and Sing Park in LaVilla stands on the historic site where brothers James Weldon and John Rosamond Johnson wrote the iconic anthem in 1900. First performed by students at the Stanton Institute, it became the NAACP's official "Black National Anthem" in 1919. Completed in 2024, the park honors the Johnsons with landscaped grounds, exhibits, and markers celebrating LaVilla's enduring legacy of Black culture, creativity, and pride. (Ennis Davis, AICP.)

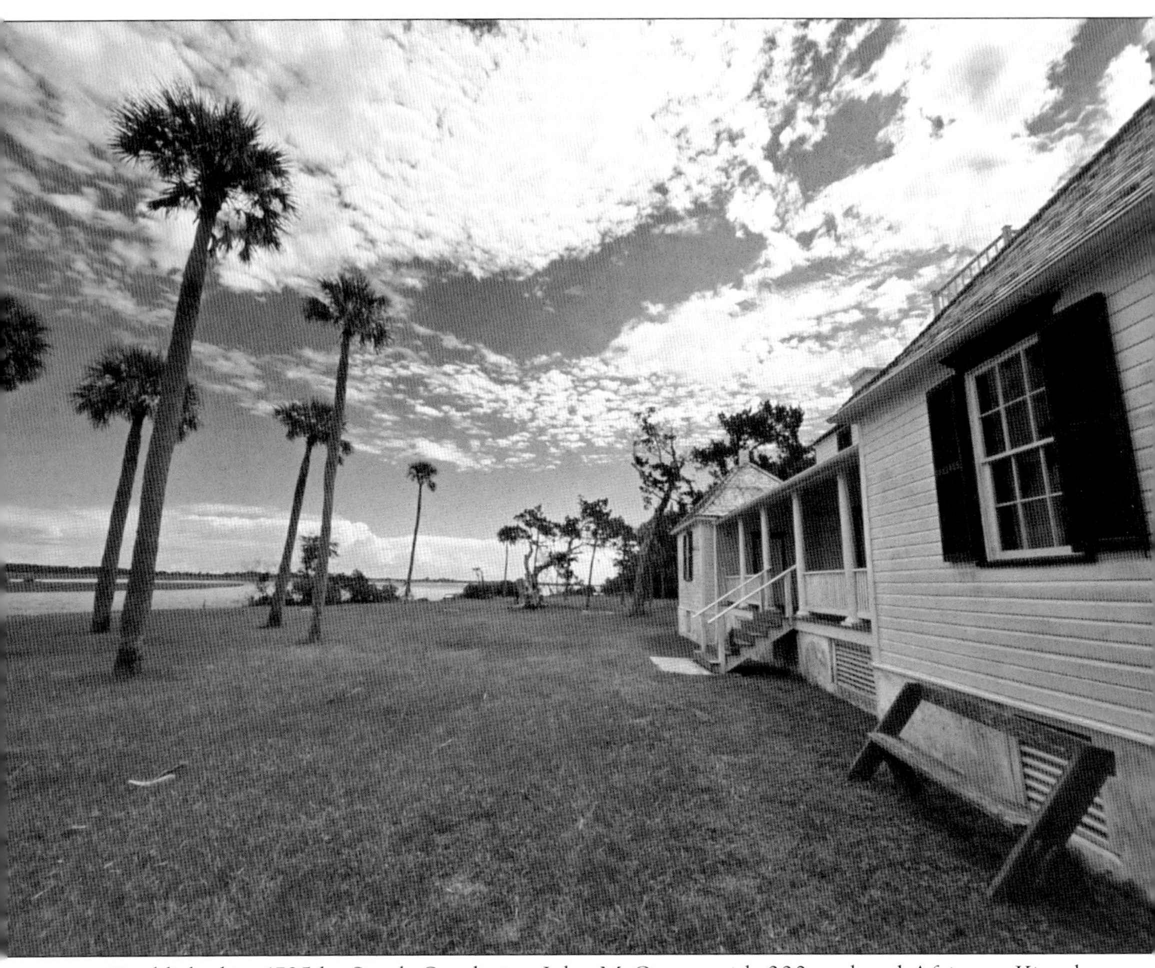

Established in 1795 by South Carolinian John McQueen with 300 enslaved Africans, Kingsley Plantation changed hands several times before Zephaniah Kingsley Jr. acquired it in 1817. Kingsley, known as one of Florida's most controversial enslavers, married Anna Madgigine Jai, a Wolof woman from present-day Senegal, who managed the plantation in his absence, cultivating Sea Island cotton, timber, and sugar. After Kingsley's death in 1843, Anna successfully defended her inheritance in a 1846 Duval County court, a rare legal victory for a Black woman in the antebellum South. With many of its structures still surviving on an isolated Sea Island, the property was acquired by the National Park Service, becoming a part of the Timucuan Ecological and Historic Preserve in 1991. (Ennis Davis, AICP.)

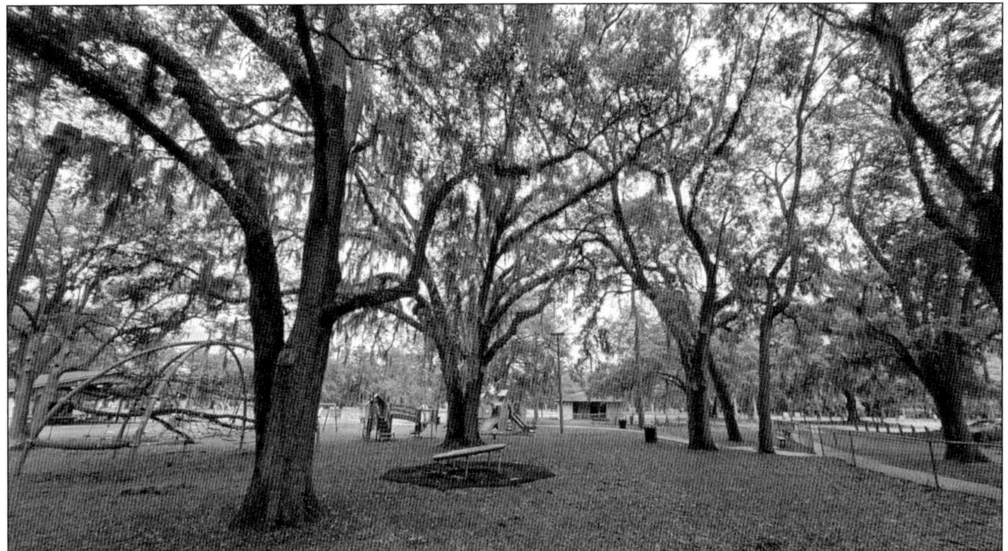

Located near Soutel Drive and Moncrief Road, Lonnie C. Miller Sr. Regional Park is a 126-acre family-friendly destination along the Ribault River in Northwest Jacksonville. Opened in 1995, it features a destination playground, splash pad, amphitheater, trails, and picnic shelters. The park sits beside the Bob Hayes Sports Complex and Legends Community Center, which offers youth athletic fields, an indoor gym, a computer lab, a fitness center, and an auditorium. (Ennis Davis, AICP.)

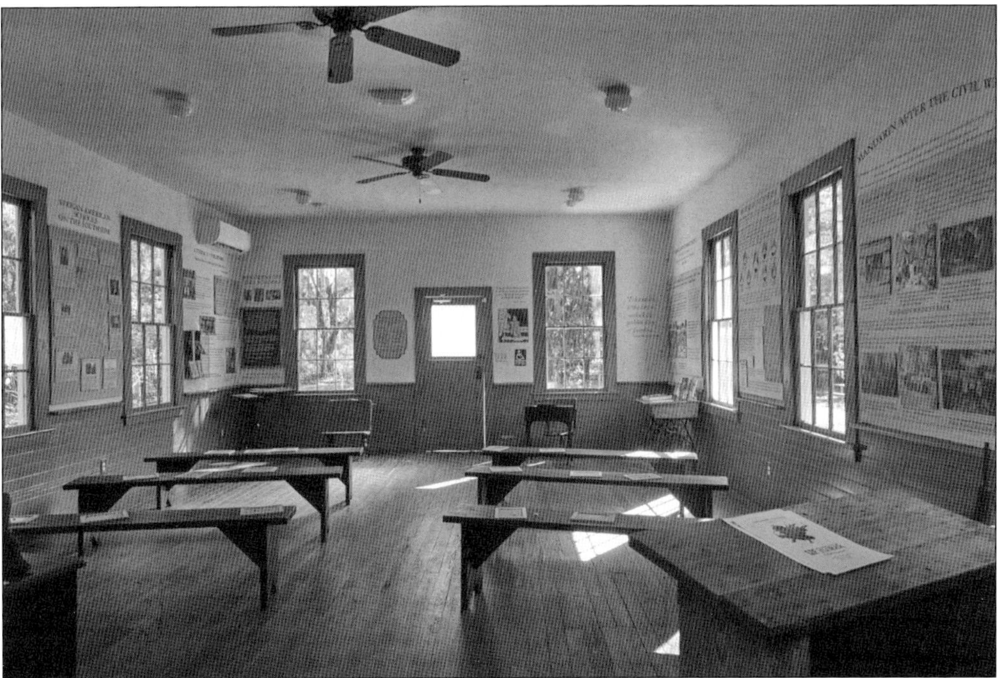

Since its 2004 opening at 11964 Mandarin Road, the Mandarin Museum & Historical Society has enhanced the original exhibits so visitors can explore some of the people and events that shaped the Mandarin community. Featured Gullah Geechee–related exhibits include the wreck of the Civil War steamboat *Maple Leaf*, the 1898 St. Joseph's Mission Schoolhouse for African American children, pictured here, and the Untold Story of Black Mandarin permanent exhibit. (Library of Congress.)

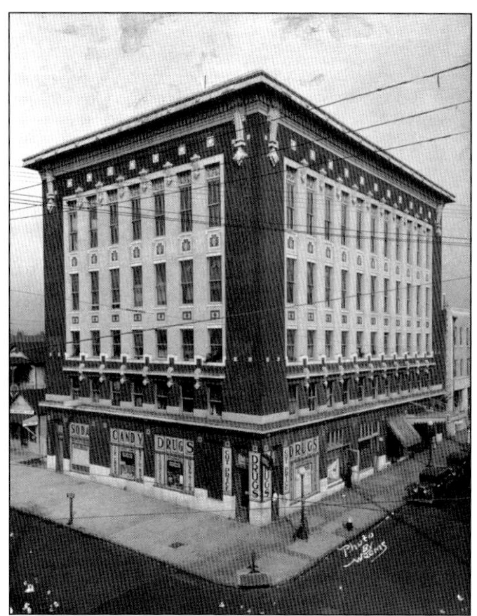

Established in 1870, the Freemasons' Most Worshipful Union Grand Lodge of Florida was founded by free people of color, formerly enslaved individuals, and US Colored Troops veterans. Completed in 1916, the Masonic Temple at 400 Broad Street in LaVilla became a cornerstone of Jacksonville's Black community. It housed businesses, professionals, and the Grand Lodge headquarters. It served as a hub of Black progress. It was added to the National Register of Historic Places in 1980. (University of Florida.)

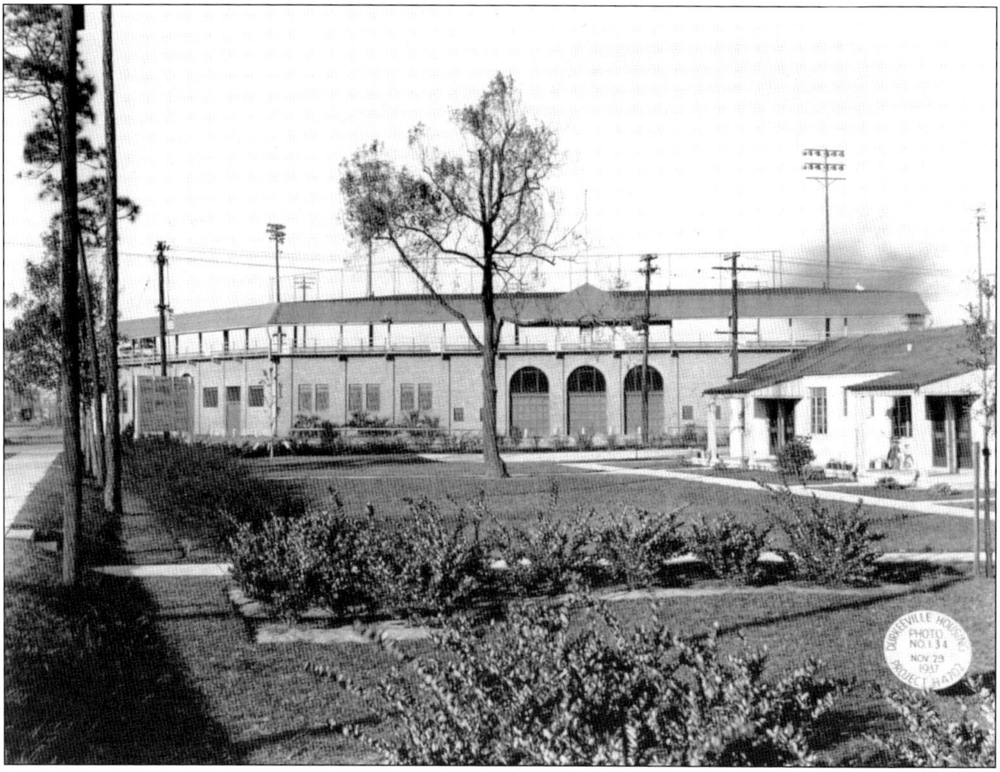

Once home to the Black-owned streetcar line known as the "Colored Man's Railroad," Myrtle Avenue remains a vital corridor linking the Gullah Geechee neighborhoods of Brooklyn, LaVilla, New Town, Durkeeville, and Moncrief. Photographed in 1937, with its walkable blocks, historic character, churches, and locally owned legacy businesses, Myrtle Avenue endures as one of Jacksonville's most authentic and culturally rich areas, preserving the spirit of the city's historic Gullah Geechee heritage. (University of Florida.)

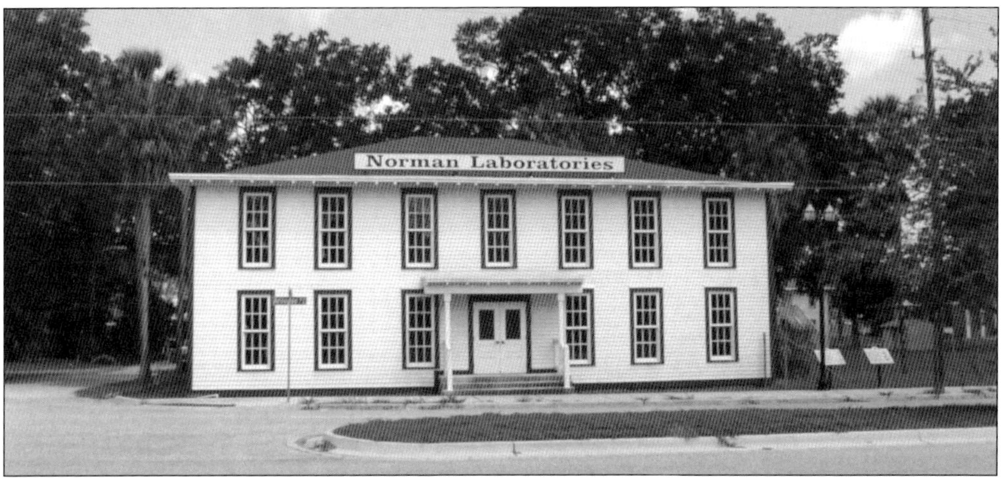

Located at 6337 Arlington Road, Norman Studios, originally the Norman Film Manufacturing Company, was founded by Richard Edward Norman and operated from 1919 to 1928, producing silent films with all-Black casts. Designated a national historic landmark, the site now serves as a museum celebrating early Black cinema and silent film history. Free public tours are offered on the first and third Saturday of each month. (State Archives of Florida.)

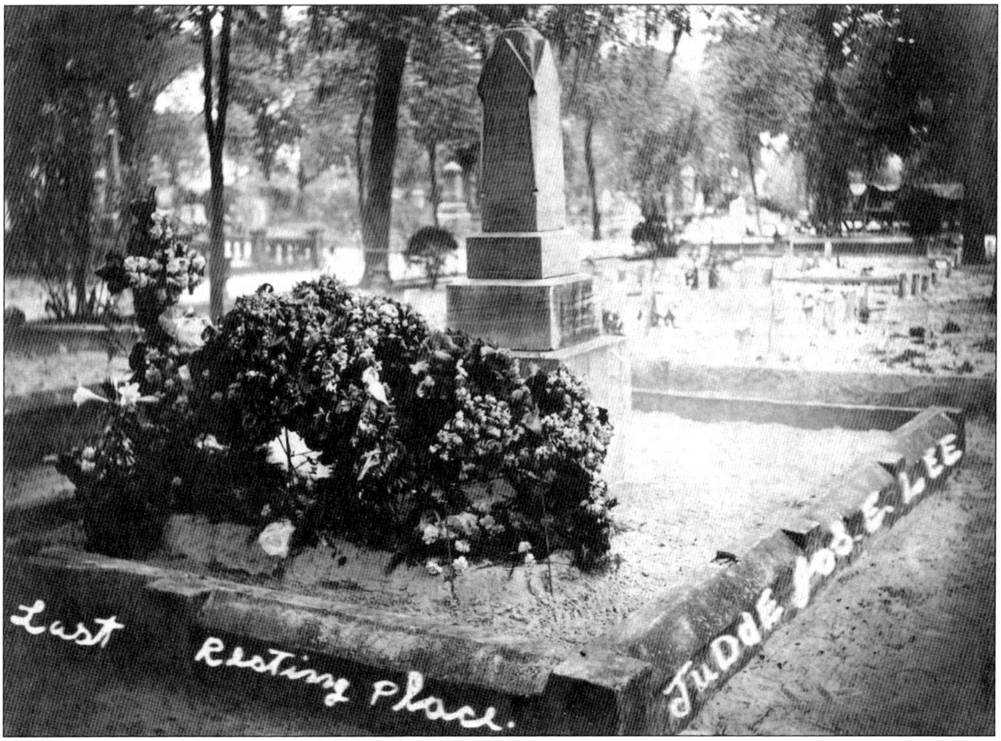

The land for Old City Cemetery, located at 911 North Washington Street, was gifted to Jacksonville in 1852 by steamboat captain Charles Willey. It dates to 1827 and has segregated Black and White sections. It is known for its ornate ironwork and hand-carved tombstones. It contains graves of prominent 19th-century citizens, freedmen, US Colored Troops, Masons, and religious groups. Notable burials include Clara and Eartha White, Dr. Alexander Darnes, and Ghanaian minister Princess Laura Adorkor Kofi. (Special Collections, Thomas G. Carpenter Library, University of North Florida.)

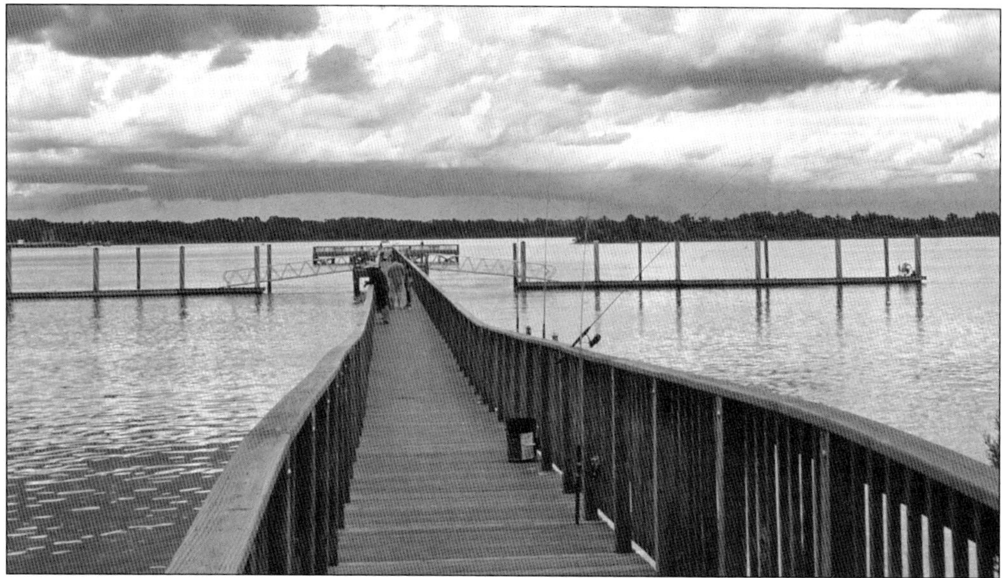

A popular fishing and hiking destination, Reddie Point Preserve's history dates to the late 1700s, when Capt. William Reddy operated an 800-acre plantation during Florida's British period. After the Civil War, the Gullah Geechee community of Chaseville emerged as Samuel Chase employed former US Colored Troops at his Reddy Point shipyard. In 2002, the 102 acres that make up Reddie Point Preserve were purchased by the City of Jacksonville. (Ennis Davis, AICP.)

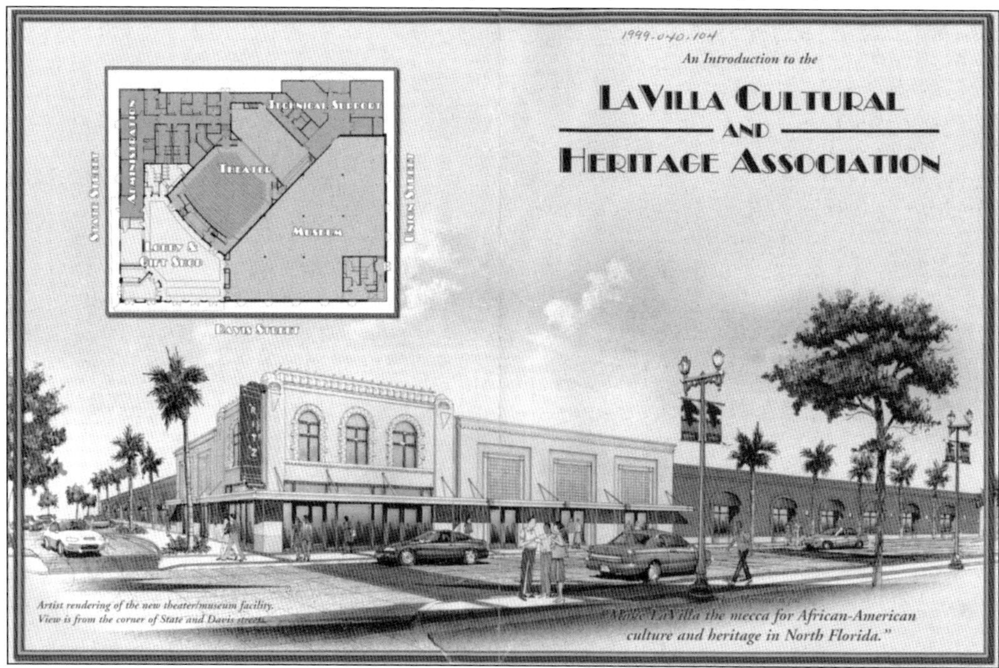

The Ritz Theatre & Museum, located at 829 North Davis Street, celebrates the city's rich Black heritage and Gullah Geechee culture. Originally opened in 1929 as a movie theater for Black audiences, it closed in 1971. Reopened in 1999 as a 32,000-square-foot, 426-seat museum and performing arts venue, the Ritz preserves and showcases African American history and life in Northeast Florida and the broader African Diaspora. (Ritz Theatre & Museum.)

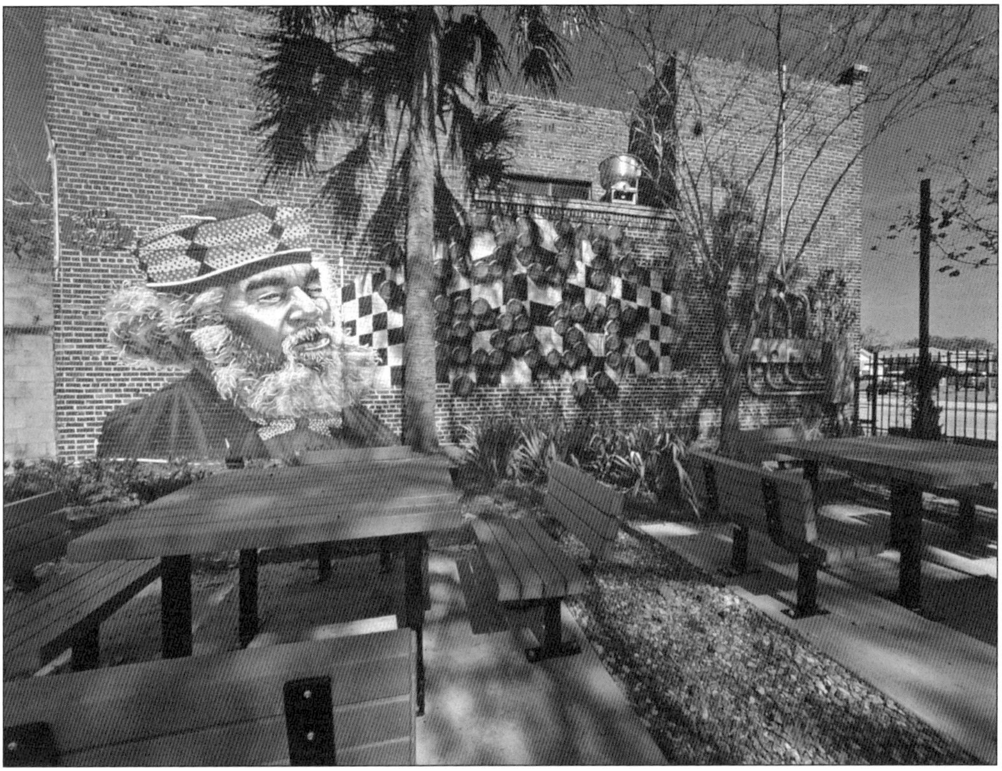

In the early 20th century, Florida Avenue became the center of Eastside Black commerce and culture. Renamed A. Philip Randolph Boulevard in 1995, "the Avenue" now hosts the lively quarterly Melanin Market. In 2024, the Florida Avenue Main Street program, the first Main Street program in Jacksonville, was established to promote preservation, local business growth, and community revitalization. It is also home to Buster Ford Checkerboard Park, pictured here, which was rehabilitated in 2025. (Ennis Davis, AICP.)

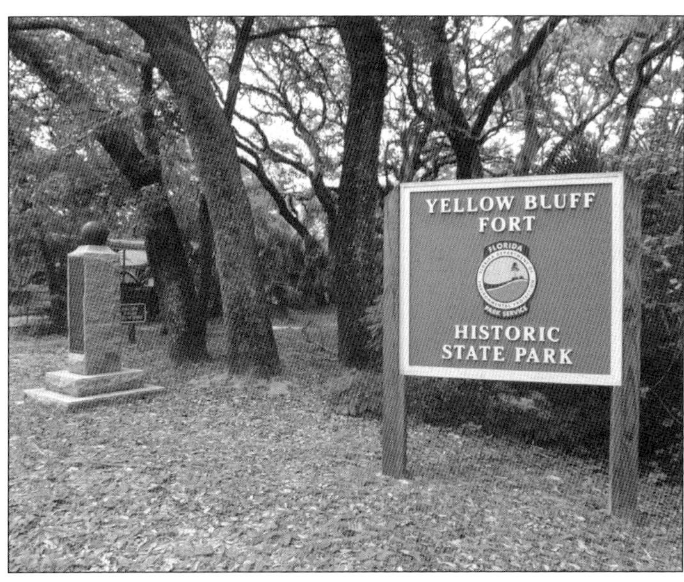

In 1861, Gen. Robert E. Lee ordered coastal defenses built to protect Florida's supply routes, leading to the construction of earthworks at Yellow Bluff. Seized by Union troops in 1862, it later housed Black Union regiments, including the 54th Massachusetts and 8th and 34th US Colored Troops, shown here. Largely intact today, the site was listed on the National Register of Historic Places in 1970 and now serves as a peaceful picnic area. (Library of Congress.)

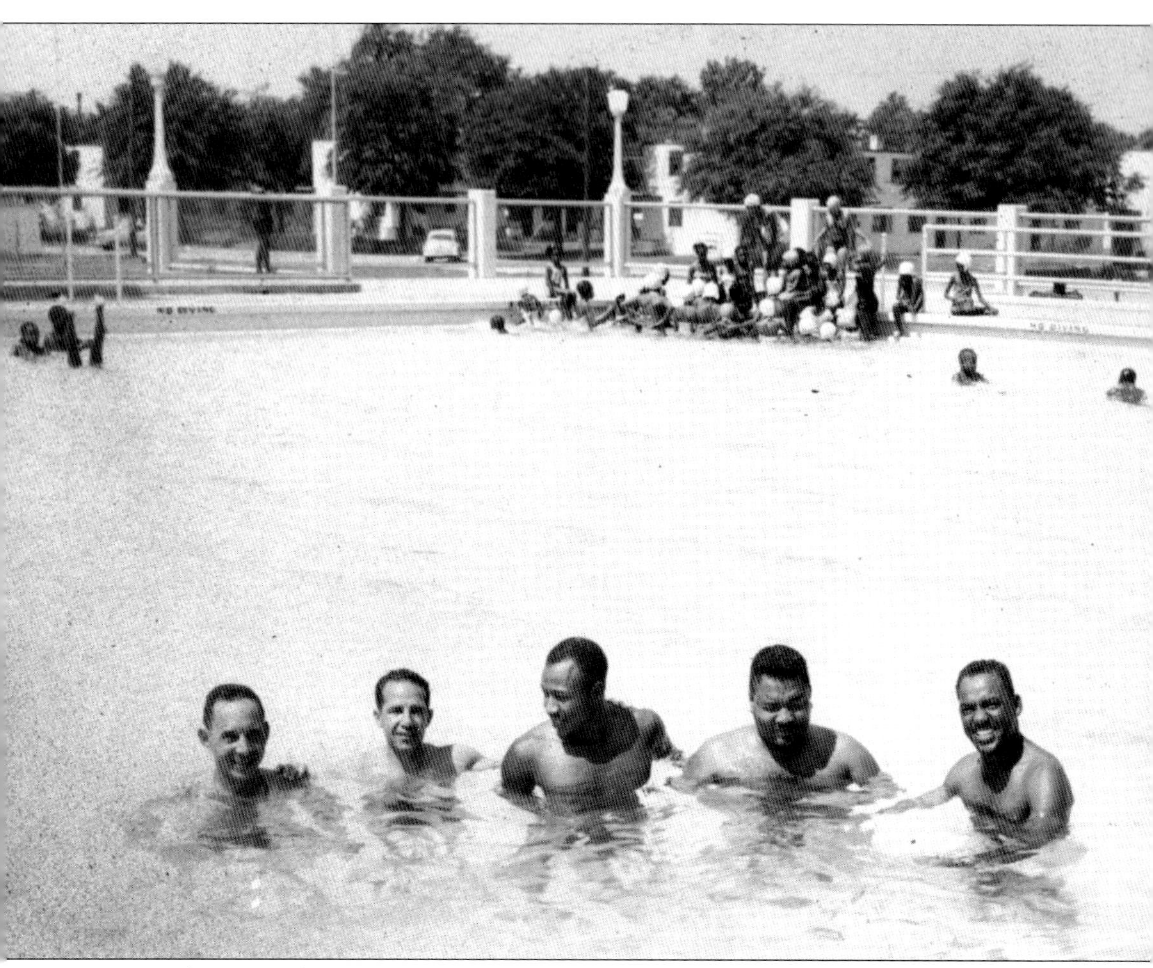

Opened in 1951, the Jefferson Street Pool, now part of Julius Guinyard Park, stands as one of Jacksonville's oldest public swimming pools opened for Black residents during segregation. The city acquired the land from the Jacksonville Housing Authority in 1949, creating a recreational hub for the surrounding Hansontown community. Originally known as the Blodgett Homes Pool, the site grew to include basketball and baseball facilities, picnic areas, and a children's playscape. Located at West Fourth and Jefferson Streets, the park underwent improvements in 1978 and a major renovation in 2001, preserving its role as a vital neighborhood gathering space. In 2006, it was renamed to honor Julius Guinyard, a longtime city parks employee whose dedication to public recreation left a lasting legacy in Jacksonville's urban landscape. (Jacksonville Public Library.)

Bibliography

Colburn, David R., and Jane L. Landers, eds. *The African American Heritage of Florida*. Gainsville: University Press of Florida, 1995.

Cross, Wilbur. *Gullah Culture in America*. Winston-Salem, NC: John F. Blair, 2008.

Geraty, Virginia Mixson. *Gullah Fuh Oonuh: A Guide to the Gullah Language*. Orangeburg, SC: Sandlapper Publishing, 2006.

Hurston, Zora Neale. *The Sanctified Church*. Berkeley, CA: Turtle Island, 1981.

The Jaxson. thejaxsonmag.com.

Johnson, James Weldon. *Along This Way*. New York: Viking Press, 1933.

Landers, Jane. *Black Society in Spanish Florida*. Urbana: University of Illinois Press, 1999.

National Park Service. *Gullah Geechee Cultural Heritage Corridor Management Plan*. Denver: US Department of the Interior, 2012.

———. *Low Country Gullah Culture Special Resource Study and Final Environmental Impact Statement*. Atlanta: US Department of the Interior, 2005.

Pinckney, Roger. *Blue Roots: African-American Folk Magic of the Gullah People*. Orangeburg, SC: Sandlapper Publishing, 2003.

Pollitzer, William S. *The Gullah People and Their African Heritage*. Athens: University of Georgia Press, 2005.

St. Pius Catholic Church. stpiusjax.org.